MW01295943

Endorsements

King Solomon was the wisest man who ever lived (1 Kings 3:12) and needed no one to advise him. Yet, in his superior intelligence he chose to surround himself with the best and the brightest minds he could find to council him in the things pertaining to leadership in government and spiritual matters (1 Kings 1). Therefore, I also felt it vital from the onset of the writing process to surround myself with the most qualified and competent people I knew who would hold me accountable to thoroughly research and properly communicate a scripturally sound and balanced approach to the gospel of Grace. These individuals are highly educated, possessing many years of life and ministry experience and are amongst my closest friends, esteemed colleagues and mentors. I highly value their insight and input into my life, not only because they believe in my ministry, but also because they know my heart. I am confident they have told me what I *needed* to hear. I also felt it critical to select individuals from different theological perspectives and denominational backgrounds to offer their unique perspectives. This was done so that the various schools of thought regarding Grace could be applied in order to present a balanced viewpoint with careful attention to caution and good judgment. Upon receiving each of their comprehensive editorials of my manuscript, their critiques addressed several significant observations and corrections that needed to be made. Therefore, I humbly submit the following endorsements as a testament to the power of wise counsel and accountability to leadership in my life (Proverbs 24:6).

"Tony Sutherland proves to be as effective a writer as he is a preacher and worship leader. I served alongside Tony in a mega-church where I witnessed first hand his sincere devotion to God and his personal, passionate pursuit of encountering the Holy Spirit's presence in his life. In the pages of this book, Tony fervently articulates with convincing persuasiveness, God's extreme and extravagant heart of love and mercy. Tony truly understands his

subject. Those readers who struggle with self-defeating perfectionism will gladly grasp the profound realities of how God views us in His amazing Grace. I highly commend this book with full assurance that you will read it through to the final chapter. Know this... You will be surprised by Grace!"

James L. Burck, Ph.D, M.Th
Southern Baptist Theological Seminary, Louisville KY
San Antonio Theological Seminary, San Antonio, TX
Pastoral Counselor
Powhatan, VA

"I have known Tony for over 20-years and I dearly love him. For nine years he served on staff with me as an Associate Pastor... all these years as a friend and colleague in ministry. In knowing Tony I have recognized three distinct qualities in him that validates those who are true ministers among us. One... He has a passion for God and the things of God. Two... He has a powerful anointing for worship. And three... He has a genuine heart for lost and hurting people. This book is a necessary read for those struggling with condemnation and failure. This work will also deeply impact those who desire to reach souls with the life-changing message of Grace. Tony's powerful insights are sure to produce a harvest of strong believers who will become instruments of God's Grace, enabling the Church of Jesus Christ to set the right standard for the last days."

Roger Bartram, M.Th
School of Theology, Cleveland TN
Senior Pastor of 30 years
Ocala, FL

"Through his unique history and experience as a seasoned minister, Tony brings a fresh and invigorating revisit to the subject of Grace vs. works, which has plagued Christians since the earliest proclamations of the gospel. Those who read this book with an open heart and mind will find a powerfully compelling case for the sovereign work of God in our lives. I have been refreshed by Tony's words, which challenge every personal tendency to fall back on self-reliance, not only for salvation, but also for the transforming of our characters to be Christ-like. Tony makes it clear: living the life of the Spirit brings total liberty

as Grace leads us through the maze of legalistic hazards and tendencies towards obsession in our personal holiness. In essence Tony underscores with passion and conviction, "If ye be led of the Spirit, ye are not under the Law. (Galatians 5:18 KJV)"

Derrel Emmerson, D.D, M.Th
Wesley Theological Seminary, Washington D.C.
Evangel Seminary, Harrisonburg VA
Retired Senior Pastor of 41-years
Professor of Pastoral Theology
Atlanta, GA

"Tony Sutherland is refreshingly passionate about God's marvelous Grace! Like the Apostle Paul, Tony's faith journey has taken him from the frustrating bondage of a legalistic, performance-based Christianity, to the joy and freedom found only in the discovery that the righteousness of God has been divinely imputed to us by faith in Christ! Therefore, we are risen with Christ and the power of sin over us has been forever broken! The realization of being in-Christ opens up a new and exciting perspective for experiencing the fullness of the Christian life. Although we still live in temporary flesh, our regenerated spirit has elevated us far above its mastery over us. Christ has provided for us an awesomely powerful, divinely engineered, devil-confounding, and eternally secure, wondrous salvation! This is why Tony has chosen in this book to go beyond his normal expertise on worship, and write about God's amazing Grace. You too will be refreshed as you breathe in the revelation from these pages!"

Lucian Gandolfo, Ph.D, M.Th.
International Seminary of Florida
Former F.B.I. Agent of 21-years
Brooklyn, NY

"I suspect that many who read this book will find themselves as quietly stunned by the timing of God's voice as I was. Tony Sutherland's relentless focus on the scandal of Grace became to me the whisper of God, pushing me farther and farther from the deadness of religion into the expansive heart of an astonishing God. For that I am grateful. Want to know God? Dive into Grace and you will know Him in joy. Thank you Tony for listening to the Spirit so that we could so

powerfully hear the Father's heart in The Word of Scripture. I believe this book will be of great benefit to those long on the journey of faith and to new believers looking for the first time on the horizons of God's love. May the embrace of Grace make us ever more alive in Christ."

Drew Shofner, Ph.D, S.T.M, M.Div
Baylor University, Yale University
Southwestern Baptist Theological Seminary
Lead Pastor, The Church at Severn Run
Severn Run, MD

"I have been a Licensed Professional Christian Counselor for 20 years working with hundreds of individuals dealing with addictions, co-dependency, psychological & social disorders, devastated marriages, grief, career & ministry failures and many more too sensitive to mention here. I was astonished at Tony's incredible insight regarding condemnation and how it directly relates to the marred self-image. It is God's healing Grace alone that truly puts broken lives back on the road to recovery (3 John 1:2). From now on this book will be considered mandatory reading for every person I counsel."

Tracy Hurst, M.A., LPC
Argosy University
Atlanta, GA

"After being married to Tony for 24 years, I can say with certainty that he lives a life of integrity and demonstrates the walk of Grace. He is an awesome husband and father to our two children and consistently displays a heartfelt compassion for the lost and hurting. The one mainstay in his life has always been his passion for God and leading others into His presence. After seeing first hand the immobilizing effects of condemnation and anxiety, we desperately want to see people set free. A revelation of God's amazing Grace is the only way. Anyone who struggles with fear or self-doubt in their relationship with God must get their hands on this book!"

Sherri Sutherland, M.SLP
Marshall University, Huntington WV
Speech Language Pathologist
Atlanta, GA

"My grace is sufficient for you."
- Jesus Christ

GRACE WORKS.

tony sutherland

All scripture quotations marked NASB, are taken from the *New American Standard Bible*®. © 1960, 1962, 1963, 1968, 1971, 1972, 1973, 1975, 1977, 1995 by the Lockman Foundation. Used by permission. All rights reserved (www.Lockman.org). All rights reserved. All Scripture quotations marked KJV are taken from the *King James Version of the Holy Bible*®. © 1979, 1980, 1982, 1984 by Thomas Nelson, Inc. Used by permission. All rights reserved. All Scripture quotations marked NIV are taken from the *New International Version*®. © 1973, 1978, 1984 by the International Bible Society. Used by permission of Zondervan. All rights reserved. All Scripture quotations marked NKJV are taken from the *New King James Version*®. © 1982 by Thomas Nelson, Inc. Used by permission. All rights reserved. All Scripture quotations marked THE MESSAGE are taken from *The Message*®. © 1993, 1994, 1995, 1996, 2000, 2001. Used by permission of NavPress Publishing Group. All rights reserved. All Scripture quotations marked NLT are taken from the *New Living Translation*®. © 1996, 2004. Used by permission of Tyndale House Publisher, Inc., Wheaton Illinois 60198. All rights reserved. All Scripture quotations marked AMP are taken from the *Amplified*® Bible. © 1962, 1964, 1965, 1987 by the Lockman Foundation. Used by permission. (www.Lockman.org). All rights reserved. Unless otherwise noted, all Hebrew & Greek word translations are taken from *www.blueletterbible.org*.

GRACE WORKS.

© 2014 Tony Sutherland Ministries, Inc.
All rights reserved.
ISBN 978-1-503-29877-4 (Second Edition)

Cover Art, Direction, Layout and Design by Michael Hamilton
www.mchcreative.com

Summary: "Helps believers overcome fear and condemnation by reinforcing their position in Christ. Our salvation is fully substantiated only through the finished work of Jesus and not of any self-effort!" – Provided by publisher
ISBN: 978-1-503-29877-4 (6X9 U.S. Trade Paperback)

No part of this book may be reproduced or transmitted in any form or by any means electronic or mechanical—including photocopying, recording or by any information storage and retrieval system—without permission in writing from the publisher. Please direct your inquiries to permissioneditor@tonysutherland.com.

Acknowledgements

Sherri... I marvel as I reflect on how God has displayed His marvelous Grace through your life towards me. I could never have written this book nor be the man I am today without you. Your unconditional love and acceptance has held me up when I didn't think I could stand anymore. Your strength, patience and faith in me have kept me going when no one else believed in me. I am totally devoted to you and love you deeply!

Asher & Anna... This book is a huge part of my legacy to you. I desperately want you to know that God will never leave you or let you go no matter what. His Grace is far greater than your greatest failures. You belong to Him forever. If there's one thing I want to instill in you is that there is nothing more important than surrendering your lives to Jesus for the sake of your future here on this earth! My deepest desire for you is that you become the man & woman of God that He has destined you to be!

My Parents, Frank & Glenda... Thanks you for your sacrificial love and for believing in me and raising me to be what God destined me to be. Know that all your efforts to instill a desire in me to pursue God's purposes for my life mean everything to me. I am proud to be your son!

My In-Laws Harold & Norma... Your genuine support for Sherri and I have been a source of great strength as we fulfill the call of God for our lives. I am forever grateful to you both for all you have done, especially for our children!

My Late Grandmother Ormie Sutherland... Although you're dancing the streets of Heaven, your legacy of Grace lives on in me. You were a truly devout woman of God. Yet, the inner source of your holiness flowed from your fiery love for Jesus and a life submitted to God's will. You well taught me what it means to be IN CHRIST and your Godly example has helped shape the man that I am today.

Pastor Jentezen Franklin & Pastor Tracy Page... It has been a great honor to be a part of what God is doing through your leadership. Thanks for believing in me and supporting me!

My friends and partners around the world... You have been a tremendous encouragement to me over the years. Your loyalty, generosity and support continually inspire me to stay true to my God given mission. I consider it a privilege to be an influence in your lives.

Lalanda Harrell... Your heart to serve during the formative years of my ministry and helping me navigate through the complexities of administration has truly been a Godsend. Of course, the completion of this book is also in part accredited to your ability to troubleshoot the formatting process. I will never forget your labor of love and faith. You life speaks volumes of what it means to be a loyal and Godly servant.

Pastor Joseph Prince... I've never had the opportunity to meet you. Yet, your books and teachings have profoundly changed my life and continue to deeply inspire me to live in the abundance of God's Grace. You have been a major contributing factor in the writing of this book! I pray God will one day allow me the great honor to share with you in person the incredible impact your ministry has had upon my life!

JESUS... Son of God, hope of all I am and will ever be. This book is my humble offering to You. Eternity cannot contain the volumes that could be written about Your great love for me! Your Grace is simply astonishing! You never cease to take my breath away and leave me speechless. To the only wise God be all the glory forever... Amen!

Contents

Introduction
    GRACE WORKS 15

Chapter 1
    THE HEART TRUTH 27

Chapter 2
    GRACE COLORED GLASSES 31

Chapter 3
    GROW IN 35

Chapter 4
    BULLETPROOF 47

Chapter 5
    A LETHAL MIXTURE 53

Chapter 6
    MAN IN THE MIRROR 63

Chapter 7
    MISSION 'INCROSSABLE' 69

Chapter 8
    NULL AND VOID 73

Chapter 9
    THE ROLLING STONES 89

Chapter 10

WHAT'S RIGHT ABOUT YOU 99

Chapter 11

GRACE MARKS THE SPOT 107

Chapter 12

REPAINT AND THIN NO MORE 117

Chapter 13

FAILURE COMES FIRST 135

Chapter 14

MARKED FOR DELETION 149

Chapter 15

IT'S ALL IN YOUR HEAD 161

Chapter 16

STRESSED TO IMPRESS 173

Chapter 17

GET A GRACE LIFT 181

Chapter 18

'SINGING' IS BELIEVING 187

Chapter 19

THE 'S' WORD 193

Chapter 20

GRACE BASED WORSHIP 205

Chapter 21

THE ENCHANTED KINGDOM 211

Chapter 22

THE GRACE AWAKENING 219

Chapter 23

212 DEGREES 229

Chapter 24

BLUE COLLAR GRACE 235

Chapter 25

DISORDER IN THE COURT 243

Chapter 26

THE ELEPHANT AND THE FLEA 253

Chapter 27

GRACE SPEAKS OUT 263

Chapter 28

SUPERGLUED 273

Chapter 29

HERE LIES WORKS 281

Chapter 30

THE GRACE REVOLUTION 293

Chapter 31

FROM HERE TO HAPPY 301

About the Author 307

APPENDIX I (Early Refutations of Grace) 309

APPENDIX II (Arminianism and Calvinism)........................... 315

Endnotes 319

Introduction

GRACE WORKS.

"But I do not consider my life of any account as dear to myself, so that I may finish my course and the ministry which I received from the Lord Jesus, to testify solemnly of the gospel of the Grace of God." (Acts 20:24 NASB)

Right from the start I want to get something out of the way. I don't know everything nor do I have all the answers to life's questions. I must make it clear that I am not coming from a place of, as the Apostle Paul said, *"having it all together"* (Philippians 3:13). I can't just tell you a story about Grace. I *am* the story of Grace. Grace is my song! I owe everything I am to the glory of God's amazing Grace. I can't imagine where I would be without the love and acceptance of God. He took the *mess* of my life and made it my *message*... a message of how Grace changed me!

About a year prior to writing this book, I began to walk through one of the fieriest trials of my life. I was out on travel, during a weekend ministry trip. As I was settling down for the evening in my hotel room following the first night of services, just as my head hit the pillow, right out of nowhere, I began to hear whispers of condemnation, past regrets, failures and defeats from years gone-by that were already under the blood of Jesus. Yet, for some unexplainable reason I felt such intense fear as if these things had happened just yesterday. For the next several months, at random moments, these same "whispers" would pursue me and the more they occurred the more my feelings of panic increased. The anxiety was so strong at times to the point where I couldn't sleep for days at a time. I remember many nights even stepping up to the platform, preparing to minister, barely mustering up the strength to stand before the people due to the overwhelming feelings of fear and condemnation. Eventually, the anxiety became more than I could bear. The frequency of these *feelings* of condemnation increased to almost a constant level. I am not exaggerating when I say, there were times when it felt like I was suffocating. The anxiety seemed to stalk me everywhere I went: while

I was waiting to board the airplane, cruise the interstate, sleeping in hotels, and even simple things like watching T.V. or brushing my teeth. Worship and prayer was a constant struggle. The only way I could explain it is I *felt like* I was being tormented. The war was ensuing: a battle for my peace of mind... my ministry... my future... my life!

After a prolonged season of this, I started encountering these *episodes* for seemingly no reason at all. It got to the point where I wasn't even sure where the fear was coming from nor could I trace it to any specific cause. I was for certain that it was a demonic attack but my awareness of this didn't help to relieve the anxiety. Often I dreaded being alone with my thoughts and made it a point (as I do now) to always travel with a companion on ministry trips. This is wise advice for anyone who regularly travels in business or ministry (Luke 10:1). Those closest to me (including my wife and a very few of my dearest lifelong friends) who knew what I was walking through were standing with me in prayer and believing with me for a breakthrough. Thank God for these people in my life!

It was during this time that the Holy Spirit began to speak to me and lead me deep into God's Word particularly into the realms of His marvelous Grace *(God has the full remedy for all of our ails)*. I believe the Apostle Paul experienced the very same thing in his life. Many times, he had to endure such harsh treatment from his opposition spending days, weeks, months and even years in a cold dungeon, being forced to face his fears alone. That's why even Paul had to call for someone to come and comfort him (2 Timothy 4:9-13). The scriptures tell us exactly what Paul faced. Many think that his *"thorn in the flesh"* was vague and open ended, left for us to decide for ourselves what it was. However, the scriptures tell us clearly that it was a *"messenger of satan"* sent to stalk and harass him (2 Corinthians 12:7). The NASB says it was sent to *"torment"* him. In response to these overwhelming satanic attacks, Paul asked God three separate times to take this *"thorn"* away. God's response to Paul is amazing...

"And He has said to me, "My Grace is sufficient for you, for power is perfected in weakness." (2 Corinthians 12:9 NASB)

What was the remedy for satan's harassment?[20] It was God's Grace. That is why I believe God led me into the all-out pursuit of His Grace. Through the revelation of the Grace of God, I have put a permanent restraining order on satan from stalking me. No matter what you are facing, God's Grace is the answer for every dilemma. In my battle with condemnation and fear, I have found that when I am focused on receiving and dwelling in the abundant goodness of God's Grace, anxiety and self-defeating thoughts lose their power over me. God's wondrous Grace is empowering me like never before to take hold of life's challenges with fearless determination to overcome IN CHRIST'S victory. This is precisely why I believe you are holding this book in your hands. It is a living testament of the profound effect of God's Grace in my life.

Confessions of a Perfectionist

Many of you reading this book may not know who I am or what it is that I do. Therefore I need to tell you a little bit about myself in order to further establish my motive for writing this book. First of all you must know that for most of my life I have been a person who has chased after God with all my heart. I was saved at an early age and had a definite experience with God being called into the ministry when I was just 8-years old. I haven't always done everything right but one thing is true; I remain to this day dedicated to the purposes of God and have seen much success in my life and ministry.

For most of my Christian walk (these past 35 years), I have been disciplined in prayer and diligent in my personal devotion to God. That hasn't changed much and I will continue to live my life for Jesus in extravagant ways because of all He means to me. However, as I have been pursuing God's Grace it has become evident to me that over the years, without realizing it, I worked overtime to try and *impress* God through my self-efforts to be Godly. Now to be sure, I have always been genuinely and sincerely passionate for the things of God. My intentions were noble to try and please the Lord and live my life for His renown and for the most part I know that I have remained true to that. Yet after all my *self-strivings*, at the end of the day, I still found myself failing to keep to the *letter of the Law*. To my discontent I wore myself out trying to please God when He was already pleased with me. After an in-depth search of God's heart and the scriptures, I now believe that the compulsions to the high standards of perfectionism I had set for myself were a major leading cause to encountering this season of condemnation that I afore mentioned. God's Grace has brought me into a whole new way of living and rather than decrease my passion and dedication it has taken my intensity to serve the Lord to a whole new level. Grace is the elevating factor of my newfound joy IN CHRIST! You must know that I am still not perfect and fail often. However, through God's Grace I have learned how to more effectively deal with condemnation and fear and move forward in Christ's confidence *in* me and His great love *for* me! Surrendering to Grace is the single most important thing I have ever done or ever will do!

As you read this book, you must know that it is not my intention to try and prove a *doctrine* but rather to share the liberating truths that have empowered me to live the fullness of the God life through His amazing Grace. This book is a *testament* of How God's Grace has brought me through life's *tests*, out of my self-striving towards perfectionism and into a whole new world of freedom IN CHRIST. I sincerely hope to lead you to that same liberty I have found in God's Grace! The impact that God's Grace has had upon me is indescribable. My old performance-based mentality has been entirely shattered and I have discovered an exciting new way to live (or should I say *to allow God to live through me*). The revelation of Grace empowers us to live. Is it any wonder why they call it *amazing*!

The Cogs of Grace

Living in the power of God's Grace is like the cogs of two machine wheels perfectly aligned setting freedom in infinite motion. When you trust God's Grace, all the working parts of your *life's mechanism* will be function properly in God's purposes. As a result things will *turn* effortlessly the way God intended. It doesn't mean you won't have problems and challenges to overcome. It means that you won't wear YOURSELF out trying to crank things up in YOUR OWN STRENGTH. You don't have to perform for God. God wants to perform THROUGH you. That's the way He designed you. As you surrender to and rely on God's Grace, you'll soon find yourself propelling forward with great momentum as the Holy Spirit (the oil) helps things operate much more smoothly. When you connect (with all cylinders) to God's Grace, your life will come into proper balance. Conversely, when you trust in your own efforts to save you and earn favor with God, everything falls out of sync and eventually breaks down. That's why so many *clunk*, *clink* and *crash* on the side of life's road trying to *thumb it* to the finish line. Experiencing the power of Grace is like a well-oiled machine. Life works as it should when you trust in God's promise that you are made righteous by Christ's *finished* work. After all, Christ's finished work is the ONLY THING that works!

Style & Approach

The original draft of this book started from a collection of blogs on Grace that I had posted over a period of time on my website. However, after months of extensive research, judicious examination and scrupulous revisions I arrived at the final manuscript you now hold in your hands. Please know that this book is not intended to be an exhaustive, definitive, argumentative or expository work on the subject of Grace. That would be a daunting task to be sure. Over the centuries, the study of Grace has sparked many controversies that have sadly split much of the Body of Christ right down the middle. This book is not an attempt to prove or disprove any one side of the 'doctrinal' argument on Grace. It's a shame that such an amazing gift from God has become grounds for holy wars among the saints. In order to present God's Grace in a LIFE-GIVING manner, this work was birthed out of a deep desire to reveal *God's heart* to hurting, condemned and broken people. Therefore I have chosen to present the material herein from an inspirational, devotional, conversational and practical approach. I have also attempted to combine a radical presentation of the subject of Grace while at the same time maintaining a consistent balance throughout. Radical yet balanced! However, I tilt more towards the side of the radical. In order to help people experience God's extreme Grace I must preach extreme Grace! Therefore, you should know from the start that I am being anything but *casual* about God's Grace!

Condemnation Kills

Now-a-days people are confused, troubled, and desperately hard-pressed for help. A doctrine or expose' won't fix broken lives. Desperate people don't need a *word*. They need a *ROPE*! God's

Grace is that rope! Carrying guilt is destructive. In fact, CONDEMNATION KILLS! Most people have enough trouble in their life without having to bear the heavy guilt from not doing enough for God or failing Him altogether. Recently a very close friend actually told me that when he goes to bed at night he feels like he didn't do enough for God that day. Our Heavenly Father does not want His children to live under guilt and condemnation (Romans 8:1). I truly believe we can live guilt and worry free lives through the power of God's Grace!

As you read this book you should have your Bible beside you as I have made many direct scripture references in parenthesis that are not directly printed. There will be times when you find yourself scratching your head and saying, *"I never thought of it that way before,"* or *"I'm going to have to ponder that one."* There may even be some things you *strongly* disagree with. However, *please commit to read this book in its entirety* and bring your questions and concerns before the Lord before making ANY assumptions or drawing concrete conclusions! At the end of each chapter make a resolution to keep reading until you finish. It is not possible for me to introduce every concept or supportive scripture reference in every chapter. That is why it has taken me 31 chapters and over 300 pages to pave a prayerfully plotted path that will lead you to greater plateaus of peace in God's Grace (That's a lot of *P's* in one mouthful). Also take into consideration that this book should be studied in balance with the many great books out there on other powerful subjects such as worship, prayer, evangelism, parenting, discipleship, prophecy, etc. As strong as my convictions are, this is just one book on Grace and should not be singled out as the end-all literary work for the Christian faith. No one person has a corner on the scriptures including me.

Keep Reading

As you commit to journey through this book, I humbly ask you to consider the nuggets of truth that inspire you, take them before the Lord in prayer and tuck them away in your spirit. As for the things that you're not sure of, seek God's wisdom and revelation on the matter. Just don't throw the baby out with the bath water. Remember, you cannot receive what you reject. In other words, if you reject everything because you disagree with a few things you will miss out on some exciting things God wants to do in your life. If you read this book with an open heart and with anticipation for God to give you a mighty revelation of Grace, you will never be the same. I will assure you of one thing... This book will only get richer with each unfolding chapter! I am fully aware that with the reading of any book comes some disagreement and difference of opinion. Even I am privy to this when I read other's writings and I expect it to be no different with this book, particularly a book about Grace. Throughout the centuries many controversies have ensued surrounding the story of Grace. Grace infuriates the religious and fixes the ruined. In fact, much opposition regarding the perplexities of Grace has surfaced among good "church going" people more than anyone else. The pure message of Grace frustrates and irritates religious people because they are immediately forced to deal with their self-righteousness. Their motto is *"Self is king. Long live the king."* Religion always says you must *try* but Grace says you must *rely*. The Bible declares that Jesus was a stumbling block of *"offense"* (1 Peter 2:8). The Greek word for *"offense"* is *skandalon*, which is where we get our English word *scandal*. Grace causes so much of a scandal in the religious church because the underlying message is that you can be saved (initially and ongoing) without working for it. Yet, like Paul I am not ashamed of the scandalous gospel of Grace, for it is the power of God that saves the sinner and keeps on saving the saint. In writing this book, I have become well prepared to defend the gospel of Grace (Philippians 1:16 NASB)! However, my intent is not to stir up a hornet's nest but rather to give hope to the hurting and help lead the believer into full maturity (1 Peter 3:18). Grace works EVERYWHERE it hurts!

A Head-On Collision with Grace

When I first encountered the vast and dynamic implications of God's Grace it completely altered my life forever. It was like having a head on collision with a Mack Truck. Discovering true Grace for the first time shattered so many false perceptions I had about how God related to me and how I should relate to Him. In many ways it made me feel like I was starting all over again just like Paul did in Acts 9. The glory of God's Grace complete threw me off my *high horse* of pride and turned my life around 180-degrees in a brand new direction. Through Grace I am now living a more meaningful life, experiencing deeper intimacy with my Heavenly Father, breathing the crisp, cool air of freedom and soaring to higher peaks of victory than I ever imagined. I can never go back to the old life I once knew before my eyes were opened to the wonders of God's Grace.

After looking back over the last two-decades of my ministry, I truly believe that I could have made a more significant impact in people's lives if I had understood the principles that I am about to share with you. As of late I cannot tell you the number of people who have approached after ministering on the subject of God's Grace and told me their life will *never* be the same. Now more than ever, I realize that God doesn't want me to just have a successful ministry. He wants me to *truly minister* His Grace to a broken and hurting world. Some who know me as a worship leader, thought it more fitting for me to write on the subject of worship. Recently I asked the Lord, *"Why a book about Grace?"* His answer was simple, *"Because My Grace inspires real worship."* It then occurred to me that so often we focus on the *way* we worship rather than on the *One* we worship. In other words, the emphasis is on the mechanics of worship rather than on the Lord of our worship. It is sad to say but many times we give more attention to *creativity* than we do the *Creator*! We're not supposed to worship the worship! Jesus alone is the object of our fondest affection! When Jesus (the person of Grace) is exalted, people from every walk of life will respond to His unconditional love and surrender to His uncontested Lordship (John 12:32). Hearts that have been forever changed by Grace will surely worship!

True intimacy with God is birthed from a place of Grace. This is because in our inadequacy and our failure God still beckons us to come into His presence and enjoy friendship with Him. God's holy perfection reminds us of how imperfect we are and His holiness alone potentially can drive us away. Yet, His Grace is the drawing factor that welcomes us as we are and it is His holiness that transforms us. Our ability to be holy isn't what gives us access into His presence. We would never be able to experience the beauty of His holiness without His Grace. Grace bids us into His Holiness and by His holiness we are partakers of His divine nature (1 Peter 1:2-4). Therefore, considering all these things, from now on every song I write, sermon I preach and book I author must flow from the revelation of God's Grace. Grace is where true worship begins!

Why the Title: Grace works?

Why do I call this book GRACE WORKS? Well if you know anything about Grace you know that *works* is the polar opposite of *Grace*. The title of this book is a purposeful play on words. Works do not make us righteous nor do they help to maintain our righteousness. Self-effort is futility! The only thing that works to make us righteous is Grace. When all else fails... Grace works... PERIOD. Grace is not a concept or an allowance for bad behavior. Grace is the WORK of God in the believer's life. I like to think of Grace as the brute strength of God that heaves out the weight of anything that hinders God's purposes from coming to pass in our lives. Grace works is a collection of *works* (volumes) on my scriptural study, revelation, divine encounter and ongoing experience with the power of God's Grace (in that order). Grace is the only thing that gives us the power to reign in life. Therefore, I dub this book *Grace Works* because only God's Grace produces anything of notable value in our lives.

In the pages of this book, there will be much that will be left to the reader to pray through and work out in their personal relationship with God (Philippians 2:12). Again, this is NOT THE DEFINITIVE WORK on Grace. The purpose of this particular work is to hammer several revelatory support beams into your understanding of New Testament Grace. Another way to look at it is that I'm simply inserting another rung into the ladder or adding another stair step of Biblical perspective in order that you may ascend into the limitless heights of the marvelous mystery of God's Grace. It is important to understand that it took Paul nearly two-thirds of the New Testament to defend the Grace message. That's precisely how you should filter his writings (through the lens of Grace). Over the years, many well-meaning preachers (including myself) have drawn messages out of Paul's writings in the New Testament that had nothing to do with the context in which He wrote them. Therefore, as you read this book, continue to keep in mind that everything Paul wrote flowed from his revelation of Grace. Paul's life mission was to defend the gospel of Grace...

"I am put here for the defense of the gospel." (Philippians 1:16 NIV)

"So that I may finish my course and the ministry which I received from the Lord Jesus, to testify solemnly of the gospel of the Grace of God." (Acts 20:24 NASB)

Wash, Rinse & Repeat

The pure gospel of Grace doesn't bring the picture into focus... It completely changes the picture altogether! That's why throughout the pages of this book there is much purposeful repetition and necessary overlapping. Therefore, you will often find yourself reading the same citations of scripture and repeating of familiar concepts. The pure message of Grace will wash and rinse your mind of old concepts that have held you in bondage. However, washing and rinsing once isn't enough. Therefore, I repeat the same fundamental concepts to reinforce the powerful truths of the Pauline gospel of Grace. To embrace the message of Grace you first must receive a *revelation* of Grace. To receive a revelation on any Biblical truth it is vital that the same scriptures and topics be readdressed several times until insight is comprehended (Romans 10:17). Once you make a valiant effort to grasp the truths of God's Grace you are on your way to receiving the spiritual revelation. Often it takes twice as long to learn about Grace because you must first be deprogrammed from legalistic teaching that has long been imbedded in your heart and mind. Over the years, we have developed philosophies that are like iron fortresses around our thinking. In order to break down false teaching and ingrained doctrines of self-efforts toward righteousness the same teachings and scriptures on Grace must be reapplied until it has penetrated those mindsets. Although God's Word is the foundation of learning about Grace, it must be *experienced* to more fully comprehend its purpose and power in the life of the believer. Merely *studying* or *intellectually processing* Grace is not enough. It must flow from a personal revelation and consistent walk in the knowledge of God's heart. Grace is not a doctrine; it's a *relationship* with a real person.

Opening a Can of Worms

Much of what I have written about in this book comes from painful life encounters regarding my own serious struggles with fear and condemnation from failing God. All throughout my Christian life I have learned valuable insights that have helped me deal with condemnation (subtle or profound) that I face on a regular basis as most believers do (whether they want to admit it or not). I long to share these secrets of the *overcoming life* with you. Thus, this book was designed to help those who desire to enjoy their relationship with

God to the fullest and progress in their pursuit of holiness! Please be advised that when the message of Grace is presented in the correct way (the way that Jesus and Paul did) it will stir up serious questions and concerns. Paul had this same problem (Romans 3:8; 6:1). However, as I previously mentioned, my heart is not to open a can of worms but rather to uncover the marvelous truths of God's awesome Grace. The primary purpose of this book is to minister encouragement to those who struggle with their failures, feel separated from God through their inability to be perfect and lead them to a greater dimension of their full liberty IN CHRIST! From the beginning I want to firmly emphasize that this book does not endorse sin nor to license people to live like Hell (Romans 6:1-5). Rather, I wrote this book to help people encounter more of HEAVEN in their lives. Grace does not set us free TO sin. Grace gives us power OVER sin. And although we are not saved BY good works; we are saved UNTO good works. As St. Augustine once said, *"Grace is given not because we have done good works, but in order that we may be able to do them."* Paul's message was the most radical of his day. He was ministering to Gentile converts who knew nothing of the Law and yet, they were coerced by the religious leaders to dutifully observe it. At the same time he rebuked the Judaizers for pressuring these precious new converts towards strict observance of the Law. But at NO TIME did Paul (or any of the New Testament writers for that matter) condone that the Grace message gives people permission to live anyway they want. Sadly, there are those who misinterpret the Grace message using it to make allowances for their sinful behavior. The "scandal of Grace" does not justify living sinfully (Galatians 5:13). Be strongly advised; Grace does not *redefine* sin. Rather, Grace *redeems* us from sin. From the start you should clearly understand that Grace does not excuse nor endorse sinful and harmful conduct in our lives. Grace cleanses and heals it. Hallelujah! Real Grace is, by it's very nature transformational. The bullet that hits you pierces you. In the same way, Grace cannot *hit* you (be authentically received) without changing you! Reaching for Grace as a cover for the continued love of sin reveals a heart that never truly received Grace in the first place.

Caution: Grace Up Ahead

Many ministers are overtly cautious to preach the pure gospel of Grace for fear that people will interpret it as a license to sin. To Believe this shows a lack of understand of God's Grace. Have you noticed that people don't need permission to sin? They sin daily without license anyway! The Grace message doesn't cause us to sin. Our *carnal desire* entices us to sin. Once we are lured by our *own lust*, sin is conceived. It is impossible for Grace to produce sin. Cat's don't birth dogs. Likewise, Sin isn't birthed from Grace. Sin is birthed by *lust*...

> **"But each one is tempted when he is carried away and enticed by his own lust. Then when lust has conceived, it gives birth to sin; and when sin is accomplished, it brings forth death."**
> **(James 1:14-15 NASB)**

The central theme of this book is that through Grace, we win the battle for holiness only as we rest IN CHRIST'S finished work. As you read this book, I hope you will more fully embrace Grace and find a deeper confidence in your Heavenly Father's perfect love for you. May Grace be YOUR story! That is my prayer!

Chapter 1

THE HEART TRUTH

"For I am not ashamed of the gospel, for it is the power of God for salvation to everyone who believes..."
(Romans 1:16 NASB)

The Gospel is without a doubt the secret power of the universe that forever vanquishes sin and guilt and releases unimaginable possibilities of freedom. It is a glorious Gospel indeed. And although the mystery of the Gospel has been revealed to us through Jesus it yet remains a mystery because of its vast implications. It is uncanny how the very gospel that forever set us free from the chains of the past, present and future is still shrouded in disbelief and incredulity to even the most devout follower of Christ...

"But we speak God's wisdom in a mystery, the hidden wisdom which God predestined before the ages to our glory."
(1 Corinthians 2:7 NASB)

When I discovered the truth of the gospel, and all the treasures that it uncovered, it completely revolutionized my life and radically transformed my ministry! As a result I have become overwhelmed with a greater passion for Jesus and awakened to a whole new way of living! It has truly had that profound of an effect upon me! This powerful revelation that I speak of is the key to salvation, healing, victory, financial breakthrough, deliverance, overcoming bondages and the fullness of the abundant life that is available to everyone at Christ's expense (G.R.A.C.E. = **G**od's **R**iches **A**t **C**hrist's **E**xpense). Note that our key passage doesn't say that the gospel *"has the power"* or that it is *"a power."* It says that it is *"THE power of God for salvation."* This small word *(the)* implies that the gospel is the SOLE power that brings us into Christ's marvelous salvation. The hope for the world is the gospel. I am tired of seeing God's people condemned, desperately defeated, sick, depressed, discouraged, confused, afraid, anxious, worried and burned out! God is moving in the earth today and yet so many aren't experiencing the victory that is available to them. I believe when the Gospel is preached rightly the power of God will be released in a more unprecedented way! Therefore, it's time for the Body of Christ to rediscover the truth of the gospel!

Too Good to Be True

The definition of The Gospel is *The Good News*. The Greek word for *gospel* is *'euaggelion'* which literally means *too-good-to-be-true-news.*[3] And the good news is the bad news is over. The scriptures tell us that the very power of God is THE GOSPEL (Good News) and the *Good News* alone is the power that saves us. Not only is it the power that saves us; it is also the ongoing power that maintains us in righteousness and takes us from victory to victory. In other words, the Gospel not only saves us; it KEEPS ON SAVING US! Grace not only brought us into freedom; it is the power that keeps us in that freedom! The Greek word for *'salvation'* in our key passage is *soteria,* which includes all the benefits of the "saved" life (forgiveness, healing, deliverance, prosperity, etc.). Salvation not only guarantees that our soul is secured in a vault in Heaven, but is also the secret to experiencing the abundant, victorious life God promised us *here* on earth. The gospel is the GOOD NEWS OF GOD'S GRACE!

"That I may finish my course and the ministry which I received from the Lord Jesus, to testify solemnly of the GOSPEL OF THE GRACE of God." (Acts 20:24 NASB)

Jesus Himself commissioned Paul to proclaim the ministry of Grace. In fact, many scholars refer to him to as the Apostle of Grace. Paul's writings (Pauline Grace) systematically explain and defend the gospel of Grace (comprising three-fourths of the entire New Testament) According to Paul, a revelation of *God's Grace alone* contains the power to save us and keep on saving us. It was a radical message of its day (and still is) Paul was harshly persecuted because he preached the gospel of Grace to a staunch, religious generation who believed the way to attain and maintain righteousness was through self-effort and ongoing perfect behavior.

Con of the Centuries

In order to fully understand Paul's writings you have to filter them through the lens of Grace, otherwise you will take what he says out of context. Many preachers create sermons from Paul's writings that have nothing to do with what He is talking about. Everything Paul wrote about was in defense of the gospel of Grace. When you take the 'text' out of the 'context' all you get is a 'con.'[1] For years, people (sinners and saints) have been conned out of walking in the fullness of the power of God because they have a skewed understanding of true Biblical Grace. The results are tragic causing them to needlessly suffer under the bondage of sin, condemnation and all manner of sickness, disease, addiction and poverty. Therefore, in order for people to be truly set free we must consistently minister (in abundance) through the spirit and power of God's Grace...

"For if by the transgression of the one, death reigned through the one, much more THOSE WHO RECEIVE THE ABUNDANCE OF GRACE and of the gift of righteousness will REIGN IN LIFE through the One, Jesus Christ." (Romans 5:17 NASB)

God's Grace doesn't even remotely give license to sin. In fact, it's quite the opposite. Along with my recent discoveries, this profound revelation of Grace has enabled me to stand firm in my righteousness IN CHRIST. As a result I am experiencing deeper intimacy with God's love and A far greater success in overcoming sinful tendencies. Look again at our key verse and the verse that directly follows...

"For I am not ashamed of the gospel, for it is the power of God for salvation to everyone who believes. FOR IN IT THE RIGHTEOUSNESS OF GOD IS REVEALED." (Romans 1:17 NASB)

Why is Grace Such a Big Deal?

The next question we must answer is, "WHAT IS GRACE?" After all, if the Gospel is the *Good News of God's Grace,* we must be able to grasp the true Biblical concept of Grace in order to comprehend the depths of this glorious good news. I believe the following passage best summarizes my definition of Grace...

"So that in the ages to come He might show the surpassing riches of His Grace in kindness toward us IN CHRIST Jesus. For by Grace you have been saved through faith; and that not of yourselves, it is the gift of God; not as a result of works, so that no one may boast."
(Ephesians 2:7-9 NASB)

Grace is the DEAL of a lifetime. Just think; the *free* gift of righteousness (perfect standing with God) is completely granted to us apart from our own effort. It cannot be earned or merited. It can only be received by believing in the finished work of Jesus. All that Christ is and all that He has done for us is for FREE! It comes without expense. We get the very best that God has to offer at NO COST to us. That's a BIG DEAL if you ask me. Grace is the *heart truth* that God sent His Son to break the curse of our slavery to the Law; thus fulfilling our inability and futility to perfectly obey it's impossible standard. The natural mind cannot comprehend this. It must be received through supernatural revelation of the Holy Spirit (1 Corinthians 2:9-14). It is impossible to earn your way into Heaven. If it were, then Grace would not be necessary. George Whitfield, the famous Anglican itinerant minister who's powerful preaching helped spread the Great Awakening in Great Britain, once said, *"What! Get to heaven on your own strength? Why, you might as well try to climb to the moon on a rope of sand."*

The Gospel is the GOOD NEWS that we don't have to earn favor with God. God's Grace alone makes us righteous. Simply accepting God's free gift of righteousness through the perfect sacrifice of Jesus is what makes us acceptable in His sight and qualifies us for the promise of eternal life and all His blessings here and now! Grace is not religion... It's a *relationship* with Jesus. Sometimes the truth just FEELS GREAT... That's Grace!

Chapter 2

GRACE COLORED GLASSES

"Blessed is the man whose sin the Lord will never count against him." (Romans 4:8 KJV)

On the Day of Atonement, the Jewish people would sojourn from every region across the nation of Israel bringing their sacrifices to the capital city of Jerusalem to atone for their sins that year. Talk about the circle of life. Every year they would have to circle back around towards Jerusalem because the sacrifice wasn't a once-and-for-all sacrifice. It was a never-ending cycle. Thus is the futility of living in the frustrating cycle of the Law and self-works *(The wandering of the children of Israel in the wilderness for 40-years also so adequately illustrates this futile cycle).* As soon as they would return home from Jerusalem after sacrificing I can imagine that they began thinking about making the journey all over again next year. This is because their sin wasn't truly cleansed; it was only atoned for (covered until the next appointed time). The bloody ritual only served as a temporary covering for sin, it wasn't fully eradicated. Only Jesus can permanently remove our sin (John 1:29).

A 'Sheep' Shape Inspection

The KJV version of our key passage (Romans 4:8) says, *"Blessed is the man to whom the Lord Does not impute sin."* The word *impute* means *to attribute, give full credit to, place blame or hold accountable for.* The Greek word *logidzomai* means to keep a mental record of events for the sake of some future action. To better understand this, we must look closely at the ancient method of priestly sacrificial inspection. When people presented a sacrifice to the priest, he carefully examined it. First the lamb had to be spotless without blemishes. Then the priest proceeded to meticulously run his fingers through the wool, checking for tumors or defects. Next he glared into the lamb's eyes to inspect for cataracts or blindness. Next he wrapped his fingers around each leg to observe for signs of bone degeneration. Finally, he set the Lamb on its feet assuring it wasn't crippled and could stand on its own. Once completed, the priest handed the knife to the person bringing the lamb and he would cut its throat, offering it as a sacrifice. Sins Absolved! Carefully notice that during the entire examination, the priest's focus wasn't on the person offering the sacrifice but on the sacrifice being offered. His gaze was steadfastly fixed on the lamb. If the lamb met the legal requirements, the sins of the person were imputed (transferred to) the lamb and the innocence of the lamb was imputed to the sinner. Remember that an earthly sacrifice was never perfect; it was accepted based on its *close proximity* to the Law's requirements. Note also that the lamb wasn't being punished for it's own imperfections but rather for the person's imperfections. The sinner's blemishes were transferred to the unblemished lamb and the "perfection" of the Lamb was transferred to the sinner. Likewise, in the New Covenant of Grace, our sins are transferred to the spotless, flawless and innocent Christ and His flawless perfection is transferred to us. Forgiven once and for all, God reckons us as never having sinned (2 Corinthians 5:19). God sees us as righteous AS HE IS RIGHTEOUS. When we believe in the name of Jesus and receive His free gift of salvation, God does not hold us accountable for our sin. Paul uses Abraham as an example of how this applies to the believer...

"Even as (the same way) Abraham BELIEVED God, and it was accounted (credited) to him for righteousness. Know ye therefore that they which are of faith (not works) the same are the children of Abraham (we are righteous just like Abraham was made righteous because of his faith not performance of the Law). So then they which be of faith (not works) are blessed with faithful Abraham (we have the same righteousness, blessings and promises as Abraham)." (Galatians 3:6-7 KJV)[37]

Note that Abraham lived four hundred years before the Law was given at Mount Sinai. He simply believed God and God granted him complete righteousness. That's the way it works for us.

The Overpayment

You may ask, *"Does all this mean I can't do anything to be righteous?"* There is nothing you could ever do to be righteous. That's why God sent His Son who knew NO sin to become sin FOR you so you could become the very righteousness of God...

"He (God) made Him (Jesus) who knew no sin to be sin on our behalf, so that we might become the righteousness of God in Him." (2 Corinthians 5:21 NASB)[37]

Jesus wasn't merely the payment for our sins; He was the OVERPAYMENT! Jesus' sacrifice isn't enough. It's MORE than enough! His redemptive work doesn't just cover us for the period between now until the next time we fail. In His finished work we are righteous PERIOD! All our sins (past, present and future) are swallowed up in His precious blood (Hebrews 10:12). When we come to God broken by sin, God doesn't see us. Just like the priest He looks at Jesus, the perfect sacrifice and because of Jesus' perfect sacrifice we are pardoned from punishment, condemnation and the imputation of sin. This doesn't mean God goes soft on sin. God is holy and righteous and in His justice He must severely punish sin. Yet, God loved us so much that He chose to brutally punish His only Son in our place. Unfathomable! God punished sin once and for all, and since He is just, He cannot punish sin twice otherwise He would not be just...

"Through His own blood, He entered the holy place ONCE FOR ALL having obtained eternal redemption." (Hebrews 9:12 NASB)

When we believe in the finished work of Christ and surrender to His Lordship we are made fully righteous and acceptable to God! One of the main reasons so many constantly fall into patterns of sin and condemnation is not so much that preachers *go light* on sin but because they *go light* on the efficacy of the sacrifice of Jesus. When we place all our emphasis on Christ's fully acceptable sacrifice and atoning blood, we can experience the fullness of freedom it provides.

A Dream Gift

Imagine for a moment that I have given my wife a ten-carat diamond ring. As she puts the ring on her finger she is breathless. What an indescribable gift! This HUGE rock demonstrates my great love for her (not to mention my enormous bank account). It is a gift. She is totally free from any obligation to pay me back. It is my gift for her to ENJOY. Soon, before I know it, she starts sending me monthly payments for it. Ridiculous! She would never enjoy the gift because of feeling the needless guilt and unnecessary obligation. Sooner or later, life for her would be insufferable! Likewise, many Christians cannot accept that God's gift of righteousness is *free*. After all, how could something priceless be free? That's why Paul called it an INDESCRIBABLE GIFT! (2 Corinthians 9:15). Likewise many Christians feel they must enter a lifetime of indentured service to repay their sin debt. As a result, there remains a subconscious guilt and abiding fear that their righteousness might be recalled if they fail to *walk the line*. However, Paul boldly addresses this misconception...

"The gifts and calling of God are IRREVOCABLE."
(Romans 11:29 NASB)

Here Paul wasn't talking about talents and ministry abilities (as many misinterpret it). The context of this passage (and all of Romans for that matter) is specifically dealing with the *free gift of righteousness* that we receive by faith through Grace. The word *'irrevocable'* in this passage means *incapable of being retracted or revoked*. In other words, God will NEVER take back your righteousness. As you meditate on this passage, revelation-truth will explode within you. When you believe, without a shred of doubt, that your righteousness cannot be rescinded (officially canceled), it will completely set you free from fear when you fall short or even fail miserably and will greatly empower you to overcome the bondages that have held you captive. Hallelujah! God sees you through Grace colored glasses!

Chapter 3

GROW IN

"But grow in Grace, and in the knowledge of our Lord and Savior Jesus Christ." (2 Peter 3:18 NASB)

When I was in middle school my science class conducted an experiment to see if chicken eggs would hatch under an electric warmer or incubator. The incubator was actually nothing more than a glorified heat lamp. The hypothesis was that that if we could reproduce the natural warm and nurturing environment of a mother hen, then the embryos would come to full term and hatch. I'm not sure if it ever worked for other science classes, but as you probably already guessed, it never worked for ours. This is because we were unsuccessful at recreating the proper environment under the heated light. The eggs couldn't foster life under the improper environment and thus never reached their maturation. This illustrates how many Christians never reach their full potential. It is because they are not in the proper environment for growth. Just like flowers need the perfect conditions of light, water and soil; likewise we spiritually mature in the love, joy and peace-filled environment of Grace. Most of us want to reach higher levels of spiritual maturity yet many times we find ourselves still acting like infants and living way beneath our means as the children of God. When we learn to rest in the knowledge of God's Grace and cease from striving to live perfectly under the standard of the Law we will begin to mature to levels of growth IN CHRIST we never thought imaginable. Growing in the knowledge of our Lord and Savior can only be realized through an ongoing experiential relationship with Him. We can only experience the abundant life promised us (John 10:10) by growing in a vital union with our Lord and Savior. A deepening relationship with Jesus is based on love and trust. This means we must receive God's free gift of righteousness without fear that He will *bail* when we *fail*. If we perform for God in order to achieve friendship with Him then we do not really trust His steadfast love. Thus, our good performance will always be based out of fear. The truth is that none of us are lovable; but the good new is God loves us anyway. Noted author and scholar

C.S. Lewis once said, *"God doesn't love us because we are lovable, but because He is love."* Friend, faith isn't produced through fear, but by love (Galatians 5:6). Our chapter key verse says we *grow in Grace and in the knowledge of OUR LORD AND SAVIOR JESUS CHRIST.* Many think that this verse means we grow in Grace *accompanied with* an intellectual understanding and application of the *scriptures.* This is in part true. However, while I am not demeaning the importance of consistent Biblical application, the way we truly ascend the heights of spiritual maturity is through the knowledge of (deep intimacy with) a person. We will never experience growth through religious formulas, but through a loving relationship with Jesus! Receiving GRACE and having a KNOWLEDGE OF JESUS is one-in-the-same. Once we understand and fully believe this nothing will be able to stop us from becoming all God designed us to be. We will be unstoppable!

Stoned to Death

"The Law was given by Moses but Grace and TRUTH came by Jesus Christ." (John 1:17 NASB)

Only Moses was allowed to draw near to God. The very image of Moses carrying the cold, stone tablets down from Sinai to the people denotes a distant, unapproachable God. Many still worship God from a fearful, foreboding distance. However, the words in the above passage *"Grace and truth came"* show a Savior that is touchable. Grace came as a person. It may sound strange at first but when Moses descended from Mount Sinai, he was literally carrying our death sentence in His hands...

"But if the MINISTRY OF DEATH, IN LETTER ENGRAVED ON STONES, came with glory, so that the sons of Israel could not look intently at the face of Moses because of the glory of His face, fading as it was how will the ministry of the Spirit fail to be even more with glory? For if the ministry of condemnation has glory, much more does the ministry of righteousness abound in glory. For indeed what had glory, in this case has no glory because of the glory that surpasses it. For if that which fades away was with glory, much more that which remains is in glory."
(2 Corinthians 3:7-11 NASB)

Paul calls the Law the *ministry of death* and *condemnation.* He again states in 2 Corinthians 3:6 that the *letter* (the Law) kills but the *Spirit*

(Grace) gives life. I believe many Christians needlessly suffer because they are living under the condemnation of the Law that only administers death and anything associated with it (i.e. illness, disease, depression, etc.).[35] The tablets of the Law were engraved in stone. The harsh preaching of the Law (unbendable and unyielding) has the same results as being stoned to death. The Law doesn't save us. Rather, it shows us our desperate need for a Savior. There is only one *Law* that saves, heals and sets us free: the Law of the Spirit (Grace).

"For the LAW OF THE SPIRIT of life IN CHRIST Jesus has set you free from the Law of sin and of death." (Romans 8:2 NASB)

In these passages the *Law of condemnation* and the *ministry of death* (the Old Covenant) has faded away and the *ministry of the Spirit* and the *ministry of righteousness* (the new covenant of Grace) has surpassed it. The following will help you see these contrasts more clearly...

THE LAW

Ministry of Death

Ministry of Condemnation

GRACE

Ministry of the Spirit

Ministry of Righteousness

The Law is the ministry of condemnation (2 Corinthians 3:9). Grace is the ministry of AFFIRMATION! (Ephesians 1:6). Under the Law we are never acceptable. Under Grace we are completely acceptable. Only the *Law of the Spirit* (Grace) can minister righteousness (life) to us. Grace takes us out from under the Law & ritual and places us into love & relationship (Ezekiel 36:26). Only Jesus can do what the Law could never do for us...

"For what THE LAW COULD NOT DO, weak as it was through the flesh, God did: sending His own Son in the likeness of sinful flesh and as an offering for sin, He condemned sin in the flesh." (Romans 8:3 NASB)

The Power of Sin: The Law

"The sting of death is sin, and THE STRENGTH OF SIN IS THE LAW." (1 Corinthians 15:56 NKJV)

Did you know the Law actually fuels our desire to sin? That's right! The Law literally empowers our carnal nature, reminding it of what it naturally wants to do. Living under the Law only causes us to fall further into sin. While the Law is holy and good it cannot *make* us holy and good. Please understand I am not saying the Law isn't important. The Law is extremely necessary, however, not for the reasons that many of us think. The Law isn't what corrects our behavior. On the contrary, it only reminds us of how far we have fallen from perfection. I am not advocating *antinomianism* (the doctrine or belief that Grace frees Christians from required obedience to any Law, whether scriptural, civil or moral). It is important to obey God's Law (I deal with this more in subsequent chapters). However, the solution to our sin is not preaching more of God's Law. Many believe that the prescription for sin is to administer more teaching on obeying the Law. However, pointing to the Law only leads to more frustration because it reminds us of what we are incapable of doing in the first place. In other words, when you draw people's attention to obeying the Law it backfires. The Commandments do not help us overcome sin. They only reveal our inability to keep them. The Law is incapable of setting us free. Again, that's why the Law is called the "*ministry of death*" (2 Corinthians 3:7).

Pink Elephants in the Room

For a moment consider this... Try not to think about pink elephants for the next 30 seconds. What is the result? You automatically think about pink elephants. No matter how hard you try you cannot erase the image of a big, pink Dumbo in your head. This is because by nature we break the rules. That is why we must live by Grace. If we are constantly self-conscious about breaking God's Laws we'll eventually break them. The only way to remove the image of the pink elephant is to replace it with another image. For instance, instead of pink elephants, now picture an iron cross in front of you. What happened? You stopped thinking about the pink elephant didn't you? Likewise, whenever we focus on God's mercy and forgiveness the images of failure dissolve with the truth of God's love towards us, and in doing so, we reinforce strong confidence and a settled assurance in our wondrous salvation. This ultimately results in a changed lifestyle of obedience and fruitfulness. Imagine that!

Think of this in terms of how children naturally respond to rules. When you tell a child not to do something, it only arouses his curiosity to do the very thing he has been told not to do. When you tell Billy not to write on the wall, what does Billy do? He scribbles on the wall. When you tell Johnny not to pull Sally's ponytail, what happens? Sally tattles on Johnny for yanking her ponytail. Get the picture? Truth be told, that's the way adults are too. We all have that hidden desire to do what we're told not to do and many times we end up doing it. Many of you are saying, *"But I don't actually sin, I'm just being tempted."* (I will deal with this further in chapter 25). However, for now, remember the Bible teaches us that when we imagine sinning it is the same thing as actually sinning. When there is a constant emphasis on striving to obey the Law, it literally gives fuel to the fire of sin. In fact, the Bible teaches us that the purpose of the Law was to show us our utter hopelessness and desperate need for a Savior. St. Augustine once said, *"The usefulness of the Law lies in convicting man of his infirmity and moving him to call upon the remedy of Grace in Christ."* In other words, the Law is like a strict schoolmaster (tutor, taskmaster, slave driver, slave master) sent to drive us to futility in order to force us to surrender to Grace through faith in Jesus Christ...

"Wherefore THE LAW WAS OUR SCHOOL MASTER to bring us unto Christ, that we might be justified by faith. But after that faith is come, we are no longer under a schoolmaster. For ye are all the children of God BY FAITH IN CHRIST JESUS." (Galatians 3:24-26 KJV)

Once we were slaves under that brutal taskmaster called *The Law* but now we are free under the new and loving *Life of Grace* through Jesus. We don't maintain our righteousness by *obeying* the Law. We become children of God by *believing* in Jesus and accepting His free gift of righteousness. It is not difficult to be righteous, as many believe. Why? Because we are not saved by strict performance of the Law! We are saved by simple faith in Jesus! IN CHRIST we are made fully righteous, totally justified and forever free through the finished work of Jesus. That's what it means to live on the side of Grace. According to John 8:32, when you *"know the truth"* (embracing it with full acceptance) only then are you able to experience true freedom (John 8:32). In this verse, the Greek word for *"know"* is *ginosko*. It is a Jewish idiom describing the sexual relations between a man and a woman. It denotes deep intimacy and close relationship. When you become deeply intimate and fully confident in the *knowledge* of what

Christ has done for you through His finished work, nothing will be able to convince you otherwise. As you become rooted and steadfastly settled in your righteousness it will have a profound effect upon the way you live your life (Ephesians 3:17-20). *Knowing* that nothing can separate you from the love of God calms every doubt and soothes every fear. Only this kind of assurance can break the power of sin in your life. The *"truth"* spoken of in John 8:23 is not talking about the Law. Rather, it is speaking of the *truth of God's Grace* that sets us free. The Children of Israel were under the Law for 1500 years and were always in bondage to it. They were never free under the Law. So the 'truth' spoken of in John 8:32 could not be talking about the Ten Commandments. Only Grace releases the power that truly sets us free from the guilt, condemnation and imputation of sin. Hallelujah!

Social Grace

There is another necessary truth to briefly interject here. Not only does the Law remind us of our *falleness* and drive us to our need for a Savior; it is also important in that it sets the standard in which society can dwell together in relative harmony. The Ten Commandments not only shows us how far we are from holiness but also provides a basis in which society can peacefully co-exist without totally caving in on and eventually destroying itself. Why do you think most people think it is wrong to murder, steal, defraud, commit adultery, etc.? It is because once the Law was revealed it aroused a moral social conscious within us. This is where the term "social Grace" comes from. Social Grace isn't just possessing good table manners or helping old ladies cross the street. Social Grace (founded on God's Laws) prevents injustice. While it is true that there have been many cases (small and extreme) when humankind has committed horrible social injustices (i.e. world wars, attempted genocide, prejudice, etc.), man knows the consequences of breaking these Laws and therefore has sought as best as humanly possible to create protective means of promoting peace from domestic and local government all the way to international and world affairs. However, the Law, pure and holy as it is, cannot ultimately save society. God only can offer full salvation to humankind through faith in Jesus Christ alone. Grace will ultimately save the nations through God's Kingdom rule (Matthew 6:10).

A Brief Grammar Lesson[4]

"The Law was given by Moses but Grace and truth CAME by Jesus Christ." (John 1:17 NASB)

Adjust your microscope and take a closer look again at John 1:17 above. Notice I have emphasized the word *'came'* by highlighting it in **bold**. One Greek rendering of *'came'* is the word *'subsists'* (notice the letter *'s'* on the end of the word). *Subsists* means *to exist in*. Jesus was the epitome of Grace and truth (John 1:14 KJV). It is important to note that the word *subsists* is a singular verb. Thus, according to the rules of grammar, a singular noun must precede it. However, at first glance it appears that *"Grace and truth"* are plural (two different things). If this were so, the correct rendering should be, *"Grace and truth subsist"* (no *'s'* on the end of the word). For example you don't say, *"Sam and Sally **sings**.* Rather you say*, "Sam and Sally **sing.***" Therefore, the word *subsists* (singular verb) denotes that *Grace and truth* are singular! This means that *Grace and truth* are functionally equivalent (one-in-the-same thing). In other words, Grace and truth are synonymous with each other. Another possible rendering would be *"the truth about God's Grace."* It is the truth about God's Grace that sets us free. Jesus said in John 14:6, *"I am the truth."* Jesus is truth (Romans 9:1). When you know the truth you know Grace. When you know Grace you know the truth. This is the gospel that saves and delivers the broken and the lost (Romans 1:16).

Truth is Grace! Living in Grace is living in the truth. Truth isn't just a collection of facts or information. It's something you *know* deep in your heart. When you *know* truth you know a person. Jesus said, *"I am the truth"* (John 14:6). You can actually have a relationship with the truth. Truth isn't a list of rules to obey. Truth is experiencing the love of Jesus. Truth is love. To know the love of Christ that surpasses all cerebral knowledge will cause us to be filled with all of God's fullness. And when you are filled with all of God there is no room for sin to assume residency and exercise power over you...

"And to know the love of Christ which surpasses knowledge, that you may be filled up to all the fullness of God." (Ephesians 3:19 NASB)

A Stark Contrast

Look carefully again at John 1:17. *"The Law was given by Moses but Grace and truth CAME by Jesus Christ."* Now compare the contrasts below. Notice that TRUTH and GRACE are on the same side.

THE LAW	GRACE & TRUTH
Moses	Jesus Christ
Given	Came

The first miracle that was performed under the Law was the turning of the Nile into blood, signifying judgment and death (Exodus 17:19-25). However, the first miracle of Jesus (the person of Grace) was the turning of water into wine at the wedding of Cana, signifying joy, celebration and newness of life in the Spirit (John 2:1-11). Under the Law, Moses had to take off his shoes because of the awesome dread and unapproachable holiness of God (Exodus 3:5). Under Grace, the father of the prodigal son tells his servants to put shoes on his son's feet, signifying that we are made worthy and welcome to stand in the father's presence (Luke 15:22). Compare the ending verses of the Old and New Testament. The last verse in the Old Testament is, *"Lest I come and strike the earth with a CURSE"* (Malachi 4:6). The last verse of the New Testament is, *"The GRACE of our Lord Jesus Christ be with you all. Amen."* (Revelation 22:21) By the way, the last book of the Bible (God's final word on the matter) is called Revelation not *Regulations*. Jesus is known as Immanuel not *a manual* (Isaiah 7:14).

Why is all of this so this important? It is because many feel that when you preach Grace, you must also preach the *"truth."* This meaning you must abide by the regulations of the Law and receive Grace to maintain a perfect standard of holiness. In other words, you have to teach people to *"live right"* or else it will not properly balance the message of Grace. In essence this tells us that Grace needs "balancing" because it cannot stand alone. The purpose of teaching of the Law is to more fully illustrate the futility of the Law in order that Grace can be accurately seen and truthfully discerned. However, we must be clear. we are only saved by Grace and not the works of the Law (Ephesians 2:7-8). No one was or will ever be set free by teaching the rules or the condition of man's soul. When you tell someone that they are a sinner and are going to hell, you are preaching the *condition*, not the *good news*. This only makes people angry and more determined to rebel against God. Next time you see someone in bondage to sin, tell him that he is going to hell and see what it accomplishes. Pastor Tullian Tchvidjian says it like this, *"If you want people outside the church to be mad, preach the Law. If you want people inside the church to be mad, preach Grace."*

The fact is people are inherently aware of their moral depravity (although they won't admit it). Paul calls it being *"without excuse"* (Romans 1:18-20 & 5:13). However, when people are constantly reminded of their sin it usually infuriates them and prompts a negative or defensive response. I am not talking about the real need for people to confront their sin. It is absolutely necessary for people to confront their sin head on in order to properly deal with it. Living in denial is potentially deadly. On the other hand I am not advocating that we analyze our sin to the point of frustration. We must remember that to deal with sin head on we must run into Jesus head on. That is the best way to overcome our sin. We overcome in HIS victory. The truth is, when we preach the message of Jesus in harsh and condemning tones it ultimately doesn't serve toward our benefit or the transformation of the sinner. As a general rule, most sinners (even though they can't explain it) feel an inner sense of emptiness and guilt because they know that somewhere deep down they are separated from their Creator. This explains why so many actors, musicians and wealthy philanthropists work overtime to appease their moral conscious by creating charities for the poor and diseased in futile attempts to relieve their guilt. Don't be deceived; much of what some deem as "humanitarian effort" is not birthed out of a true sense of compassion and moral conviction but rather motivated by some self-promoting form of ethical penitence. The truth is, when the Law is preached people come under greater bondage (1 Corinthians 15:56). When you accentuate the depraved condition of a sinner's soul it pushes him farther away. People need to hear the good news of great joy that God loves them so much He sent His only Son to save them from their sin and offer them the promise of eternal salvation. There is something about Grace that is hard for people to resist. We need to trust God's Grace above trying to stir up contention in people's hearts. Manipulation and fear tactics usually backfire anyway. Notice, God didn't give an ultimatum to the world. Rather he sent His Son to die in order to captivate sinners and compel them to respond to His love…

"For God so greatly loved and dearly prized the world that He [even] gave up His only begotten (unique) Son, so that whoever believes in (trusts in, clings to, relies on) Him shall not perish (come to destruction, be lost) but have eternal (everlasting) life."
(John 3:16 AMP)

IN CHRIST Status[15]

It is important to have a supernatural revelation and a solid Biblical understanding of our IN CHRIST status because everything He is, we are also. Having such knowledge of all Christ is will cause us to have the confidence to stand firm. As God's love is perfected in us, we escape the judgment from condemnation IN CHRIST. In other words, since Christ is perfectly acceptable in God's sight; so are we…

"Herein is our love made PERFECT, that we may have boldness in the day of judgment: because AS HE IS SO ARE WE IN THIS WORLD."
(1 John 4:17 KJV)

The *"day of judgment"* here refers to the *moment* we feel judged. Knowing we've been made perfect IN CHRIST empowers us with boldness and releases us from judgment. As Jesus is, so are we: perfect, blameless, and well pleasing to God. That's how God sees us. Matthew 3:16-17 tells us when Jesus was baptized the Heavens opened and His Father declared, *"This is My beloved Son with whom I am well pleased."* Immediately after this in Matthew 4:10, satan began to tempt and revile Jesus by saying, *"If You are the Son of God…"* Notice satan said, *"IF"* and also left out a very important word: BELOVED! Satan tried to make Jesus doubt that He was His Father's BELOVED son. If Satan can deceive you into doubting that you are not loved and accepted he'll have you right where he wants you: discouraged, disappointed, and defeated. However, when you realize that the Heavens ARE opened above you and that you ARE fully loved and accepted by God, His BELOVED, you will begin to live and operate in confidence, power and authority.

44

> "To the praise of the glory of His Grace, which He freely bestowed on us in the BELOVED. In Him we have redemption through His blood, the forgiveness of our trespasses, according to the riches of His Grace, which He lavished on us. In all wisdom and insight."
> (Ephesians 1:6-8 NASB)

Condemnation has no power over you when you believe you are God's BELOVED! Confidence in God's love for you destroys the power of condemnation and fear. God is not just pleased with you. He is WELL PLEASED with you because you are IN CHRIST. We can confidently approach God even though we may have failed or struggle with certain sin issues in our lives...

> "In whom we have boldness and access with confidence through faith in Him." (Ephesians 3:12 KJV)

Grow In – Grow Up

IN CHRIST you are ALL that He is and can have all He has (1 John 4:17). As you receive the abundance of this truth, you will mature in every aspect of His character. The scriptures tell us that we can actually reflect Jesus' very nature.

> "We are to GROW UP in all aspects INTO HIM who is the head, even CHRIST." (Ephesians 4:15 NASB)

In order to grasp this you must realize that you don't grow by *striving* to be perfect! When you realize you are ALREADY perfect IN CHRIST, life transformation is imminent. There is no such thing as *spiritual growth.* Many would argue this but consider for a moment... When you are born again you are born of Heaven. Even as a brand new believer you are mighty IN CHRIST. It is not a baby Jesus that dwells inside of you. Your SPIRIT man is incorruptible, fully mature, and fully loaded with all the spiritual DNA you need to become all God has created you to be. This revelation will revolutionize your life. You don't receive embryonic righteousness when you are born again then grow to adolescent and then on to adult righteousness. NO! The moment you receive Christ into your life you take on ALL the divine nature of God Himself (1 Peter 1:4). Unless your eyes are opened to this truth you will never rise above substandard living (Ephesians 1:18-19). The Bible doesn't say to be transformed by the renewing of your spirit. It says to be transformed by the renewing of your MIND (Romans 12:1-2). Your mind is where most of your problems lie: you don't see yourself for who you are IN CHRIST and who He is in you (Colossians 1:7). However, when you begin to wrap your mind around the truth that you ARE the righteousness OF GOD through Christ, change naturally occurs. Beloved, you are as righteous AS GOD (1 Corinthians 1:30; 2 Corinthians 5:21; Philippians 3:9).

I've heard some say that Grace is good but at some point we need to grow up. Friend, it is impossible to grow apart from Grace. It isn't get Grace and then move on to more lofty spiritual heights. Grace isn't the primer or the ABC's of the gospel. It's the A to Z! We never graduate from Grace. To GROW UP is to GROW IN the revelation of who Jesus is and who He is IN YOU. Having a greater enlightenment and deeper appreciation of the impact that Grace has already made in you is the key to maturity in every area of your life.

Chapter 4

BULLETPROOF

**"And having put on the breastplate of righteousness."
(Ephesians 6:14 NASB)**

Our righteousness (right-standing) with God has been made complete by Jesus' finished work on the cross. It is not what we do for God but it is what God has already done for us. We cannot earn favor with God. When we live in this truth we will find ourselves living better for God accidentally than we ever could on purpose.[3] As we allow God's Grace to invade our hearts His holiness becomes irresistible. In other words, through Grace we simply won't be able to resist living holy lives. The truth is, we don't get good to be righteous. We get righteousness to be good. We must arm ourselves with the knowledge that we are righteous and that only by Grace can we stand confidently before God with a clear conscious...

**"Stand firm therefore, HAVING GIRDED YOUR LOINS WITH TRUTH, and HAVING PUT ON THE BREASTPLATE OF RIGHTEOUSNESS..."
(Ephesians 6:14 NASB)**

Paul clearly instructs us that we are to arm ourselves with the breastplate of righteousness. The Roman breastplate protected the vital organs (including the heart) from injury and also the back from undetected attacks. Today it would be like wearing a bulletproof vest. When our heart (mind, will & emotions) tells us that we have lost our righteousness from spiritual misdemeanors we can stand firm in the armor of Christ's righteousness regardless of our poor performance.

Please understand I am not advocating that Grace gives us permission to sin (Romans 6:1-4). This book was not written to justify the sinner to continue in his sin, but to encourage precious believers who struggle with condemnation and help them hunger after a deeper relationship with Jesus and a passionate desire for holiness. I want to make abundantly clear that I hate sin and what it does to people. Sin is devastating and ruins lives. Yet we have a consolation IN CHRIST and because of God's Grace we can have TOTAL VICTORY over the devil in every area of our lives.[20] It is when we try to live for God in our own strength that we eventually run out of energy and end up failing miserably. My teachings on Grace are not intended to lift the boundaries or warnings against a sinful *lifestyle.*

The gospel of Grace is extremely difficult to grasp, especially for religious people who claim they have *mastered* victory over failure. This may sound foolish, but if I were to ask some people if they had sinned this past week, they would say with proud conviction, *"No, not me!"* Spiritual pride seriously misguides us into thinking that we are made Godly by our good works (1 John 1:10). However, through Grace, the new convert is as Godly as the person who has been a Christian for many years. How? Why? Because good works do not make us Godly (Ephesians 2:7-9)! Only the blood of Jesus cleanses us of unrighteousness, keeps us perpetually clean and makes us worthy to stand in God's presence...

"And the blood of Jesus His Son cleanses us from all sin."
(1 John 1:7 NASB)

Christ's blood cleanses us from ALL sin. Be sure that we can NEVER be righteous by our goodness towards God but by GOD'S goodness towards us. That's why Jesus did for us what we could never do...

"Therefore there is now no condemnation for those who are IN CHRIST Jesus. For the Law of the Spirit of life IN CHRIST Jesus has set you free from the Law of sin and of death. FOR WHAT THE LAW COULD NOT DO, WEAK AS IT WAS THROUGH THE FLESH, GOD DID SENDING HIS OWN SON IN THE LIKENESS OF SINFUL FLESH AND AS AN OFFERING FOR SIN, He condemned sin in the flesh so that the requirement of the Law might be fulfilled in us, who do not walk according to the flesh but according to the Spirit." (Romans 8:1-4 NASB)

Paul tells us here that we are free from Sin's power over us. True, we may fail from time to time, but Sin can never *master* us again. Jesus is our master now. Sin can never have power over those who live on the side of Grace...

"For SIN SHALL NOT BE MASTER OVER YOU, for you are not under Law but UNDER GRACE." (Romans 6:14 NASB)

The Greek word for *'master'* is *'kyrieuo,'* which means to *exercise influence upon.* When we quit trying to live holy in order to be acceptable to God, sin loses its power over us, our desire for sin weakens and our desire for God increases. To get OVER sin we must get UNDER Grace. In his writings, the apostle Paul constantly drove home the truth of being made righteous by God's Grace alone. He was also trying to retrain the minds of those who had been heckled by the Judaizers that righteousness came only through good works. Therefore, Paul warned them to arm themselves with the constant reassurance that they were acceptable to God simply by believing in His Grace. Having faith in God's Grace deflects the bullets of fear and condemnation the enemy discharges in our direction. Rest assured, the devil will hurl rounds of guilt our way but when we are confident in the truth that we are righteous apart from our own efforts, we stand bulletproof in the line of fire!

The Armor of Grace

Using the items of the Roman soldier's armor, Paul powerfully illustrated how we are to arm ourselves against condemnation (Ephesians 6:10-17). We typically refer to it as the 'Armor of God.' However, in context of Paul's defense of the gospel and the theme of this book, I submit that it *could* be called the Armor of *Grace.*

> **"Finally, be strong in the Lord and in the strength of His might. Put on the full armor of God, so that you will be able to stand firm against the schemes of the devil. For our struggle is not against flesh and blood, but against the rulers, against the powers, against the world forces of this darkness, against the spiritual forces of wickedness in the heavenly places." (Ephesians 6:10-13 NASB)**

The scheme of the devil has never changed. He has always used the handwritten requirements of the Law (Colossians 2:14-15) as a weapon against God's people to discourage and demobilize us. But God has seized the weapon of condemnation out of his hand and spoiled his strategy, making a public mockery out of him. Nevertheless, the enemy is relentless in his efforts to frustrate our peace and obstruct our progress. This is why we must, as verses 11-13 tell us, *"stand firm"* in the liberty of God's Grace.

The Holster of Truth

"Therefore, take up the full armor of God, so that you will be able to resist in the evil day, and having done everything, to stand firm. Stand firm therefore, HAVING GIRDED YOUR LOINS WITH TRUTH..."
(Ephesians 6:14a NASB)

The truth is not the moral code of the Law (as we have previously discussed). The truth Paul is speaking of here is the buckle (if you will) that *fastens* or holds us together in God's Grace. It literally keeps us from falling apart under condemnation and fear. Also, remember that the Law never set anyone free. Jesus is THE truth (John 8:32) that sets us free from bondage to the Law and empowers us to live above reproach to sin. The truth of God's Grace prevents us from dropping our protective armor thereby exposing our hearts to the enemy's attacks.

The Bulletproof Vest of Righteousness

"Having put on the breastplate of righteousness..."
(Ephesians 6:14b NASB)

As previously mentioned, the Roman soldier's breastplate covered him front-to-back thereby protecting his vital organs, particularly his heart. The enemy will shoot his fiery darts our way attempting to *dishearten* us when we fail God. However, when we stand behind our breastplate of righteousness, believing that we are righteous based on Christ's finished work alone, nothing the enemy can say or do can convince us otherwise.

The Combat Boots of Peace

"And having shod your feet with the preparation of the gospel of peace..."(Ephesians 6:15 NASB)

Paul often began his letters with salutations of *"Grace and Peace"* (13 different times in the New Testament to be exact). The gospel (the good news of God's Grace) produces a calm reassurance that we are at peace with God in spite of our failure to measure up to His perfect standard. We will never be at peace trying to be perfect. That's why

God gave us Jesus. Only Jesus meets God's standard of perfection. When we walk in the steadfast confidence that we are IN CHRIST and that God looks at us with pleasure in His eyes it will cause us to fall in love with Him over and over again! How can we keep falling into sin if we are constantly falling in love with Jesus? God's peace negates all fear of condemnation and keeps us from doubting in our salvation!

The Shield of Faith

"In addition to all, taking up the shield of faith with which you will be able to extinguish all the flaming arrows of the evil one..."
(Ephesians 6:16 NASB)

King David proclaimed that God's truth was his buckler (Psalms 91:4). A Roman shield (or *buckler* as it was called) was perfect for close hand-to-hand combat. Firmly strapped to the arm of the soldier, it was just the right size and weight for fending off an opponent's blows while allowing full dexterity to *return them.* Faith in God's Grace is how we fight off satan's attacks. Paul instructed us to fight the GOOD fight of FAITH (1 Timothy 6:12). Sometimes it's a fight to stand firm in God's Grace. However, it is a GOOD fight because the enemy cannot defeat us when we spiritually secure IN CHRIST'S victory!

The Helmet of Salvation

"And take THE HELMET OF SALVATION..." (Ephesians 6:17a NASB)

Our mind is the primary battlefield where the arguments rage regarding our peace with God and the assurance of our salvation (2 Corinthians 10:4-5). It is difficult to wrap our minds around the truth that we are acceptable to God even when we fall short in certain areas of our lives. However, when we settle in our minds once and for all that we are made righteous by faith we receive the power to overcome sin through Christ's finished work.

The Sword of the Spirit

"And the sword of the Spirit, which is the word of God."
(Ephesians 6:17b NASB)

The pieces of armor described so far are protective gear designed to defend us against the enemy from fear and condemnation. They deflect the bullets of satan's lies fired against us. However, there is one more item that is an offensive weapon against the devil: The Word of God. We must consistently believe and receive what the scriptures say about our righteousness in order to cut off the attack of the *father of lies* and the *accuser of the brethren* (Revelation 12:10). We don't study the Bible to make God pleased with us. God *already* takes great pleasure in us (Psalms 149:4). The reason we study the Bible is because we need to thoroughly understand our New Covenant IN CHRIST. Though the devil may empty his arsenal of artillery on us, when we are full of the Word of God regarding who we are, what we have and what we can do IN CHRIST, satan's condemnation ricochets off our bulletproof armor right back in His direction.

"No weapon that is formed against you will prosper; and every tongue that accuses you in judgment you will condemn. This is the heritage of the servants of the LORD, and their vindication is from Me, declares the LORD." (Isaiah 54:17 NASB)

IN CHRIST'S total sufficiency we are protected by impenetrable Grace. Although we may feel the blunt, bruising force of the battle of life on the outside, inside we are completely invulnerable and safe from vital spiritual defeat. Grace seals all possible entry points of sin's piercing and permanent damage (Ephesians 4:7).

Chapter 5

A LETHAL MIXTURE

"Nor do people put new wine into old wineskins; otherwise the wineskins burst and the wine pours out and the wineskins are ruined." (Matthew 9:17 NASB)

Throughout the scriptures it is evident that certain mixtures are detestable to God. For instance, God would not allow Ishmael (man made schemes) to dwell in the same tent with Isaac (God's way to the promise). Jesus Himself said in our key passage when we put new wine (new covenant of Grace) into old wine skins (Old Covenant of the Law) the wineskins will burst and all the good wine (Grace) will spill out and be wasted. The book of Revelation further supports this idea of God's distaste for certain mixtures.

"I know your works, that you are neither cold nor hot. I could wish you were cold or hot. So then, because you are lukewarm, and neither cold nor hot, I will vomit you out of My mouth." (Revelation 3:15-16 NASB)

Here God clearly addresses the Laodicean church's *lukewarmness* issue. Look carefully again... He says, *"I know your WORKS that you are neither hot nor cold."* God is pointing directly at the *reason* they are lukewarm. Reliance on self-works always produces lukewarm living. Hot and cold water both serve a specific purpose. Hot water purifies while cold water refreshes. However, lukewarmness doesn't serve any purpose but to be poured out on the ground (or vomited as is the case). When we stop striving to earn favor with God through self-effort and live on the side of Grace we will be ablaze for God while at the same time appealing to a world desperately looking for hope. When the church learns to embrace Grace we will be the envy of the nations. God desires His people to experience and model the extremely abundant Life He has promised through His Grace.

Religion is a putrid concoction of man-made formulas created to earn God's approval. God abhors such sickening brews. The story of the Tower of Babel is such an example (Genesis 11:1-9). The people committed to reach the Heavens on their own initiative in order to *get to God.* God was not impressed and steadfastly resisted their pride. The result? Total catastrophe! Their efforts only ended in confusion, frustration and futility. Nothing but a big pile of dirt equivalent to a modern day landfill remains. That is what our self-efforts to become Godly produce. Rubbish! Often the church demands of its people that they ascribe to certain credos outside of simple faith in Jesus to become acceptable to God. As a born again believer, you will never be more acceptable to God than you are right now. The Old Covenant system of rules and regulation to attain holiness involved intense personal effort in order to be accepted by God. However, since Christ has come, in order to have a relationship with God, all you must do is trust in Jesus by simple faith. Religion makes it hard to know God. Jesus makes it easy! Look what the Apostle Peter said about people going back to live under the Old Covenant system of the Law once they had been introduced to the New Covenant of Grace.

> "**If they have escaped the corruption of the world by knowing our Lord and Savior Jesus Christ (The person of Grace not a doctrine) and are again entangled in it and overcome, they are worse off at the end than they were at the beginning. It would have been better for them not to have known the way of righteousness (being saved by Grace through faith not of works), than to have known it and then to turn their backs on the sacred command that was passed on to them. Of them the proverbs are true: 'A dog returns to its vomit,' (the old system of the Law) and, 'A sow that is washed goes back to her wallowing in the mud (trying to be righteous through self-effort)" (2 Peter 2:20-2 NIV)**[37]

The very thought of the putrid mixture of Law and Grace is nauseating to God. In light of this, there is another implication of Revelation 3:15-16 regarding *hot and cold* that we need to consider. God would prefer we live by the Law (cold) because at least eventually we would come to the end of our own self-efforts to be righteous and be driven by our need for a Savior and accept His free gift of Grace (or) He would much rather we be hot (accept Grace) and fully embrace the love that saves us apart from our own striving. God will not puke us out because WE make Him nauseous. Rather it's the rancid TASTE of Law and Grace mixed together that He despises.

Falling From Grace

Paul clearly pointed out in his writings that when we try to maintain holiness through obedience to the Law we mix the Law and Grace together which in effect, cancels out the power of Grace. Paul used the words *"fallen from Grace"* to further explain this. Let's closely examine what this phrase means in the following passage.

> **"Christ is become of no effect unto you (Grace is neutralized), whosoever of you are justified by the Law (think you are justified by what you do for God). You are fallen from Grace (returned to the old system of the Law)... You were running so well (embracing Grace and experiencing spiritual fruitfulness); who hindered you from obeying the truth (the truth of God's Grace)... A little leaven (living by the religious teachings of the Old Covenant) leavens the whole lump (neutralizes the effects of Grace)." (Galatians 5:4-9 KJV)[37]**

This passage is often misused when teaching Grace. I used to believe that *"falling from Grace,"* meant losing my righteousness. Not so! When understood in it's proper context this passage is talking about *losing your grip* and *letting go* of God's GRACE, thus *sliding back* into the old system of WORKS. Look what happens when we walk in the *flesh* (work to earn God's favor).

> **"But I say, walk by the spirit (live on the side of God's Grace), and you will not carry out the desire of the flesh (end up wearing out from self effort). For the flesh sets its desire against the Spirit and the Spirit against the flesh (Law and Grace are polar opposites of each other); for these are in opposition to one another (Law and Grace don't mix), so that you may not do the things that you please (do the right thing). But if you are led by the Spirit (the way of Grace) you are not under the Law (obligated to perform perfectly) to gain God's favor). Now the deeds of the flesh (self-effort) are evident, which are immorality, impurity, sensuality, idolatry sorcery, enmities, strife, jealousy, outbursts of anger, disputes, dissensions, factions, envying, drunkenness, carousing and things like these... (Galatians 5:16-25 NASB)[37]**

I always thought this passage taught us to strive for holiness so that the fruit of the Holy Spirit would manifest in our lives. Yet so many people find themselves living the opposite of what they strive so hard for. Ironic! How is it that so many people fail to produce spiritual fruit in their lives after being so diligent to obey God? It is because when we live BY *fleshly* efforts to be righteous we produce fleshly results. The only way to bear true spiritual fruit is to be led by the Spirit (receive Grace).

But the fruit of the Spirit is (the byproduct of Grace will produce) love, joy, peace, patience, kindness, goodness, faithfulness, gentleness, self-control; against such things there is no Law (the Law could never produce this kind of life)." (Galatians 5:16-25 NASB)[37]

In high school football practice we were forced to run up a 100-foot hill of mud affectionately called *The Hill.* The coach would scream at us to dash to the top as the entire team cLawed their way to total exhaustion. Relying on self works, is like trying to run up that mound of mud in the pouring rain. Although we might make it up a few times, eventually we would *slide back* to the bottom totally covered in the soot of our self-efforts. A life of works is truly a slippery slope. No one can keep up a life of works forever. This is the reason many *backslide,* in their relationship with God even to the point of becoming a menace to themselves and others. Self-righteousness will always drag you back down into the ditch of a sinful lifestyle. Although it is impossible to slide out of God's love, we can slip so far as to lose our *sense* of connection to God, which has the potential of having devastating affects on our future here on earth. The way to keep from sliding backwards is to keep our grip on God's Grace. Besides, we can't hold God up with our efforts anyway. God's Grace holds us up. When we quit trying to work for God's love, God's love will work for us!

Don't Lean on Grace

Once after ministering in a service the pastor approached me and said, *"In my teachings I lean more towards the side of Grace."* to which I wistfully replied, *"I don't lean on the side of Grace. I LIVE on the side of Grace!"* We set ourselves up for failure if we keep one foot landlocked on the side of legalism and the other dabbling around on the side of Grace. The only way to escape the vicious cycle of defeat is to totally surrender and fully commit to living on the side of God's Grace. Thereby, we allow His power to produce the fruit of true change and explosive transformation in our lives. Living by self-effort exhausts us until we eventually give in to the very things we strive not to do. Self-reliance = God defiance. In his writings, Paul revealed his own struggle to produce righteousness through self-effort. Eventually he came to the end of himself and declared...

"For what I am doing, I do not understand (why do I keep failing God when I try to do good); for I am not practicing what I would like to do (I am not doing what I should do), but I am doing the very thing I hate (sin is overpowering me)... For I know that nothing good dwells in me, that is, in my flesh (my flesh is incapable of producing anything good no matter how hard I try)... O wretched man that I am (I'm totally frustrated) Who shall deliver me from the body of this death? (life of struggling to be righteous)... Not that we are sufficient of ourselves to think anything as of ourselves (our own strength is futile and our own efforts to perform perfectly will ultimately fail us); but our sufficiency is of God (God's Grace is the only way to have victory over sin)... And He (God) said unto me, 'My GRACE is sufficient for you; for MY strength (God's Power) is made perfect in weakness (When I stop trying God starts doing)" (Romans 7:15,18,24 & 2 Corinthians 3:5; 12:9 NASB)[37]

Grace mixed with self-righteousness is the formula for disaster. If we try to strive by the Law while trying to live in God's Grace, it will not produce the results God intended. In fact when we try to combine the two together (like two dangerous chemicals) it will blow up in our face! Just like drinking and driving don't mix... Neither does Grace and works... It's a deadly combination!

Rejecting Grace

"But the Spirit explicitly says in later times some will fall away from the faith, paying attention to deceitful spirits and doctrines of demons." (1 Timothy 4:1 NASB)

The passage above has caused much debate over the years. Many Bible teachers, through maniupulation and fear tactics, have mishandled this verse (and other like it) in an attempt to control believers and prevent them from *falling away* from their salvation. However, to better understand what Paul is saying, carefully ponder the flow of this passage and the two verses that follow it.

"But the Spirit explicitly says (Paul authoritatively speaking from deep spiritual revelation) that in later times some (religious leaders) will fall away from (completely disregard and reject) the faith (the way of

Grace), paying attention to deceitful spirits and doctrines of demons (legalistic standards imposed by religious leaders). By means of hypcocrisy of liars (religious Jews) seared in their own conscience (unable to be convinced of the legitimacy of Grace) as with a branding iron, men who forbid marriage and advocate abstaining from foods (Pharasical preservers of the Law) which God has created to be gratefully shared in by those who believe and know the truth (those who have accepted their salvation by Grace through faith)." (1 Timothy 4:1-3 NASB)[37]

The hypocritic *"liars"* Paul refers to are those religious naysayers who are seared in their conscious to the extent that they are unable to be convinced in the possibilty of the truth of the gospel of Grace. Paul also refers to the religious Pharsees as Hypocrite just as Jesus Himself did (Matthew 23:13). Verse 1 is not describing those who have accepted Christ and then reject Him. According to verse 4 it is clearly referring to those who deny and resist ALTOGETHER the notion that you can be saved by Grace through faith in Jesus alone. These religious leaders (like many today) chose from the start to reject the Grace message because they were ensnared by their own religious pracitces regarding such things as the forbidding of marriage and abstaining from certain foods, Etc. Paul called these things *"deceitful spirits and doctrines of demons."* In other words it is a demonic deception to think that ahering to regulations could save anybody. Paul goes on to say that these people *"pay attention"* (or draw attention) to their good works (which is the ultimate deception) and as a result reject putting their faith in God's Grace. Another very important thing to consider is the literal meaning of the words *"fall away."* The Greek translation is *apostesontai*, which is where we get our English word *apostasy*. Look at some of it's following meanings...

To stand off, withdraw, go away, depart from

To excite others to revolt against

To desert, become faithless

To shun or flee from

To keep or remove one's self from

Religiously *seared* people stand off, reject, shun and even cause others to revolt against the message of Grace. The apostates spoken of here do not include those who once having trusted in Christ and then turn away. They consist only those who absolutely and categorically deny the gospel of Grace. In conclusion, 1 Timothy 4:1 foretells us that many religious people will *fall* into that category.[31]

A Fungus Among Us

Jesus warned His disciples of the religious naysayers who contended with the pure message of the gospel of Grace.

"Watch out and beware of the leaven... The teaching of the Pharisees and Sadducees." (Matthew 16:6,12 NASB)

Leaven is yeast. By definition yeast is a fungi that is used in the fermenting process or for baking bread. Hello people! Did you hear me (as I tap the microphone)? Leaven is a FUNGUS! The Pharisees and Sadducees (two staunch religious sects of Jesus' day) taught that the Law and good works make us righteous. This was their primary 'doctrine.' Jesus cautioned His disciples to avoid their teachings like the plague. Paul put it this way...

"Beware of the dogs (religious leaders), beware of the evil workers (false teachers), beware of the false circumcision (teaching that the requirements of the Law save us)." (Philippians 3:2 NASB)[37]

Why avoid the doctrine that the Law makes us righteous? Because a little bit of leaven (Law teaching) leavens the whole lump (totally neutralizes Grace).

"Your boasting is not good. Do you not know that a little leaven leavens the whole lump of dough?" (1 Corinthians 5:6 NASB)

This passage regarding leaven has been used many times as an illustration of what sin does in our lives, meaning that a little sin un-dealt with will eventually overtake us and hold us captive. However, the word *leaven* in this particular context here is not being compared to sin. It is being compared to the FALSE TEACHING that good works make us righteous. It's ludicrous to think we have anything to do with making ourselves righteous. Even a *tiny little bit* of self-effort leavens (totally neutralizes) the effects of Grace. Don't misunderstand me. I am not saying we shouldn't value and teach the Ten Commandments nor am I proposing that we shouldn't do good works, live holy, serve others, be benevolent, show compassion or behave generously, courteously and charitably. Martin Luther once said, *"God doesn't need our good works but our neighbor does."* However, that being said, we shouldn't teach that the Law and good works make us holy. Rather, we should teach that the Law and good works only POINT us to a holy God. We can never live up to God's standard on our own. Only through Christ are we deemed holy in God's eyes. We are saved by Grace alone. Mixing Law and Grace works like the fermentation process: a fungus that *sours* pure grape juice. It's not, *"Yes Grace but..."* or *"Grace is good however..."* We all know what follows. Like fungous yeast, the self-righteous attitude produces a putrid, gaseous stench from our lives. We must totally rely on God's Grace to produce the purity so longed for in the life of the believer. One miniscule of legalistic teaching infused with the gospel message completely cancels out the effects Grace. Also, dough infused with yeast takes a lot of *kneading*. Simply put, baking bread is *labor intensive.* Why, because the gas that yeast produces along with SELF RISING flour causes bread to inflate. In order to prepare the dough it has to be *punched* several times before it is ready for baking. Likewise, self-righteousness produces within us an undetectable smug arrogance causing us to impose legalistic demands of perfection on others and ourselves. Simply put, self-righteousness is the source of all fear and pride. When we fail we fear we *lose* God. When we succeed we feel we *are* God. Conversely, humility is the benchmark of a life that totally relies on God's Grace. Unleavened bread represents a life of humility that rejects self-reliance and instead trusts God's Grace, which produces the lovely aroma of a grateful and contrite heart.

"But thanks be to God, Who always leads us in triumph IN CHRIST, and manifests through us the sweet aroma of the knowledge of Him in every place." (2 Corinthians 2:14 NASB)

Another powerful Old Testament illustration we can glean Grace from is the shewbread of the Mosaic Tabernacle: the large unleavened wafers that were set before the Holy Place (Exodus 29:2-4). This is extremely symbolic for the New Covenant believer. We cannot come before God boasting in our own righteousness as if to believe we have earned the right to an audience with Him (2 Corinthians 3:5). To believe this is utter nonsense. We can approach Him only through faith in the finished work of Jesus and HIS righteousness...

"And may be found IN HIM, not having a righteousness of my own derived from the Law, but that which is through faith IN CHRIST, the righteousness which comes from God on the basis of faith." (Philippians 3:9 NASB)

Just as leaven 'puffs up' bread, thinking that we have anything to do with being righteous causes us to be *puffed up* with pride when we do good and deflated when we fail. We cannot boast before God in any good we do (1 Corinthians 1:29). The Pharisees strutted around like proud peacocks, gloating in their self-righteousness. Spiritual pride is the worst pride of all! Unleavened bread is symbolic of those who have renounced their self-sufficiency to accomplish anything good in and of themselves. The problem with being *puffed up* is that all it takes is just one pinprick of failure to totally let the air out of our spiritual pride. In light of this, we must constantly live in humble recognition of our dependency on God's Grace to cover and keep us. During the Exodus God wanted the Children of Israel to remember it was HIS POWER ALONE that saved them from the death angel (self-righteousness loves to take personal credit for only what God can do). Whenever the Israelites celebrated the Passover, God wanted them to remember that it was by no effort of their own that they possessed the Promised Land.

"Do not say in your heart when the LORD your God has driven them out before you, 'Because of my righteousness the LORD has brought me in to possess this land..." (Deuteronomy 9:4 NASB)

Notice also that unleavened bread is *flat*. In the Bible, whenever people entered the presence of God, they fell *flat* on their face. God's presence *flattens* our self-righteousness. The bread of flesh (self-effort) is crusty, stale and moldy. Only Jesus is living bread.

"I am the living bread that came down out of Heaven; if anyone eats of this bread, he will live forever; and the bread also which I will give for the life of the world is My flesh." (John 6:51 NASB)

Trusting in Jesus is the same as eating the bread of life. Jesus gave His flesh so we could stop using our flesh (self-efforts) to be righteous. Relying on our flesh profits nothing.

"It is the Spirit who gives life; the flesh profits nothing; the words that I have spoken to you are spirit and are life." (John 6:63 NASB)

Chapter 6

MAN IN THE MIRROR

"But one who looks intently at the perfect Law, the Law of liberty, and abides by it, not having become a forgetful hearer but an effectual doer, this man will be blessed in what he does." (James 1:25 NASB)

When we look into a natural mirror we can clearly see the image of who we are. However, the Word of God is our spiritual mirror. It shows us the true reflection of who we are IN CHRIST. Yet, often we forget who we are and in Whose image we were created. That's why it is important for us look into the Word often so that we can be reminded of God's perception of us. The two verses preceding this passage are particularly important for us to look at. They show us that if we are not living up to the fullest potential for our lives (being doers of the Word) it is because we forget what God's Word says about us.

"For if anyone is a hearer of the word and not a doer, he is like a man who looks at his natural face in a mirror; for once he has looked at himself and gone away, he has immediately forgotten what kind of person he was." (James 1:23-24 NASB)

When we look into the wrong mirror (i.e. negative opinions of others, personal insecurities, judgment from our skeptics, etc.) we will see a distorted picture of who we are and in turn be driven to live out what we see in ourselves. The more we focus on the Law we will see our transgressions.

"The Law came in so that the transgression would increase; but where sin increased, Grace abounded all the more... I would not have come to know sin except through the Law..." (Romans 5:20 & 7:7 NASB

Assuming you are a believer, whenever you look into the old dingy and cracked mirror of the Law (or interpretively, your own failure to be right), you see a marred self-image, which negatively affects your self-esteem. Just like a natural mirror, when you focus on all your flaws you see your whole self as flawed. But Grace is calling out from the mirror of the New Covenant to remind you that your sins are forgiven and that you are white as snow. God truly sees you as the *fairest of them all* (i.e. Snow White). If you could see what God sees you would see yourself constantly being formed into the likeness of Jesus (Galatians 4:19 & Philippians 1:6 NASB). This revelation will transform your thinking. It is important to have a Godly image of yourself because what you think will determine how you act towards God and others. This reminds me of an old sitcom I used to watch growing up called *Happy Days*. During the intro, Fonzie (the loverboy of the show) stands in front of the mirror to comb his hair and realizes that his hair is already combed and perfectly in place. He gives a cocky shrug of the shoulders as if to say, "*That's right! I always look so good, I don't even have to comb my hair.*" Often we are so *down* on ourselves for our shortcomings, failures and insecurities. But God's Word clearly teaches us that we are His *beloved* and that we are always accepted (Ephesians 1:6). We are beautiful to Him and He loves us. The perfect Law that Paul is talking about in our key passage is the *perfect Law of liberty* (Grace). Remember the Old Covenant was imperfect in that it could not save us. It only served to remind us that we are hopelessly in need of a Savior.

"For what the Law could not do, weak as it was through the flesh, God did: sending His own Son in the likeness of sinful flesh and as an offering for sin, He condemned sin in the flesh, SO THAT THE REQUIREMENT OF THE LAW MIGHT BE FULLFILLED IN US, who do not walk according to the flesh but according to the Spirit."
(Romans 8:3-4 NASB)

"Because by the works of the Law, no flesh will be justified in His sight; for through the Law comes the knowledge of sin."
(Romans 3:20 NASB)

All it takes is one glance at the Ten Commandments to see where we have failed. This is why we must constantly pour over the scriptures pertaining to our NEW COVENANT in God's Grace. Grasping the truth of all we are and all we have IN CHRIST will empower us to become *more effective doers* of the word. The Greek word for 'effectual' in our key passage is *energeo,* which means, to *be mighty in*. When we trust in our self-effort (the old system of works) we end up failing miserably every time. This is why we must receive an abundance of Grace teaching so we will be filled with the faith of God to release spiritual power for success in life and service (this includes power for prayer, worship, witnessing, overcoming temptation, serving others, bearing spiritual fruit, etc.).

The Doing Part

It has been said that our *doing* flows from *being.* Knowing, without a shadow of a doubt, that we belong to God creates a continuum to *BE LONGING.* In other words the urge or longing to think right and act right comes from a deep sense of our identity IN CHRIST (belonging to Him). Be certain that the *doing* part IS important. However, the *doing* isn't what makes us righteous. Rather the *doing* proves to the world that we are truly His and convinces them of the redeeming and saving power of Jesus. We can stare at the scriptures until our eyes get crossed and our brain gets sore but no change will come until we realize we belong to God. This will produce the authentic desire to do what is right. God's Grace does not give us permission to be lazy, passive and fatalistic. Grace is God's power in us to become super productive, bountifully fruitful and abundantly blessed in every area of our lives. When we look into the Word of God we will realize that there are needful changes to be made. However, these changes will occur only when we make a *heart* decision to take the necessary steps God reveals towards effective change (i.e. balancing a budget, developing a prayer life, setting health goals, forgiving those who have hurt us, etc.). Here is a simple equation to remember:

Revelation - Application = **Frustration**

Revelation + Application = **Transformation**

We will never be able to perform to God's *perfect* standard. God knows this and that's why He gives us His Grace. God Himself wants to perform *through us.* So often we struggle pointlessly to meet God's expectations when all we need do is simply rest on His ability to work in and through us. The only way we will ever be able to experience God's supernatural force performing through our lives is to fully accept the truth of the gospel of Grace. We are not made righteous by our *doing* but by our *believing.* Our belief shapes our behavior. Having faith-filled *thoughts* in God's Grace will produce faithful *actions*! Faith in God's Grace makes us effective doers.

> "For this reason we also constantly thank God that when you received the word of God which you heard from us, you accepted it not as the word of men, but for what it really is, the word of God, which also performs its work in you who believe." (1 Thessalonians 2:13-14 NASB)

Again, our righteousness is not of doing but of *believing*. We cannot gain right of entry to the Grace of God (pre or post salvation) by working. We only have access into the marvelous Grace of God by FAITH: betting all our chips (if you will) on the Grace of God to save us and continue it's atoning work in our lives.

> "Therefore, having been justified BY FAITH, we have peace with God through our Lord Jesus Christ, through Whom also WE HAVE ACCESS BY FAITH into this Grace in which we stand, and rejoice in hope of the glory of God." (Romans 5:1-2 NKJV)

However, when you obey God you prove and reveal that you are a believer. This is because obedience requires trust. We do what God tells us to do because we fully trust Him with the circumstances and simply obey. It is easy to say you believe God but it is an entirely different thing to prove it. Being a doer of the word testifies to the world that we are believers and convinces them of the life-transforming power of the Gospel. Make no mistake; doing God's Word is the outward manifestation of the inward work of Grace!

Resisting Temptation

> "Submit yourselves therefore to God. Resist the devil, and he will flee from you." (James 4:7 KJV)

Be advised… No Christian is immune to temptation. As long as you are a flesh and blood human being you will be tempted to sin (that is unless you are an alien from outer space). Yet, the Bible is clear that we must resist any and all forms of temptation. We cannot allow the enemy permission to gain any access into our lives. However, the problem with resisting temptation isn't with the *resisting* part; it's with the *submitting* part. The Bible doesn't teach us just to resist the devil. Read James 4:7 again! It says *submit* to God first and then resist the devil. Most of our failures come from trying to fight temptation in our own strength. However, as James points out, when you submit to and rely on God's higher power (Grace) you will not only be able to escape temptation but also overcome any possible repercussions that sin may have in your life. The irony of it all is that when you submit to God's purposes and agree with His directives, instead of trying to avoid the enemy, the enemy will eventually *avoid you,* particularly in the areas where you struggle. The devil will flee FROM YOU when you turn to God for power to resist and avoid his pitfalls. The formula is simple. Submit + Resist = the devil flees! This is not to say that you will never be tempted but as you regularly learn to submit to God the devil loses his influence over you and you'll find yourself walking in victory on a more consistent basis. It's all a matter of what you are focused on. When you give your attention to the goodness of God and allow His voice to be the most prominent, the enemy won't be able to get a word or thought in edgewise. Submitting to God means having a love relationship with Jesus. This is what seals all possible entry points for the devil's schemes to try and sabotage your life.

One more thing to consider here is that when we are saved from our sin it angers Satan. You see, we used to serve satan and because we no longer belong to him he will do anything he can to destroy our lives. Before we were saved sin wasn't tempting to us because we freely served our father the devil and easily gave in to our lust. But now that we're saved, we have a new heart that wants to serve Jesus. Yet, satan will try to use our old ways to lure us back to a life of captivity. Jesus never promised us that the Christian life would be easy and free from temptation but He did promise to never abandon us in our struggle and failure.

"He Himself (Jesus) has said, "I will never leave you nor forsake you." (Hebrews 13:5 NKJV)[37]

When we are struggling with temptation and fail, we have a sure promise from the Lord that no matter what, He will NEVER leave us abandoned. The dictionary definition of *never* means *not ever, at no time, not at all, absolutely not, to no extent or degree,* and if God is always with us, who can be against us (Romans 8:31)?

Reflecting His Glory

Finally, we need to wipe the fog (clouded perceptions of who we are and who Christ is in us) off of the mirror so we can see the image of who we are IN CHRIST! Having a deep and sure revelation of Grace removes the veil from our thinking. Once our minds are renewed by the word of Grace the confusion is gone. As we continue to look into the mirror of God's Word, it clearly reveals that we *already* reflect the very glory of the Lord, and the more clearly we see the reflect of God's glory in and through our lives, we are continually transformed into that image.

"But we all, with unveiled face, beholding as in a mirror the glory of the Lord,   ARE BEING TRANSFORMED INTO THE SAME IMAGE FROM GLORY TO GLORY, just as from the Lord, the Spirit."
(2 Corinthians 3:18 NASB)

Our true reflection in the mirror of God's word is glorious. We literally radiate God's perfect glory (even in our imperfections). There is nothing imperfect about God's glory. This revelation should fill us with the confidence to face life with Holy Spirit boldness and resilient poise. So take the blinders off and see who you really are... The righteousness of God IN CHRIST.

"He made Him who knew no sin to be sin on our behalf, so that we might become the righteousness of God in Him."
(2 Corinthians 5:21 NASB)

Chapter 7

MISSION INCROSSABLE

"And Moses said unto the people, 'Fear ye not, stand still, and see the salvation of the LORD." (Exodus 14:13 KJV)

There are many Old Testament examples that point the way to Jesus and are perfect pictures of God's Grace in full effect. These "types and shadows" reveal the person or the nature of Christ and His work of redemption. The reason they are called types and shadows is because they are only hints or glimpses of the better covenant revealed in the New Testament.

"But now He has obtained a more excellent ministry, by as much as He is also the mediator of a better covenant, which has been enacted on better promises." (Hebrews 8:6 NASB)

The story of Moses at the Red Sea is a perfect real life illustration of God's Grace in action. The Egyptian army was chasing down Moses and the Children of Israel. En route they were pinned down from behind and the ONLY WAY of escape was through the Red Sea. God led them straight into an impossible situation. I call it an *incrossable* situation. It was no fault of their own or by accident that they arrived at a dead end. They were not at a crossroads. There was only ONE WAY to go. Now it was up to God alone to deliver them. All Moses could do was tell the people not to fear but to *stand still* and watch God show up and show off. Can you imagine the frustration of the people when they came to a stand still? When you come to a *stand-still* in your life then it's time to *stand still*. Besides, the Israelites couldn't out run the Egyptian army even if they wanted to. To beat it all, there was no way out but across the RED Sea. This so typifies our inability to become righteous or find true salvation by self-effort. Only the cross makes it crossable. We cannot get to heaven nor do we achieve special status with God by our own good works. Only the blood gives us connection to God and eternal life. True; God is honored by our efforts but we are not approved unto God or made righteous by doing good things for Him. Our works don't approve us. Only Christ's blood approves us. The scriptures expressly tell us that the only way to eternal life is THROUGH Jesus Christ our Lord (Romans 3:23). The gulf to righteousness in our lives was too great for us to cross it. Jesus carried the cross and placed it in our path so we could have safe passage to the other side. When Christ leads us in HIS righteousness, we bear fruit that proves our right standing with Him. Right *standing* with God makes us stand uprightly!

The Israelites had to cross *through* the murky RED waters to reach safety. The same is true for us. We have to cross *through* the RED blood of Jesus in order to stand before God as righteous. There is NO OTHER WAY! Notice that the sea completely split in two and they walked across on dry land. When Jesus died, the veil in the temple that separated us from God's glory was completely ripped in half by the power of God signifying that we now have access into His presence (Matthew 15:38; Mark 27:51). This not only stands for our initial born again experience; it also represents obtaining ongoing righteousness. We are not only saved by Grace, we are maintained by Grace. Salvation is not attained not by our own striving, but by God's power alone. When the fear of guilt hunts us down, as the Egyptian army did, and tries to drag us back under the yoke of slavery to condemnation, we don't have to fear. God has our BACK! We no longer have to feel trapped by our inability to live perfectly. We can claim our FULL righteousness through Jesus finished work. And when we do, the voices of guilt and fear are drowned under the blood of our salvation. Have you ever noticed that sometimes God purposely leads us right into impossible situations in life to show us that ONLY HE can deliver us. You can see this all throughout the Bible (I.e. Joshua, Gideon, Ester, Nehemiah, Jehoshaphat, Elijah, the list goes on). Unless Grace is steering the ship of your life you will run amuck on the rocky banks of failure. Let Grace take the wheel.

Did you know it isn't hard to live the Christian life? It's IMPOSSIBLE! That's one of the reasons why Paul called Grace the mystery of the gospel. It's so easy to be saved yet it's impossible to live it out! You may be asking, *"Then why bother with trying to live righteously?"* My friend, God gave the Law so that we would come to the end of ourselves and finally TRUST IN HIS GRACE that makes us righteous (Romans 3:20; Galatians 3:24). Grace settles the issue. We don't have to try anymore. Righteous living flows from a righteous standing. We can't be righteous apart from God's Grace!

A Burdensome Assignment

Recently I gave an assignment to my daughter. I told her to read for 40-minutes and if she could do so without complaining I would take her out for ice cream. Simple enough? Not really! You see; it is impossible for anyone not to ever complain, especially an 8-year old. Only 20 minutes later she came and asked me how much time she had left. I knew she wouldn't be happy that her time wasn't up and I waited for her to pout about it. Sure enough she sulked her shoulders, let out a heavy sigh and exclaimed, *"I'VE ONLY READ TWENTY MINUTES?!* I couldn't help but chuckle as I pointed out her complaining. She smirked and said, *"Aw man! You got me Dad."* I took her out and bought her ice cream anyway. That's Grace!

I tell this story to make the point that the system of attaining righteousness by our good efforts is impossible. The only way that we can be made holy is to receive God's free gift of Grace. You'd think after centuries of attempting to obtain favor with God through the Law that the Children of Israel would have learned that it was impossible. Not so! In all of their striving to obey God's Law the Children of Israel still fell into deep apostasy. Their feeble attempts to gaining righteousness with God through the Law failed! Only Jesus makes us acceptable to God.

"For there is one God, and one mediator also between God and men, the man Christ Jesus." (1 Timothy 2:5 NASB)

The meaning of "mediator" is very insightful. The Greek word is *mesites,* which means...

One who intervenes between two parties

To make or restore peace and friendship

To form a compact

To ratify, confirm, authorize, endorse, approve

To sanction a covenant

An arbitrator (a peace maker)

Jesus intervened to make peace, restore friendship and ratify our covenant with God. Jesus is the only way to obtain favor and right standing with God. This makes the *incrossable* crossable (Romans 3:23). When we believe we are made righteous by His blood alone, we will be divinely energized to live out our faith with true conviction and a passionate desire to pursue holiness. There is no other way to truly live Holy than for God to produce His holiness in and through us!

Holiness for Our Good

Holy living is for OUR GOOD, not for God's good. Yet, so often we wear ourselves out trying to *please* the Lord when we are already His good pleasure. The secret of Grace is that we find divine energy to fulfill God's purposes when we, by faith, simply learn to rest and enjoy being in God's good pleasure through Christ's finished work (Romans 3:28; Galatians 3:6-26; Hebrews 11:6). We must remember that God is tender lovingly patient with us. He knows we are flesh and we fail. Yet, He loves us unconditionally and is committed to lead us towards maturity by the power of His Spirit and the knowledge of His Word. This doesn't mean that God closes His eyes and turns His head when we sin. No! His eyes are continually upon us (Proverbs 15:3). Yet, when we *come to the end of ourselves* (like the Children of Israel at the Red Sea) God's Grace will make possible what was impossible.

"The sons of Israel went through the midst of the sea on the dry land, and the waters were like a wall to them on their right hand and on their left." (Exodus 14:13 NASB)[27]

Chapter 8

NULL AND VOID

"Think not that I am come to destroy the Law, or the prophets: I am not come to destroy but to fulfill." (Matthew 5:17 KJV)

When a legal contract is drawn up it only remains effective if both people abide by it. If one party fails to live up to its end of the bargain the contract becomes null and void. This is exactly what happened with the legal contract of the Old Covenant. God presented the Children of Israel with an impossible scenario. We can see this in the very addendums of the Law (I.e. Exodus and Leviticus) as well as the utter failure and eventual complete falling away of the Children of Israel later into the pages of the Old Testament. There was no way they could fulfill their part of the contract. God purposely posed a losing battle in order to prepare the way for the revealing of the true way to perfection... Jesus Christ (Romans 3:20; Galatians 3:24). Notice how God instructed the Children of Israel.

> **"Now it shall be, if you diligently obey the LORD your God, being careful to DO ALL HIS COMMANDMENTS which I command you today, the LORD your God will set you high above all the nations of the earth. "All these blessings will come upon you and overtake you if you obey the LORD your God." (Deuteronomy 28:1-2 NASB)**

The next 13 verses go on to state all the blessings that would overtake the Children of Israel if they intently listened to the voice of the Lord and obeyed ALL the commandments. All those blessings included health, prosperity, favor, success, etc. The formula was in black & white: *obey ALL the commandments and receive ALL the blessings.* In order to receive the promises of God in full, the Israelites had to fulfill *every commandment* to the letter. Unthinkable! For instance, God commanded the priests to sacrifice animals and in the meantime were not to allow any blood to stain their garments. Imagine that! The entire camp of Israel was a bloody slaughterhouse and yet God demanded the priests to remain clean. CRAZY IMPOSSIBLE!

Trying to obtain perfection by perfectly obeying God's Laws leads only to frustration and futility!

If you read Deuteronomy 28:1-2 from an Old Testament position then the blessings of God come only through obedience. It was either obey all and get *all* or disobey one and get *none*. And the truth is, we all disobey God's Laws regularly. That means none of us qualify for any of God's blessings. We're all out in the cold. Nobody is eligible for the blessings. Why? Because even in our very best behavior we still fall entirely short of God's standards (Romans 3:23). NOBODY obeys ALL God's Laws. Oh, we might be able to hold up the weight of obedience for a while but sooner or later we'll drop the bar. Nobody can hold up perfection. Perfection is unattainable outside of Jesus. Being IN CHRIST means we are perfect because of HIS perfection! Perfection isn't based on *how* we live but in WHOM we live! Christ alone is perfectly perfect and flawlessly flawless, and in Him we are also perfect! The fulfillment of our end of the contract was completed through Jesus. What was once a binding *contract* is now an everlasting *covenant* (Hebrews 13:20). Jesus bore all our condemnation and the heavy grief that accompanies it. He was brutally punished in our place. God's furious wrath for our failing to fulfill His Law was unleashed upon His son (Isaiah 53:3-6) and now we no longer have an appointment with God's wrath (1 Thessalonians 5:9). The end of Malachi proves the Israelites failed at their end of the deal. Therefore, CONTRACT NULLIFIED! In Matthew 23, Jesus rebuked the Jewish leaders by pointing out that the very Law they lived by condemned them. The Law condemns us even at our best because our best just isn't good enough. Only by faith in *Christ's obedience* can we claim perfection to God's standard, thereby qualifying for all His blessings and benefits.

"In order that in Christ Jesus the blessing of Abraham might come to the Gentiles, SO THAT WE WOULD RECEIVE THE PROMISE THROUGH FAITH." (Galatians 3:14 NASB)

Believe and Receive

Christ redeemed us from the curse of bondage to the Law. In the Old Covenant you had to *obey* in order to receive God's blessings. Now, through Christ, our righteous blessings are attained not by obeying, but by *believing* (Romans 1:17; 3:22; 3:25; 4:11; 4:13; 9:30; 10:6; Galatians 5:5; Philippians 3:9). It's simple: Believe and Receive. The following is a lengthy passage but it is critical to understand the premise that only BY FAITH in God's Grace are we justified and made righteous in order to receive the blessings and promises of God.

"Abraham BELIEVED GOD, and it was reckoned (credited) to him as righteousness. Therefore, be sure that it is THOSE WHO ARE OF FAITH who are sons of Abraham. The Scripture, foreseeing that God would justify the Gentiles BY FAITH... So then THOSE WHO ARE OF FAITH are blessed with Abraham, the believer. For as many as are of the works of the Law are under a curse... Now that no one is justified by the Law... THE RIGHTEOUS MAN SHALL LIVE BY FAITH. However, THE LAW IS NOT OF FAITH; on the contrary... Christ redeemed us from the curse of the Law, having become a curse for us in order that in Christ Jesus the blessing of Abraham might come to the Gentiles, so that we would receive the promise of the Spirit THROUGH FAITH. For if a Law had been given which was able to impart life, then righteousness would indeed have been based on Law. But the Scripture has shut up everyone under sin; so that the promise BY FAITH in Jesus Christ might be given TO THOSE WHO BELIEVE. But before faith came, we were kept in custody under (held in bondage to) the Law... Therefore the Law has become our tutor to lead us to Christ (to forcefully teach us to recognize our need for Grace) so that we may be JUSTIFIED BY FAITH. But NOW THAT FAITH HAS COME, we are no longer under a tutor. For you are all sons of God THROUGH FAITH in Christ Jesus."
(Galatians 3:6-14; 21-26 NASB)[37]

The weapon most used by the enemy against us is the Old Covenant system of the Law. Our adversary the devil shakes the Law like a rolled up newspaper (the old and bad news) in our faces to discourage us when we fail. However through Grace, Satan can no longer use the weapon of guilt and condemnation against us.

"Having wiped out the handwriting of requirements that was against us, which was contrary to us. And He has taken it out of the way, having nailed it to the cross. Having disarmed principalities and powers, He made a public spectacle of them, triumphing over them in it."
(Colossians 2:14-15 NKJV)

Distinctions of Law and Grace[6]

Our New Covenant (life in the Spirit) is far superior to the system of the Law. Below is a quick glance at the contrasts of Law vs. Grace. It's obvious that Grace is the only way to experience the fullness of the Christian life.

LAW (The Flesh)	GRACE (The Spirit)
Delights in Self (Romans 8:3)	Depends on God (Acts 1:8)
Provokes Rebellion (Romans 7:8)	Promotes Obedience (Philippians 2:13)
Prolongs Sin (Romans 5:20)	Produces Holiness (Romans 8:4)
Ends in Futility (Romans 4:15)	Endures in Fruitfulness (Galatians 5:22-23)
Relies on Works (Galatians 3:12)	Rests on Faith (2 Corinthians 5:7)
Breeds Death (2 Corinthians 3:4-6)	Births Life (Romans 8:2)

Misnomers of Grace

If this next concern of mine seems like I'm coming on strong, be advised it is my fullest intention to do so! Among the many misnomers of Grace, there is one so underhanded, so treacherous, so devious, and so maligning yet hundreds of thousands (even millions) of people are falling for it everyday. It is a demonic conspiracy twisted by the devil himself to make us believe we must do more, pay more and suffer more to earn our full rights as God's children. There are preachers that will actually tell you if you follow their self-made formulas and do ABC then God will do XYZ. Child of God, Jesus already did letter A all the way through Z. He fulfilled EVERY LETTER of the Law through His finished work and there is nothing else we can do but trust in what He already did! Your salvation, forgiveness and healing are paid for no matter how many preachers try to convince you that you have to give money so you can see yourself or your relatives saved and healed. That's the equivalent of the early Catholic Church commissioning charismatic crusaders with compelling personalities to poor, humble provinces promising wary villagers that they could shorten their loved ones' sentences in purgatory if they would only purchase indulgences (certificates of wit to escape judgment). Pure foolishness! Jesus paid for our salvation, healing, deliverance, miracles, financial breakthroughs and much more with His own blood. All our debts have been cancelled and there is no remaining balance. Don't fall for the rotten lie that we have to pay more for our forgiveness and all that our salvation entails. We don't pay for God's blessings, as it were, by our giving. We worship through our giving as a response of joy for all He has already done knowing He has fully met our needs at CHRIST'S EXPENSE! He has blessed us so that we may be a blessing. It is only by God's great generosity that we are made rich in every way (spiritually, physically, mentally, emotionally, financially, etc.). As believers we are entitled to ALL of God's blessings without exception, qualms, suspicions, misgivings, worries, doubts or reservations. The benefits of righteousness are as much a gift as the gift of righteousness itself. They can't be earned because they are GIFTS. Therefore, we must simply believe that we are full beneficiaries of all the promises of God because of what Jesus has already done; and rest assured; we are indebted to no one for any of them (Romans 13:8). The equation is simple: Receive and enjoy. Besides NO ONE on earth can keep God's covenant. So God became a man and fulfilled all our obligations Himself. Every account has been settled! (Ezekiel 22:30; Hebrews 6:13)

Annulled but Fulfilled

We are justified by faith alone. Our good works do not lead us to faith. Rather having true faith in Jesus Christ leads us to good works. Putting your full trust in the finished work of Christ will not decrease your desire to live holy; it will increase your desire and determination to taste the fruits of righteousness. Some may ask, *"Since Jesus has fulfilled the Law and granted Grace does that annul a believer's responsibility to obey the Law?"* It is true that believers are no longer subject to the condemnation and punishment of sin that the Law requires. However, we should not misunderstand that honoring your mother and father, not murdering, not committing adultery and not stealing (to name a few of them but not excluding any) are good and right commandments. However, man is not able to perfectly fulfill these Laws because they are inflexible and unyielding even to the very motive and intent of the heart (Matthew 5:21-22). In the Old Covenant, people's mindsets were governed by fear. The false perception was that obeying the commandments appeased or was somehow *good for God*. However, in our New Covenant we know that obeying God is not for *His* good. Obeying God is for *OUR* good!

Christ in Us

Not only are we in Christ but Christ is in us! Jesus secured our righteousness by *taking up* residence IN US! The Apostle Paul had the audacity to declare that we are ONE with Jesus. Therefore, if our union with Jesus is assured, then we are as secure as Jesus is.

"But he that is joined unto the Lord is ONE SPIRIT."
(1 Corinthians 6:17 KJV)

How can you separate One Spirit. It would be like trying to take red food coloring out of water. Once they are mixed they are inseparable. What was impossible through the Law is now possible through Jesus. Christ and ALL His power in us enables us to be victorious.

"To whom God willed to make known what is the riches of the glory of this mystery among the Gentiles, which is CHRIST IN YOU, the hope of glory." (Colossians 1:27 NASB)

Not only are we IN CHRIST but Christ is also IN US giving us hope instead of fear. The very glory of His presence inside of us empowers us to live in the fullness of His Spirit. Granted, we will fail at times in our obedience walk. But because of Christ's sacrifice we are no longer under the rigidity of the Law and the severity of punishment thus nullifying our end of the covenant. If you failed in the Old Covenant you immediately lost your right standing with God. In our new Covenant, when we fail, we don't lose our righteousness with God. Why? It is because we are IN CHRIST. The Law has no more power than it did in the Old Covenant to help us obey the Law. It was powerless to save us! However, what was once a *commandment* not to be broken is now a *promise* to be fulfilled.[2] Through Christ the

Law's demands are met and the power to overcome addictions and break bondages works through us to produce the life we long for. Jesus has taken full responsibility to fulfill the commandments through us. IN CHRIST we no longer have to bear the burdensome requirements of the Law. The weight of the Law's stringent demand is now on His shoulders. All we have to do is simply surrender to Grace. God has taken what was a *commandment* and turned it into a *promise*. Therefore, to those who receive God's Grace, comes the power to fulfill His promise.

"But as many as RECEIVED Him, to them gave He power to become the sons of God, even to them that BELIEVE on His name." (John 1:12 NASB)

To Obey or Not to Obey

Many feel the only way to receive righteousness is by obeying God's word. We acquire this distorted mindset from much of the *Law preaching* that prevails in our churches today. However, the scripture clearly teach us that we don't receive by doing. We receive by believing. Our righteousness comes to us by *"obedience to the faith.*

"Through Him we have received Grace and apostleship for obedience to the faith..." (Romans 1:5 NKJV)

What does *"obedience to the faith"* mean? At first, it doesn't seem to make any sense. However, when you look a little deeper it becomes clear. Paul is simply saying that believing you are already righteous is the first step to walking in obedience. One of the biggest obstacles to obedience is fear of the outcome of that obedience. Obeying God requires that you trust and leave the consequences to Him. When you settle the *trust issue,* obedience to God's will becomes much easier because you know He has your best interests at heart. Right faith always precedes right actions. Instead of trying to obey God first, we must come to the end of ourselves and lay down our own determination to serve God so that He may fill us with HIS determination to walk the walk of dedication and consecration. It's like I always say, *"We can't but God can."* Jesus perfectly obeyed God even to the point of death because He completely trusted His Father. That trust empowered Him to *go all the way* with God. When we let

THAT kind of trust fill our lives there is nothing that can stop us from living a life of purity, power and fruitfulness.

Grace is a Verb

At this point you may be asking, *"Aren't the commandments of God important and shouldn't we obey them?"* The answer is, YES; we need to obey God and yes, His Laws are important! Grace is not just a safety-catch for our salvation. Grace is a verb! I like to think of it as being R.E.A.L. = **R**eceive Grace, **E**xperience Grace, **A**ct on Grace, **L**ive Grace (in that order). Grace wasn't given to cancel out obeying God. Rather, Grace makes it possible for us to get the BEST out of life through humble obedience. Obedience is simply a positive response to God's loving directions for our success. We don't obey God to *make* Him love us. We obey God *because* He loves us. God wants us to obey Him because it ultimately makes US happy! The reason why we sin is because we are deceived into believing the lie that Sin will make us happy rather than believe in the promise that holiness will make us happy. God is also happy when we obey him not because we appease His righteous anger but because it delights Him to see us living to our fullest potential. You may have heard it said that God is concerned more about our holiness than He is our happiness. My friend, God is *equally* concerned about our happiness as He is our holiness. That's why He wants us to live holy lives. We more often experience and more fully *enjoy* the blessings God has already given us by trusting His plan and walking in it. PLEASE HEAR ME LOUD AND CLEAR! It is extremely important to obey God! However, disobedience doesn't mean you *forfeit* your righteousness. I once heard someone say, *"You can't lose your salvation, but you can forfeit it."* What's the difference? After all, when you forfeit a game, you lose it. So either way, you lose! When you disobey God, you don't lose your salvation. However, when you walk in disobedience you don't get to enjoy your righteousness and *savor* God's *conditional* blessings here and now! Once we are purchased in Christ, our salvation is *unconditional* because of what Christ has already finished for us. However, know for sure that our temporal blessings in this life are *conditional* in that they are affected by our obedience. When David prayed not to be cast from God's presence and for the Holy Spirit not to be taken from Him (Psalms 51:11) he was not referring to perdition from losing his salvation, but for God not to withdraw the temporary blessing of His anointing upon his life. Disobedience does more than *"hurt your testimony."* It causes you harm (physically and spiritually). Conversely, obedience keeps you in a circle of safety within the boundaries of God's best for your life. You can have God's blessings right in your hand and not be experiencing the delight of those blessings. Through God's Grace, His blessings empower us to obey. Once we get caught up in that cycle, it is almost impossible to get out of it.

Remember that Abraham was considered righteous nearly fourteen years before He was circumcised (Romans 4:10). And through his faith in God he was able to offer his son Isaac. Think of the immense implications of this. The extreme act of Abraham's obedience came *after* he was considered righteous for believing in God (Genesis 15:6; Romans 4:3). It wasn't his great deed that made him righteous. It was his righteousness that gave him the desire to obey God even if it meant giving up his only son in sacrificial obedience to God. Obeying the Law through Christ's power is no longer a burden of *obligation* but a response of *love.* Through the power of Grace our desires truly change as we grow in the Grace and knowledge of our Lord's love for us (2 Peter 3:18). At one time I felt as if God would love me more if I obeyed and served Him harder. Now through Grace, it is Christ's love that compels *me* to love and serve Him with everything in me (2 Corinthians 5:14).

Holy Living Attainable

I believe we can overcome a *lifestyle* of sin. However, living a holy life doesn't mean we are never going to make mistakes and never fail. When we put ourselves on the pedestal of perfectionism we set ourselves up for massive disappointment. However, when we purpose to regularly *cooperate* with the Holy Spirit, *submit* to His ways and *rely* on His power, we will be surprised just how holy we can live! Being *wholly* dependent on God's Grace produces holy living. I like to think of it as *WHOLLY* living. In other words, living a lifestyle of holiness is living a life of *WHOLEness!* When we think of *holiness* in this way, it takes the religious fear of failure out of the equation and helps us see it as a life that is God's best for us. Holy living isn't what's best for God; it's what's best for *us!* Living a life of perfect moral behavior doesn't *make* you holy. It is the other way around. Your righteousness (secured only through Christ's finished work) enables you to live *righteously.* Once you are confident and secure in your salvation; supernatural strength will surge through you. The way to *wholeness* is to completely rely on God's Grace.

"Therefore, prepare your minds for action (don't be slothful and passive in your pursuit of Christ), keep sober in spirit (don't think you are capable in your own ability), FIX YOUR HOPE COMPLETELY ON THE GRACE TO BE BROUGHT TO YOU AT THE REVELATION OF JESUS CHRIST. As obedient children, do not be conformed to the former lusts which were yours in your ignorance (living by the standard of the old regimental practices of the Law), but like the Holy One who called you, be holy yourselves also in all your behavior; because it is written, "YOU SHALL BE HOLY, FOR I AM HOLY."
(1 Peter 1:13-16 NASB)[37]

It is inevitable that you will sin (and even often). Just pinch yourself and you'll be reminded that you are flesh. And be forewarned that as long as you live in that flesh you will fail. However, God knows you are flesh and when you fall short you don't have to wallow in the misery of guilt and condemnation. Remember that the Bible says your righteousness is irrevocable and your salvation is secure (Romans 11:29).[14] Don't think for a moment that you are incapable of living in victory! Jesus fully purchased your redemption not only to reserve your *place* in eternity but also to establish your *position* here on Earth. God's Grace isn't anemic! God's Grace is His supreme omnipotence working in you, enabling you to live the overcoming life. It's simply a matter of what you're relying on. When you fail, instead of becoming anxious, simply regroup yourself and relax in God's Grace through Christ. At the same time you are resting in God's Grace, you can be fully running after God's best for you. The paradox of God's Grace is that you can *rest* and *run* at the same time. Baffling! Resting in Grace doesn't mean living sluggardly or slothfully. On the contrary, God's Grace swallows up passivity and releases passion in your life.

Holiness: A Gift

"Humble yourselves in the sight of the Lord and HE WILL LIFT YOU UP." (2 Chronicles 7:14 NASB)

A humble attitude is essential to receiving God's Grace. When we humble ourselves and trust in Jesus we in-effect declare our inability to satisfy the Law's requirements. Recognizing our weakness actually positions us to receive God's strength. Jesus came to *lift* us to God's standard of Holiness. We can't get there without Him. He is the only way we can encounter God (John 4:28). This is why Paul said...

"There is no one who does good, no, not one." (Romans 3:12 NKJV)

God's holiness is a gift not a burden. That's why the Psalmist declared that God's holiness was beautiful (Psalms 29:2). God so greatly desired to share His life with us that He gave us His son to make it possible. God invites us to enjoy the divine pleasure of his Holiness through Christ's perfection (2 Peter 1:4). Holy living doesn't enable us to experience a relationship with God. It's the other way around. Having a relationship with Jesus enables us to experience His holiness. When we humbly trust in His Grace instead of our feeble attempts towards perfect behavior we will encounter His holiness. Many believe when you fail at living holy you won't be able to encounter God's presence. This comes from years of ingrained religious teaching and a gross misinterpretation of the following passages...

"Blessed are the pure in heart for they shall see God."
(Matthew 5:8 KJV)

"Follow peace with all men and holiness, without which no man shall see the Lord." (Hebrews 12:14 KJV)

Firstly, "pure" doesn't mean *sinless*. It refers to a heart that is humble and broken. Matthew 5:3 says that the poor in *spirit* shall inherit the Kingdom of Heaven. This doesn't mean that only poor people receive God's inheritance. It means that those who possess a broken heart and wholly depend on Jesus will experience His kingdom authority to rule above the deception of the world's system. Secondly, we must remember that the passage above is in direct reference to Paul's defense of Grace. It is impossible for any man to be holy outside of God's Grace. Only through Christ are we considered completely holy and qualified to stand in God's presence. We must also consider that Paul's instruction was to *"follow peace."* We must constantly seek to establish peace with others. Judging others based on our self-imposed standards of perfection is prideful and hinders the work of Grace in our life. We must also bestow Grace to others and allow the Holy Spirit to guide them on an individual basis. Judging others doesn't define who they are. It defines who YOU are. Now to be sure, Paul advocated the necessity of holy living and totally surrendering one's life to God in all matters of conduct and conversation (Romans 6:19, 22; 2 Corinthians 7:1; Ephesians 4:24; 1 Thessalonians 4:7, etc.). He had to make this obvious because of those who felt his message entitled people to sin without consequences. However, in all of his writings, Paul made it abundantly clear that it is impossible to be holy outside of a vital and ongoing relationship with Jesus Christ. If it were possible to be holy on our own there would have been no need for Jesus. Jesus is the only way to true holiness!

Cheap Grace

In order to better appreciate the astounding implications of Grace we must also understand mercy and the difference between the two. Mercy is not getting what you deserve and Grace is getting what you don't deserve. In other words, mercy bails us out of prison and Grace allows us to move into the mansion (as it were). Mercy is the agent of *release* and Grace is the agent of *reward.* Grace is the *extension* of mercy. It goes the extra mile. Once mercy *lets us off the hook*, Grace then *blesses us off the hook* (beyond our wildest dreams). Mercy provides us full pardon and then Grace provides us full righteousness. Mercy breaks us out of jail *regardless* of our crime and then Grace blesses us *in spite of* our crime.

The question remains: Does this make God's Grace cheap? Absolutely not! Our righteousness cost JESUS everything. Truth is, we will never have enough spiritual currency to pay God back for His indescribable gift. We are at our best completely bankrupt. Therefore, let me clarify: Grace isn't cheap. It cost Jesus everything. The great and glorious news is it's FREE for us! The implications of this are unfathomable. Charles Spurgeon one said, *"Free Grace can go into the gutter and bring up a jewel."* Christ purchased our redemption IN FULL. Our freedom cost Jesus everything so it would cost us nothing! This is the astoundingly confounding miracle of mercy and Grace. We can argue and reason about it all we want. Yet, the indisputable truth is there is nothing we can do about it except to receive it! One side note... Whenever Grace is presented arguments will always ensue. Why? The devil wants people to question their salvation. Legalism always stalks Grace, but Grace is always out front, proclaiming salvation and deliverance to all men. Some make their case for Grace by presenting scriptures. God made a much stronger case by presenting a person... JESUS! Rest assured, no one with an encounter with God's Grace is ever at the mercy of someone with a *word.* Yes, scripture is extremely important as it supports truth (especially in the light of Grace). But no matter how legalists contend with Grace (Jesus), His loving, effervescent radiance outshines every argument.

Some contend that when you preach Grace you are giving people a *Get out of Jail Free* card. My friend, that's just how it works. After all, if you ended up in jail, wouldn't you want a free pass out? That's exactly what happens when we receive the infinite mercy and Grace of God. None of us have to serve even one millisecond of sin's eternal sentence. When God forgives, He forgives for good! We don't have to mope around feeling as if He still holds a grudge against us. If that were the case we would never feel forgiven. Friend, God is not mad at you. He's *madly* in love with you! True forgiveness is accompanied by a sense of relief from indebtedness. The Greek word for 'forgive' is *afeame.* The implication is to release someone from incarceration or imprisonment. Full forgiveness is the undercurrent of our freedom IN CHRIST. To be forgiven by God means to be released from any indebtedness to Him. The truth is, God's Grace is free because we simply cannot afford it. When we sin we can fall hard on the forgiveness of God and ask Him to strengthen our resolve to get back up and move forward. God's mercy never runs out and always triumphs over judgment (Psalms 100:5, James 2:13).

To fully understand what Grace is we must also understand what it is *not.* Grace is not gracious*ness,* temporary leniency, propriety or politeness. While it may include these in the giving they are not the embodiment of Grace. Grace is the permanent pardon from sin, complete dismissal of judgment, acquittal from punishment and the total cancellation of debt owed for wrongful acts committed against humanity and God... FOREVER!

No Strings Attached

Some think God's Grace is His way of giving us a little bit of extra *slack* whenever we fail or a short *window of opportunity* to make things right. This is a total misconception. For instance some financial institutions allow a "Grace period" of up to 15 days after the due date to make a payment on any bills incurred. After that, it's considered delinquent and will count against your credit score. Some view God's Grace the same way. It's *"I've forgiven you for the time being but I expect you to get your issues under control or else we'll have to revisit this forgiven business!"* Beloved, God doesn't partly pardon us until we learn to get things right. We will never get things perfectly right. God's Grace comes with no strings attached. In other words, God doesn't give us His Grace with the expectation that we will come through on our end of the *deal*. If that were the case then it wouldn't truly be Grace because it would cost us something to receive it. We often bargain with God, *"If You do this God then I'll do that."* Friend, God fulfills His promise whether or not we fulfill ours. Why? Because His promise is eternal (Hebrews 10:23). Truth is, those who deserve Grace the least are the ones who need it the most.

In the story of the prodigal son, the robe, ring, sandals and fatted calf reveal God's amazing heart of Grace (Luke 11:15-32). The robe is symbolic of high social class status and distinction. The ring: a bestowal of kingly authority. The sandals: a luxury of the day as only slaves walked barefoot. And the fattened calf: the centerpiece of customary family feasts and festivals. These symbols represent radical Grace, total forgiveness and complete restoration. Too often the religious *'church'* offers only limited or conditional Grace. It's, *"You're forgiven but we're keeping our eye on you."* Or *"You're welcome back in the church but you can never minister here again."* However, when GOD looks at us He doesn't see a prodigal failure. He sees us forgiven and whole.[28] The prodigal son never stopped belonging to his father just because he made wrong decisions. He simply became displaced from those bad choices! Many Christians are displaced today and separated from the Father's *house* by years of regret. Although they certainly still belong to God, they aren't in the PLACE they belong, living far beneath God's best for their lives.

Instead of being like the elder brother who was offended by the Father's display of affection, we must defend the wounded and help love them back to their place of acceptance in the Father's *house*. We should never look down on someone unless we're helping him up. Jesus came to defend the weak not the sleek. A strong word to ministers here: We must always remember that the pulpit is not a place of beating but a place of feeding! We must always see our people as sheep in need of shepherding. Jesus' anger was never directed toward the sinner or the hurting? It was ALWAYS directed toward the religious Pharisees, sharply rebuking them for their pompous attitude toward the downtrodden and the destitute? Jesus was drawn to the outcast. Likewise we must fully extend God's forgiveness to the fallen. The more we release mercy the more chances it has of penetrating the hardest of hearts. It's like the old saying goes; *If you want to build a bridge to your enemy you must first make him your friend.* It is difficult for broken people to resist a constant outpouring of God's love. God's love causes even the grievous of sinners to admit their failures, release bitterness, cease accusing others for their own mistakes, take personal responsibility and willingly enter the restoration process. God's Grace always triumphs over religious pride. Living on the side of Grace isn't living in denial. Rather it's living in God's *undeniable* Grace. We mustn't let our failures surprise or demobilize us. The good news is that our greatest weakness is GOD'S opportunity to reveal His perfect strength through us (2 Corinthians 12:9). Most teaching and preaching out there is all about what we must do to be better Christians or more pleasing to God. However, the key to victorious living is to quit striving to be all we can be for God and simply allow God to be all He is in us and through us.

"I have strength for all things IN CHRIST Who empowers me [I am ready for anything and equal to anything through Him Who infuses inner strength into me; I am self-sufficient IN CHRIST'S sufficiency]."
(Philippians 4:13 AMP)

The KJV translation says, *"I can do all things through Christ."* The literal translation of *"through"* is "IN." We can do all things IN CHRIST! Beloved, all the power we need to obey God and fulfill His purposes for our lives is ALREADY inside of us (Colossians 1:27). Grace is God's FULLFILABILITY! It's His *ability* to *fulfill* His promise in you. Some will use Matthew 5:48 to support our need to strive for perfection. But when Jesus said, *"Therefore you are to be perfect, as your Heavenly Father is perfect,"* He wasn't setting a goal for us to attain. He was pointing out our inability to live up to the perfect standard (Romans 3:23). The Greek word for "perfection" is *teleioi*, which means *that which is fully accomplished or finished.* Only Jesus finished the work (John 19:20). And because He alone finished the work *for us* He alone will finish the work *in us!* (Philippians 1:6) Friend, don't be anxious when you fail. You are still in God's loving grasp. When you fail to do good *for God*, remember that Christ did good *for you* and He does all things well (Mark 7:32). Know that Christ is working in you to live righteously in an unrighteous world. Trust in your right *standing* with God and it will lead you to right *living*. God is not demanding that you get everything right. Jesus IS your RIGHTness! When you *feel* insecure in your performance, rest in His security and His performance and it will produce amazing results in your life.

Chapter 9

THE ROLLING STONES

"And it will be said, 'Build up, build up, prepare the way, remove every obstacle out of the way of My people.'"
(Isaiah 57:14 NASB)

The Law was engraved by the finger of God on stone tablets. I believe God chose stone as His palate to demonstrate the futility of fulfilling the requirements of His Laws. Stone is inflexible, unbending and unyielding. It is rigid in its requirements and cold in its consequences (get hit in the head with a rock and you'll see what I mean). With one crushing blow, David brought a 9-foot giant to the ground. Not even the strongest of the giants of *the faith* is able to stand against the rigidity of the Law. All have fallen short of God's standard (Romans 3:23). It is ironic to note that although the Law (like stone) is rigid, it is at the same time fragile (easy to break). In the Old Covenant, if the Law was broken (disobeyed) the punishment was severe. So in essence, you could break the Law but in turn it would *break* you.

As I have afore mentioned, the Ten Commandments are called the *'ministry of death'* (2 Corinthians 3:7). This is why it says in Romans 3:23 that the wages of sin is death. Trying to earn our salvation is futility resulting in the opposite of what we work for... Death! Conversely, eternal life is a free gift and the way we receive it is through faith in the finished work of Jesus Christ. When we receive the free gift of Grace, God turns our heart of stone into a heart of flesh and writes His Law on our hearts giving us power to overcome sin and break its grip on our lives.

"Clearly you are an epistle (letter) of Christ, ministered by us, written not with ink but by the Spirit of the living God, not on tablets of stone but on tablets of flesh, that is, of the heart." (2 Corinthians 3:3 NKJV)[37]

The prophet Jeremiah prophesied that a day would come when God would write His Law on our hearts.

"But this is the covenant which I will make with the house of Israel after those days," declares the LORD, "I WILL PUT MY LAW WITHING THEM AND ON THEIR HEART I WILL WRITE IT; and I will be their God, and they shall be My people." (Jeremiah 33:31 NASB)

Jeremiah envisioned a day when we would no longer have to live by the standard of the Law. Instead God would put His heart of holiness inside of us to help us live consecrated lives. This is not some dream. This is reality for us in God's Grace. When Jesus raised Lazarus from the dead in John 11, He first asked the people to remove the stone covering that blocked the entrance to his grave. He did this so the people could experience the awesome miracle that was about to take place. How powerful an illustration this is for us. The Old Covenant Law is like a stone that covers the resurrection power of Grace. We will never truly know the miracle working power of God's Grace until we allow the 'stone' of the Law to be moved out of our way. Likewise, the stone had to be rolled away from Jesus' grave so that the world could be witness to the promise of redemption by His finished work. Through Jesus, God wiped out the requirements of the Law so that Grace could have its perfect work in our lives.

"Having wiped out the handwriting of requirements that was against us, which was contrary to us. AND HE HAS TAKEN IT OUT OF THE WAY, having nailed it to the cross." (Colossians 2:14 NKJV)

Notice this passage of scripture teaches us that the *'handwriting of requirements'* (the Old Covenant Law) actually worked contrary or against us. In other words the Law actually fights against us making it impossible to achieve favor with God. We could not get to God so God had to reach down and get us. That's the work of Grace. Moses was known as the most humble man on earth (Numbers 12:3). Yet it says of him in Hebrews 12:2 When he approached the mountain of God *"So terrifying was the sight"* he said, *"I am exceedingly afraid and trembling."* Even the meekest man on earth didn't feel as if he was worthy enough to approach the flaming fire of God on the mountain. The Law condemns us at our best but Grace saves us at our worst! Hallelujah!

There are countless people trapped beneath the rubble of sin and are desperately crying out for someone to save them from the carnage. They don't need someone to pile more debris on them.

"Then Jesus spoke to the crowds and to His disciples, therefore all that they tell you, do and observe, but do not do according to their deeds; for they (the religious leaders) say things and do not do them. They tie up heavy burdens and lay them on men's shoulders, but they themselves are unwilling to move them with so much as a finger. (Matthew 23:1-4 NASB)[37]

A word to ministers... I believe it is our high calling and privilege as new covenant ministers of the gospel of Grace to remove the *stone of the Law* from the people's hearts whenever we preach. Often we subtly teach Law and Grace together. Together these produce hazardous results; much like a boulder falling on a passing car. This is what Jesus meant when He said...

"And whosoever shall fall on this stone (Jesus) shall be broken: but on whomsoever it (the Law) shall fall, it will grind him to powder." (Matthew 21:44 NASB)[37]

This passage is repeated word for word in Luke 20:18. This means that it is double important for us to remember. God receives broken hearts that fall upon His Grace (Psalms 34:18). But those who live under the heavy burden of the Law (stone tablets) will be crushed (unable to fulfill righteousness ending in futility). We should never flaunt our spiritual pride like the Pharisees, declaring how much we pray, fast or labor for the gospel. Often, when we boast of our works, we subtly present them as Medals of Honor to others (rather than a privilege from the Lord). Those things are well and good, but the level in which we do them should remain a private issue (Matthew 6:1-8)!

When we parade our good works it is like placing a huge boulder (obstacle if you will) in front of people saying, *"If you can achieve spiritual status through great effort, like I have, then you can be as Godly as I am."* This is religious pride at it's best. Some people actually think they have achieved their spirituality with God. However, when we're too quick to point our finger and pass judgment on other's failures we need to remind ourselves that if it weren't for the Grace of God, we'd all be in the same sinking boat. For instance, there are many people who find it hard to pray merely five-minutes daily, but those same people (who have been purchased by the blood of Jesus) are precious and valuable to God. I can just imagine the mother of five young children struggling to have 'quiet' time with God everyday! In our zeal to please the Lord we often impose such high standards of spiritual discipline *across the board* as the only way to lay up favor with God. This causes many to become despondent to the point of giving up because they feel they must meet the same requirements as someone who has had more time to mature in the things of God. This shouldn't be so. God loves and favors the person who wrestles with being diligent in spiritual disciplines as much as the person who is fervent in their devotion to God.

The bottom line is when you remove works from the equation of Grace it makes religious people mad. This is because it places them at the same spiritual level as everyone else. After all their self-effort to appear righteous, at the end of the day, they are no more Godly than the newborn Christian. There is no such thing as being *more saved* than the next person. Paul encouraged the Roman Church (a gentile church) that they were righteous based on simple faith. At the same time he scolded the religious Jews, who having practiced the Law their entire lives, didn't even come close to the true meaning of righteousness.

"In other words, it is not the natural children who are God's children, but it is the children of the promise who are regarded as Abraham's offspring." (Romans 9:8 NIV)

The *"natural children"* Paul referred to were the Jews. The *"children of the promise"* were those who, by faith IN CHRIST, had accepted the free gift of righteousness. Also notice that Paul called them *"Abraham's offspring"* instead of Moses offspring? Many religious Jews put more emphasis in Moses and the Law than they did the true Father of Judaism (Abraham). They had become so steeped in the Law that they actually forgot their roots. However, Paul didn't miss a chance to remind them of it either. Remember that Abraham believed God (400 years before the giving of the Law) and God considered Him righteous. Paul was always pointing back to Abraham. Can you imagine how mad this made the Jewish leaders? Livid! Religious people hate when their spiritual arrogance is exposed! Although Paul wrote his letter to encourage the church in Rome, when you read between the lines, he is also firmly dealing with the Jews' religious pride and their attitude of spiritual superiority toward these gentile believers.

"For we maintain that a man is justified by faith apart from works of the Law. Or is God the God of Jews only? Is He not the God of Gentiles also? Yes, of Gentiles also? (Romans 3:28 NASB)

The Vineyard Owner

In Matthew 20:1-16, Jesus told a parable of a vineyard owner who went out to invite workers to labor in his vineyard (this vineyard owner represented Jesus). As he went out early in the morning he found some lined up and eager to work. So he hired them and promised them a penny for their day's wages. These early birds represented those of Jewish lineage who lived their whole lives under the Old Covenant Law. Then he found some others at noon and dusk standing around idle in the market place. These represent the Jews who weren't orthodox in their practice and had gone astray from the Law yet were coming into the new revelation of Jesus' teaching on the Kingdom of God. Then he found some slothful derelicts late at night half-heartedly agreeing to work (these represented the pagan gentiles). Yet, at the end of the day all three groups received the SAME WAGE (one penny). The point Jesus was trying to make in this story is that accepting the invitation to come into the vineyard (the Kingdom of God) is the reward. When anyone accepts the free gift of righteousness by faith through Grace he gets the same favor and access to all God has and all He is. IN CHRIST'S economy WE ALL GET PAID THE SAME. It doesn't matter how long we've been saved. We all have been given Grace, which is favor undeserved and there is no other favor to be handed out. The only favor we will ever get is UNDESERVED favor. None of us has been given the option of favor earned. God's favor is a free gift that all of us receive by faith alone! Think about how God has blessed you when you should have been cut off. Even when we are at our best we're not good enough for God's righteousness. Newborn convert to veteran saint; Grace levels the playing field!

No Lack in Grace[4]

Religion teaches us that strict adherence to Christian duty entitles us to more of God's provision. Some think that if we read the Bible more and pray more passionately then God's blessings will abound more for us. I DO believe in the power of prayer & worship and I deal with it more in chapter 12. However, many think that in order to have *"more of God"* we must scurry about with much religious activity to maintain God's presence. Yet, in Grace, it matters not *how long* we read the Bible or *how feverishly* we pray, God's presence abounds in our lives all the more. Even the Old Testament proves this...

"When the layer of dew evaporated, behold, on the surface of the wilderness there was a fine flake-like thing, fine as the frost on the ground. When the sons of Israel saw it, they said to one another, "What is it?" For they did not know what it was. And Moses said to them, 'It is the bread which the LORD has given you to eat. This is what the LORD has commanded, "Gather of it every man as much as he should eat; you shall take an omer apiece according to the number of persons each of you has in his tent." The sons of Israel did so, AND SOME GATHERED MUCH AND SOME LITTLE. WHEN THEY MEASURED IT WITH AN OMER, HE WHO HAD GATHERED MUCH HAD NO EXCESS, AND HE WHO HAD GATHERED LITTLE HAD NO LACK; EVERY MAN GATHERED AS MUCH AS HE SHOULD EAT."
(Exodus 16:14-18 NASB)

God's provision of manna powerfully teaches us about His marvelous Grace. Notice the manna fell *on the surface of the wilderness.* In the dry seasons of our lives it often feels like God has abandoned us but all the while He is still right there, loving and providing for us. Manna was God's *very best* for the Children of Israel. God gives us His best even when we are at our worst. Jesus became sin for us so we could become His righteousness. In Grace, Jesus got what we deserved and we got what He deserved. Incomprehensible! (Psalms 103:10) We can only receive God's Grace *by faith.* There is no other way to righteousness! God's Grace alone saves us! Also, notice that each day some of the Israelites collected *much* manna and some collected *little*; but in the end everyone's measurement was totally sufficient for their needs. No one among them lacked! This shows us another powerful principle of Grace. Some people may barely get enough time in their day to pray and read the Bible, while others spend hours with God in private devotion. However, when we are covered in God's Grace, *whatever we do unto the Lord,* God makes up for our lack! IN CHRIST we will always have *all we need* because our sufficiency is not of our works but of God's Grace.

"And God is able to make all Grace abound to you, so that always having all sufficiency in everything, you may have an abundance for every good deed." (2 Corinthians 9:8 NASB)

True Godliness

"Since you died with Christ to the basic principles of this world, why, as though you still belonged to it, do you submit to its rules: "Do not handle! Do not taste! Do not touch!?" These are all destined to perish with use, because they are based on human commands and teachings. Such regulations indeed have an appearance of wisdom, with their self-imposed worship, their false humility and their harsh treatment of the body, but they lack any value in restraining sensual indulgence."
(Colossians 2:20-24 NIV)

Paul was addressing religious people who felt that their commitment to piety gave them more personal value to God. Some even felt that they were Godlier than others because of their strict adherence to religious duty. However, in God's Grace, there is no such thing as someone being more *Godly* than someone else. Grace evens the score. The person who has faithfully served God all their life is no Godlier than the person who has recently accepted Christ as Savior. The blood of Jesus is the ONLY THING that makes us acceptable to God. Truth is, when Grace is presented many reject it lest their pride be exposed and their self-righteousness dealt a swift deathblow. Those who have received Grace cannot revel in their self-effort. Their attitude should be, *"If not for Grace; there go I."* Through His eyes of Grace, God loves us all the same, never holds us in contempt and shows no favoritism to one more than another.

"Then Peter replied, 'I see very clearly that GOD SHOWS NO FAVORITISM.' " (Acts 10:34 NLT)

Most of us judge others based on their level of 'spirituality.' We say things like, *"My, isn't he a Godly man"* or *"He's a good Christian"* as if there are *bad* Christians and *good* Christians. There is only one kind of Christian and that is one who is saved by the blood of Jesus. There is no other way to be a Christian. Good works do not make you a certain type Christian (at any level). While God is honored by our devoutness it doesn't make us *Godly.* I'm not downplaying the importance of being passionate, devoted followers of Christ. However, many are at different stages of their spiritual journey. We should never judge others based on their level of behavior or Christian service. Paul realized that he was not able, in his own sufficiency, to keep his commitment to God. However, he was FULLY persuaded that God would keep HIS end of the deal thus ending the fear of failure. Through Grace, God is the one that keeps our commitment to Him.

"For I know whom I have believed and am persuaded that HE IS ABLE TO KEEP WHAT I HAVE COMMITTED TO HIM until that Day."
(2 Timothy 1:12 NKJV)

Think of this. If I were to purchase a new Ferrari (I can dream), I would have to ensure that I could make ALL the payments. That's a steep commitment. I would be considered an idiot if looked across the desk at the banker and said, *"I realize I am committing to make my payments faithfully each month. However, there may be a few months where things are tight and I may not be able to fulfill my obligations to the bank. Would you be willing to take care of my payments when there's too much month at the end of the money?"* Can you imagine his reaction? He would think I'd lost my mind! In comparison, God knew that there was no way we would be able to keep our end of the covenant we made to Him. That's why Paul made it clear that even he was not able to keep his end of the deal at ANYTIME. Jesus paid our debt in full and we are free to live in the endless possibilities of what only His Grace can afford. In the equation of Grace as it pertains to the Christian life, it's not up to us. It's up to God. We must embrace this to have peace with God. What HE started HE ALONE is able to finish (Philippians 1:6; Hebrews 12:2). This may be hard to grasp but it is a powerful truth we must believe nevertheless. This unshakable confidence in God's ability to keep His promise TO US, in spite of our failure, gives us peace when we aren't *"measuring up"* and strengthens our resolve to keep moving in a *Godward* direction. Our Godliness isn't dependent on us. Only Christ's blood makes us Godly. Goodness doesn't define us. GRACE defines us! For too long *Godliness* has been a term reserved only for the *spiritually elite.* This fallacy has led us to label people based on their level of piety. Paul was among the most devout men who ever lived, yet he admitted that he was still the *chief of sinners* (1 Timothy 1:15). It takes a truly Godly person to humble himself enough to admit He is the *worst* of sinners. A Godly attitude is a humble attitude. Our Lord Himself, who was full of Grace and truth, modeled ultimate humility (Philippians 2:3-8).

Humility is the defining disposition of a Godly life that is forged in the fires of Grace.

Wheat or Chaff

All our works (even the good ones) won't get us into Heaven. Only the blood of Jesus secures our reservation. All our self-attempts to earn right standing with God will be burned up like straw.

"John (the Baptist) answered and said to them all, 'As for me, I baptize you with water; but One is coming who is mightier than I, and I am not fit to untie the thong of His sandals; He will baptize you with the Holy Spirit and fire. HIS WINNOWING FORK IS IN HIS HAND TO THOROUGHLY CLEAR HIS THRESHING FLOOR, AND TO GATHER THE WHEAT INTO HIS BARN; BUT HE WILL BURN UP THE CHAFF WITH UNQUENCHABLE FIRE.'" (Luke 3:16-17 NASB)[37]

We often think this passage means that Jesus is going to take His holy machete' and slice away at sinners, separating them from the rank of the saints. This is not what it is saying. John the Baptist prophesied this while baptizing converts from Judaism. These converts (followers of John) were those who believed and anxiously anticipating the promise of the coming Messiah. While he was baptizing them, there were Jewish leaders watching nearby, waiting for the chance to falsely accuse him. However, John indignantly preached against the Pharisees, declaring that Jesus was coming to divide the wheat (true followers of Jesus) from the chaff (the religious Jews who put their faith in the Law) and burn up all their self-efforts like straw with unquenchable fire. Many think John the Baptist was a *clothesline* preacher; ripping people up and down with legalistic fervor. Quite the contrary; John was a defender of the weak and the rejected. He preached that Jesus was coming to take away the sins of the world and bring true repentance (John 1:29).

Prudent or Passionate

We must have the fiery zeal of John the Baptist, preparing this generation to receive the gospel of Grace. Do we want to be known for our prudence or our *passion?* We must live a live as to be remembered for being tenderhearted yet *tenacious,* benevolent yet *bold,* empathetic yet *edgy.* We must be compassionate yet *compelling,* daring enough to pay the price, breaking through religious barriers and reaching out with the love of Jesus to rescue a desperate generation. God is looking for rolling stones, those who will roll the stone away from people's hearts so they can know the love of the resurrected Savior!

"Go through the gates, CLEAR THE WAY FOR THE PEOPLE; build up, build up the highway, REMOVE THE STONES, lift up a standard over the peoples." (Isaiah 62:10 NASB)

Chapter 10

WHAT'S RIGHT ABOUT YOU

"And He, when He comes, will convict the world concerning sin and righteousness and judgment." (John 16:8 NASB)

Have you ever heard someone say, *"What's wrong with you?"* As soon as they mutter the words it feels like a cloud comes over the top of you and dumps a ton of rain on your parade. Its demeaning and slanderous tone seems to bring all emotional insecurity to the surface like a geyser. It reminds me of the scene on the *Truman Show* with Jim Carey when he was sulking on the beach and all of the sudden a rain cloud appeared out of nowhere and started raining on him and no one else. That's how I feel when someone says, *"What's wrong with you?"*

This is the devil's typical shenanigan. He loves to make a detailed inventory of all that's *wrong* with you and every area where you are failing. On the other hand, the Holy Spirit reminds you of what's right about you! According to our key passage the Holy Spirit doesn't convict the believer of sin; He convicts the WORLD of sin. The word *'convict'* in our theme verse means *'to declare guilty'*. The Holy Spirit does not pronounce the harsh sentence of guilt upon believers. Rather He *convinces* us of our righteousness. When we believe on the name of Jesus we are made righteous and the Holy Spirit convinces us of our righteousness! Although there may be tension in the relationship due to our disobedience, the Holy Spirit does not pass sentence on us (convict). It is the devil's mission to convince us that the Holy Spirit is condemning us, while all the time it is the voice of the enemy harassing and accusing us

"For the accuser of our brethren has been thrown down, he who accuses them before our God day and night. And they overcame him because of the blood of the Lamb and because of the word of their testimony..." (Revelation 12:10-11 NASB)

It is vitally important to understand the truth of God's Grace that sets us free (John 8:32). When we are confident that God's Grace makes us righteous apart from our works, we will be able to rightly discern whose *voice* is *convicting* us when we fail. The way we overcome the voices of accusation hurled against us is to confess (sometimes shout out loud) the truth that Christ's blood alone has made us righteousness apart from our performance perfectly to the standard of the Law. As the passage above reiterates, we can continually experience the transforming power of Grace (the overcoming life) when we boldly testify of the work of the cross.

The 'Grace' Escape

> "...When the enemy shall come in like a flood, the Spirit of the LORD shall lift up a standard against him." (Isaiah 59:19 KJV)

The Hebrew word for '*standard*' is *nuwc* (pronounced *nus*), which means to *flee or escape.* God's awesome mercy made a way of escape for us. The standard spoken of here is a direct prophetic reference to Jesus. The way of escape is Jesus! God sent Jesus to be sin's sacrifice for us. When the enemy comes looking for us, he can't find us. We've escaped. We have escaped the judgment of God and any possibility of condemnation. Through Jesus we slip by the enemy unaware and unnoticed. We are forever free from the imputation of sin.

> "...They have escaped the pollutions of the world through the knowledge of the Lord and Savior Jesus Christ." (2 Peter 2:20 NKJV)

Not of This World

We need to get a revelation of what *'not of this world'* means in order to be confident when the enemy comes to condemn us. The Kingdom of God is not of this world. Therefore, since we are citizens of the kingdom of God we are not of this world. While we are not convicted of our sin (as our key passage says), we are being *convinced* of our righteousness. Remember that the Holy Spirit convicts the *world* of sin. When you become a believer you are taken out of the kingdom of darkness (this world's system) and are transferred into the Kingdom of God and His light.

> "Giving thanks to the Father, Who has qualified us to share in the inheritance of the SAINTS IN LIGHT. For HE RESCUED US FROM THE DOMAIN OF DARKNESS, AND TRANSFERRED US TO THE KINGDOM OF HIS BELOVED SON." (Colossians 1:13-14 NASB)

This means you are an official citizen of Heaven. As a believer you are subject to a totally different jurisdiction than those who are in the world and are still under bondage to sin and condemnation. We are not of this world.

> "If you were of the world, the world would love its own; but because YOU ARE NOT OF THE WORLD, but I chose you out of the world, because of this the world hates you." (John 15:19 NASB)

> "Jesus answered, 'MY KINGDOM IS NOT OF THIS WORLD.'"
> (John 18:36 NASB)

There is nothing but light all around you. This is why you won't hear harsh words from the Holy Spirit when you fail or fall short. The Holy Spirit believes in you and is cheering you on! He is your most loyal fan. When you're down He won't throw mud at you. He lifts you OUT of the mud. Condemning and discouraging words come from of the darkness. The kingdom of this world is a dark place; but when you are IN CHRIST there is no darkness AT ALL.

> "God is Light, and in Him there is NO DARKNESS AT ALL."
> (1 John 1:5 NASB)

When we fail, the devil is the one who immediately condemns us, attempting to bring disappointment and discouragement. On the other hand, the Holy Spirit is the One who encourages us to run Jesus and fall upon the forgiveness God has *already given* to us.

> "In whom WE HAVE redemption, the forgiveness of sins."
> (Colossians 1:14 NASB)

Who Are You Listening To?

Although we have this awesome redemption (the forgiveness of sins) IN CHRIST, the devil still deceives us into thinking that we must bear judgment when we fail. He does this in order to *push us away* from

God. Yet all the while the Holy Spirit is pointing us to the Father heart of God. When you fail, don't run away from God… Run TO Him! The Holy Spirit is not against us. He is our helper.

"But when the HELPER comes, whom I shall send to you from the Father, the Spirit of truth who proceeds from the Father, He will testify of Me." (John 15:26 NKJV)

Another word for *Helper* is *'comforter'.* The Greek word is *Parakletos* meaning *'One who comes along side.'* In other words, the Holy Spirit comes along side of us and helps us to fulfill our potential and strengthen us when we are weak. He is literally ON OUR SIDE. He is not against us; He is FOR US! (Romans 8:31) This is why He never convicts the believer. The Holy Spirit comes to *convince* us of our righteousness IN CHRIST (John 16:8-10). The Holy Spirit tells us we're *O.K.* but meanwhile the devil tells us we're *KO'd.* Who's voice are you listening to?

Many times when we enter into worship and prayer, the devil does everything he can to drive us out of God's presence with condemnation and self-doubt. To be sure, when we sin we will feel grieved. However, the Holy Spirit beckons us to run TO Jesus, not away from him. We do not have to *cower fearfully* under the cloud of condemnation. We can *come fearlessly* before the throne of Grace (Hebrews 4:16). The Holy Spirit never condemns those who are IN CHRIST! He is our *Encourager.* When we feel discouraged it is not the voice of the Holy Spirit. When we pray, the enemy immediately pulls out our *bad rap* sheet and proceeds to tear us down, but the Holy Spirit *always* builds us up.

"But you, beloved, building yourselves up on your most holy faith, praying in the Holy Spirit." (Jude 1:20 NASB)

1 Peter 5:5 says, God resists the proud (self-righteous) but gives Grace to the humble (broken & repentant). And the truth is we all desperately need Grace. Even in our best efforts none of us *have it all together.* God doesn't give us Grace *when* we need it. He gives us Grace BECAUSE we need it. We need Grace every single second of every single day. If we didn't need Grace, God wouldn't have sent His Son into our broken world. Because of Grace, nothing is missing and nothing is broken. We are complete in Him (Colossians 2:10). Grace

takes our broken pieces and turns us into *masterpieces*. Romans 8:1 says, *"There is therefore NOW NO CONDEMNATION for those who are IN CHRIST Jesus."* The word *"now"* means *right this very second* there is no reason for you to feel condemned. Look all you want but you won't find a trace of condemnation in Jesus. Jesus was already condemned for us (Isaiah 53). And since we are IN CHRIST we too are no longer condemned.

When Jesus prepared to depart the earth, I'm sure the disciples didn't have clue what they would do without their mentor, best friend and faithful Shepherd. The disciples needed comfort and reassurance. Therefore, Jesus lovingly addressed their fears and uncertainty. He promised them the Holy Spirit would come and convince them of His presence and continually reveal His true character to them. The purpose of The Holy Spirit in our lives is to convince us of the nature of Jesus' love and total commitment to us. This is what John 15:26 means when it says, *"He (the Holy Spirit) will testify of Me (tell the truth about our identity in Christ)."*

Jesus' final sentence to His disciples is also of critical importance to note. If you had just a few minutes left on this earth with your loved ones what would you say? Would you tell them to remember to take out the trash, keep the house spotless and all the dishes washed? Would you make sure they knew how to divide your estate and liquidate your assets? Or would you desperately try to convey your affinity and deep affection for them? The answer here is obvious. You would certainly share your most profound love and desire for them to succeed in life. Many think that last thing Jesus said was, *"Go into all the world and preach..."* Without reading to the very end of what He said many charge out to fulfill His directives and work feverishly to make sure every creature hears the gospel. This is what we call the *Great Commission.* It is an extremely important call and I'm not demeaning its importance. I myself am deeply committed to this call. However, Jesus didn't leave us with an *imperative.* He left us with a *promise...*

"I am with you ALWAYS, even to the end of the age."
(Matthew 28:20 NASB)

This verse is crystal clear and needs no Greek translation. Jesus simply and affectionately said, as He was ascending into the heavens,

"I will be with you ALWAYS... TO THE END...!" Jesus wasn't being flippant. He carefully chose His words to assure the disciples and future generations of His everlasting love and His steadfast commitment to remain with them no matter what! You must allow this to sink deep into your soul as revelation truth. Otherwise, you'll never trust the possibility that Jesus will *never* leave you and will never fully embrace your purpose! We must receive His promise before we can fulfill His purpose. Vital to our commission is His abiding presence. Jesus is referred to in scriptures as The GOOD SHEPHERD and the Good Shepherd doesn't abandon His flock to the wolves (John 10:11-14). What kind of shepherd would Jesus be if He lost track of His sheep and wasn't able to rescue them? Be certain: if one single little lamb strays. He will go after it not to return empty handed (Matt 18:11-14). To this, all our insecurities are swallowed up in the constant awareness that we are never forgotten, never alone, never abandoned and never disowned.

"I will not leave you as orphans..." (John 14:18 NASB)

"And I give eternal life to them, and they will never perish; and NO ONE WILL SNATCH THEM OUT OF MY HAND." (John 10:28 NASB)

You may say, *"But there are so many issues and shortcomings in my life."* There is good-news for you! God doesn't see you the way you see yourself. He sees you through the finished work of HIS SON! Therefore, He sees you as perfect because He sees you IN CHRIST. Therefore, since Christ is perfect, He also sees YOU as perfect.

"By this, love is perfected with us (we are made perfect IN CHRIST'S love) so that we may have confidence (not fear) in the day of judgment (the very moment we feel judged); because as He is, so also are we in this world (God sees us the way He sees Jesus)." (1 John 4:17 NASB)[37]

We all have issues but God isn't focused on your issues. God eyes are fixed on Jesus. Therefore, He sees you as blameless IN CHRIST. Don't worry, God also sees the issues and intends on dealing with them in His time and in His way. You are being perfected daily. However, God sees you as a finished work because you are hidden deep in the finished work of His Son. You can rest secure and confident in Christ's eternal love for you. The enemy cannot hit a HIDDEN target.

"Your life is hidden with Christ in God." (Colossians 3:3 NASB)

We are not only hidden from the devil but we are also hidden from God's judgment and wrath. Our lives are securely hidden inside of Christ. God cannot see the failures of our lives because we are hidden IN CHRIST. God doesn't see us as weaklings.

"And He said to me, "My Grace is sufficient for you, for My strength is made perfect in weakness." Therefore most gladly I will rather boast in my infirmities, that the power of Christ may rest upon me." (2 Corinthians 12:9 NASB)

We are perfect in God's eyes even in our weaknesses. That's why the Bible says, *"Let the weak say I am strong"* (Joel 3:10). Be sure that God would never tell us to lie. When you say, *"I am perfectly strong IN CHRIST "* you are speaking the gospel truth (1 Timothy 2:7). The more you believe and speak this the more God's strength will manifest in your life. Because of God's Grace we have been enriched in everything (especially in the weak areas of our lives). Jesus makes up for all of our deficiencies.

I thank my God always concerning you for the Grace of God which was given you IN CHRIST Jesus, that in everything you were enriched in Him, in all speech and all knowledge, even as the testimony concerning Christ was confirmed in you, so that you are not lacking in any gift, awaiting eagerly the revelation of our Lord Jesus Christ, WHO WILL ALSO CONFIRM YOU TO THE END, BLAMELESS in the day of our Lord Jesus Christ." (1 Corinthians 1:4-8 NASB)

IN CHRIST we lack nothing! Yet, so many times we see ourselves on the wrong side of tracks. You may say, *"But I have so many sinful, weak areas in my life and I am constantly falling short."* Child of God you must see yourself as a complete work IN CHRIST. Many think that if they remain squeaky-clean and perfectly pure to the end then Jesus will confirm them in the end. This is not what it says. Read 1 Corinthians 1:4-8 again, it says that He would continue to confirm us *"to the end."* From the moment we put our trust IN CHRIST until the day we see Him face to face, Jesus *confirms* us as blameless before the Father! By faith we need to receive Christ's *confirmation* instead of the devil's *condemnation.* God's sees us as a finished work because He sees us IN CHRIST'S finished work. As long as we believe rightly about ourselves we will eventually find ourselves living rightly.

Victorious living flows from victorious thinking. Paul was confident when he said that God would finish what He started *until the day of Christ Jesus.*

For I am confident of this very thing, that He who began a good work in you WILL PERFECT IT UNTIL THE DAY OF CHRIST JESUS."
(Philippians 1:6 NASB)

You may see yourself as a work in progress but God sees you as a finished work IN CHRIST!

Now that's what's RIGHT about you!

Chapter 11

GRACE MARKS THE SPOT

"But He gives more Grace. Therefore it says, 'God resists the proud, but gives Grace to the humble.'"
(James 4:6 NKJV)

The spirit of religion deceives us into thinking that we are capable of performing perfectly to the standard of the Law. This is the fallacy of legalistic teaching: that we can actually get to the place where we NEVER give into temptation and are able to avoid sin at EVERY turn. Ludicrous! The Jewish legalists despised and reviled Paul because he reminded them of their inability to live a Godly life apart from God's Grace. While it may not appear it at first, when you observe religious folks or talk with them long enough, they always point toward their own 'devoutness' and 'piety.' Religion always spoils the fragrance of humility. No matter how holy we think we are the spirit of the world will constantly challenge us. Yet, James says that God gives more Grace to us in those times. When we finally humble ourselves and admit that we can't do anything apart from God's Grace that is when the power of God takes hold and begins to work in our lives. According to our key passage, God resists a spirit of pride and self-sufficiency. The Greek word for 'resists' is *antitasso* which means *to set one's self in battle against another*. It is where we get our English word antihistamine. (Like an antihistamine fighting against the symptoms of a virus). God literally sets Himself against pride. Those who think they can achieve righteousness through works and impose those same self-righteous standards on others will eventually have a rude awakening. Why? Because Grace does not work for those who think they are beyond the need for it. The fact is, no matter where we are in our relationship with Jesus, we will desperately need radical Grace until the day we die.

My wife and I own a Boston Terrier named Jazz who just turned ten-years old. We absolutely adore her. Jazz follows us wherever we go and never let's us out of her sight. No matter how many times Jazz makes a *mishap* on the floor we instantly and lovingly forgive her. As

Jazz looks up with sad eyes, ears slumped down, trembling in fear we tell her that we love her and that everything is alright. Then Jazz gleefully bounds around vivaciously wagging her tail in appreciation. Now be certain, the stains never come out completely clean. But whenever we see the spots on the carpet our love completely overrides her *failure* to be perfect. In fact, we still let her hop on our lap, sleep beside us on the couch and toss treats out to her as if nothing ever happened. Think of this... Jazz isn't even capable of *apologizing* and yet we release forgiveness regardless. Now if we love a dog that much how much more does our Heavenly Father love and forgive us when we make a mess of things.

Think of God's Grace in these terms... When my children disobey me I don't tear up their birth certificates. No failure in their lives is too great for me to no longer consider them my children. They don't forfeit my last name just because they fail to obey my rules. I will always love them and they will always be mine. And so it is with our Heavenly Father. I know this is a hard pill to swallow for some religious people. However, for the broken and humble who need God's Grace it is good news. The most amazing thing about God's Grace is that we belong to Him forever. Hallelujah! When this truth grasps you, it won't cause you to go out and sin! It will make you want to love and live for Him even more than ever. Guaranteed!

I don't care how long you have been serving God; there will always be a *worldly pull* on you. These carnal tendencies or points of concern (I call them *sin spots*) will be something that we will continually deal with. Notice that God didn't take away Paul's *thorn*. No one seems to know what this *thorn* was. Some scholars claim it was depression, suicidal tendencies or an unknown sin vice (see page 2 for my possible explanation). One thing is for sure, no matter what it was (or what ours is for that matter) the Bible teaches us that God's Grace is more than sufficient enough to cover us. Our weakness is the perfect platform for God's strength to work in us..."And He has said to me, 'My Grace is sufficient for you, for **power is perfected in weakness.'** Most gladly, therefore, I will rather boast about my weaknesses, so that the power of Christ may dwell in me." (2 Corinthians 12:9 NASB)

This gives us hope because although we struggle in certain areas of our lives, God's Grace completely and permanently removes the condemnation, punishment and imputation of sin. These sin-spots I refer to can be: temper, lust, envy, jealousy, selfishness, conceit, doubt, anger, impatience or _____ (I purposely put the blank here for you to fill in with your sin-spot). The Bible teaches us that sin is always crouching at our door (Genesis 4:7) and the truth is (more often than we'd like to admit) we are vulnerable to be pounced on. But the very moment we put our faith in God's Grace we will begin to experience the victory that overcomes ANY sin *issue* in our life (1 John 5:4). We must also understand that Grace cannot be manufactured or forced to work by our self-efforts. It is born (naturally flows) from God. If I've said it once, I've said it a thousand times, *"When we stop; God starts!"* It's that simple! Grace folds its arms when we operate in our own strength. Paul called this *"frustrating the Grace of God"* (Galatians 2:21). When a victim is drowning he must first stop thrashing about before the lifeguard will jump in and save him otherwise they will both be dragged to their watery grave. The same is true of exerting our self-effort to be righteous. Only when we learn to rest in the power of God's Grace will we begin to savor the victory of the overcoming life. Victorious living is a *by-product* of God's Grace. Instead of anxiously *running about* to be perfect we should be diligent to *rest* in God's Grace.

"So there remains a Sabbath rest for the people of God. For the one who has entered His rest has Himself also rested from his works, as God did from His. THEREFORE LET US BE DILIGENT TO ENTER THAT REST, SO THAT NO ONE WILL FALL, through following the same example of disobedience." (Hebrews 4:9-11 NASB)

God's arms are the only arms you can rest in while He's working at the same time. Therefore, our work is to *rest* in God's Grace and simply *believe* in His steadfast love (John 6:29). This is how to enjoy our peace with Him. The Jews of Paul's time had great difficulty accepting the fact that they no longer had to meet the expectations of the Law in order to be righteous before God. That's why Paul emphasized that in order to avoid falling into disobedience we must learn how to rest in Jesus' finished work. Jesus is our Sabbath. Once we cease from striving in our own efforts to be righteous and simply rest in His Grace, we will experience God's power to overcome sin.

God's Grace ALWAYS overcomes the world. It is by God's might alone that our sinful tendencies are brought under submission (Zechariah 4:6). When we trust in God's Grace sin loses its power to hold us under its tyranny (Romans 6:14). Some people (who aren't what we call *'good'*) struggle their whole lives with certain vices and pestering habits. However, even for those who consider themselves *good enough* not to fall into sin still have need of great Grace. It isn't our inability or ability to perform to God's standard of the Law that determines our favor with God. Grace gives us approval from God thereby instantly canceling out the condemnation of Sin. Jesus alone is acceptable to God and therefore so are we (1 John 4:17). Even in our best we will always come up *very short* from God's standard of perfection (Romans 3:23). Religious people find it difficult to admit they are incapable of living the Christian life. They feel as if *holy living* qualifies them for God's Grace. Actuality it's the other way around. God's Grace gives us power to live holy. However, when we miss the mark, just like a trapeze artist missing the swinging bar, we will always fall into the net of Grace. Sin loses no matter what. We win no matter what. Hallelujah! (1 Corinthians 15:54-55)

Grace atones for all our sin issues. This is not to say that we shouldn't make significant strides toward maturity or that we can't regularly experience consistent victory over sin (1 Corinthians 15:57; Romans 6:14). However, it is impossible for us to ever think in this life that we will be sinless. That's why God gives us the gift of Grace. If we could *save* ourselves we wouldn't need a *Savior*. Our righteousness isn't based on whether we succeed or fail at performing perfectly to the standard of the Law. Rather it's based upon Christ's finished work and His free gift of Righteousness.

"I have been crucified with Christ; and it is no longer I who live, but Christ lives in me; and the life which I now live in the flesh I live by faith IN THE SON OF GOD, who loved me and gave Himself up for me."
(Galatians 2:20 KJV)

We no longer have to work to become righteous. Every time I meditate on this amazing truth it makes me sigh in overwhelming relief. Righteousness isn't something we *achieve;* it is something we *receive!* Through Christ's finished work we can stand before God with sincere hearts, fully washed and assured that we are perfectly acceptable to Him (Hebrews 10:22; Revelation 1:5).

Communion Unworthy

Much of what we believe about righteousness is based mostly upon *our ability* to live holy. In other words, if we live holy then we'll be righteous. Yet, we still sing the song *"Oh, how I love Jesus because He first loved me."* If many of us sang what we really believe it might sound like, *"Oh how I love Jesus because He loves me for doing everything right!"* The sad truth is many actually believe that! Take for instance the Holy Communion. The communion is a living sermon illustration that Jesus gave us both to be seen and experienced. Many modern day illustrated sermons are seen from a one-dimensional view. However, the Lord's Supper is a masterful visual to be partaken of in a personal way. It was not given to become another religious ordinance (as so many treat it). The Holy Communion isn't holy *in and of itself.* There is only ONE who is holy. The bread and the wine we partake of in communion aren't holy. These *elements* are merely a representation of the Holy One. We must remember that communion wasn't meant to be a *religious* observance but rather a *reminder* of God's Grace. Communion is an invitation of mercy extended to ALL who need Christ's love, forgiveness and healing.

When communion is administered in some churches there is often fear attached to it. You'll hear statements such as: *"If you have any sin in your life you shouldn't take this communion or you'll bring damnation on yourself"* or *"If you take communion with sin in your heart you trample God's Grace under foot."* This makes many parishioners feel *communion unworthy* and thus will allow the communion plate to pass right on by. Paul's letter to the Hebrews addressed a growing number of Jewish Christians who were forsaking the joy of their newfound salvation and reverting back to their Jewish traditions. Note: I didn't say they were forsaking their salvation. They were forsaking the JOY of their salvation *(salvation is joyous when you quit relying on your own miserable ability to be perfect).* The phrase, *"trampling the Son of God under foot"* refers to the Jews who chose self-righteous works over receiving Grace. When we reject God's Grace we in effect treat Christ's sacrifice as a common thing. It is far less reverent to reject God's Grace than it is to fail at living holy.

"How much more severely do you think a man deserves to be punished who has trampled the Son of God under foot, who has treated as an

unholy thing the blood of the covenant that sanctified him, and who has INSULTED THE SPIRIT OF GRACE?" (Hebrews 10:29 NIV)

It's like a slap in God's face to choose self-righteous works over the precious blood of His dear Son. After all Jesus endured, people will still choose works over Grace. Unbelievable! What a blatant disregard to God's gift. It's horribly degrading to God to say that the blood of Jesus isn't powerful enough to save us. My friend, there isn't anyone who is ever "good enough" to receive communion. We all regularly fail and yet we are all invited to the communion table, especially when we are struggling. Jesus welcomes us to come and find total forgiveness without fear of being turned away (John 6:37). When we sin it is not the time to reject God's Grace. The perfect time to come to the throne of Grace is when we are IN NEED (Hebrews 4:16). Remember, even on our best day we are still not good enough...

"For whenever you eat this bread and drink this cup, you proclaim the Lord's death until He comes, therefore whoever eats the bread or drinks the cup of the Lord in an unworthy manner will be guilty of sinning against the body and blood of the Lord. A man ought to examine himself before he eats of the bread and drinks of the cup. For anyone who eats and drinks without recognizing the body of the Lord eats and drinks judgment on himself. That is why many among you are weak and sick, and a number of you have fallen asleep."
(1 Corinthians 11:26-30 NIV)

Whenever we partake of the communion we proclaim (illustrate) the Grace of God. Partaking of the communion in an *unworthy manner* is to *feel* or perceive ourselves as unworthy. We should never think or claim that Jesus' blood wasn't enough to save us. The KJV says when we partake of communion with feelings of unworthiness we literally *"drink damnation to ourselves."* Believing we are unworthy of God's goodness causes us to ultimately refuse His goodness. Partaking of the communion *unworthily* is an adverb that describes *how* we partake of it. Verse 29 says if you *eat and drink* unworthily. It doesn't say that YOU are unworthy. Rather it's in the WAY in which we partake of it. If we partake *as if* we are unworthy then we will have a difficult time receiving. However, if we partake as if we ARE worthy (by Christ's finished work) then we will have the faith to receive all that Jesus' blood and body provides (forgiveness, health and wholeness).

Receiving from God isn't based on our worthiness anyway. It's based on CHRIST'S worthiness. We receive all God has to offer not based on what we do but on what Jesus has already done. Paul says we *should* examine ourselves (verse 28). By this he doesn't mean that we should pull out a checklist of all our past and present mistakes. Rather we should bring our sins TO Him in order that we may receive His Grace, mercy and forgiveness. There is an old worship chorus we used to sing that says, *"Just forget about yourself. Concentrate on Him and worship Him."* This is truly the key to breakthrough. When we focus on our self and our sin it drags us deeper down. Besides, if God forgets all our sins why would He want us to shine the spotlight on them? When we hear voices reminding us of all our weaknesses it is not the voice of the Holy Spirit. In order to focus on the bright future God has for us (Jeremiah 29:11) we must quit turning around and looking back into our past. Besides, God's Grace constantly follows us and clears our trail of mistakes.

"Surely goodness and mercy shall follow me all the days of my life."
(Psalms 23:5 NKJV)

Broken for Our Brokenness

Paul goes on to say in 1 Corinthians 11:28 that immediately after we have examined ourselves *we should freely eat of the bread and drink of the cup."* To be sure, we aren't to live in denial of our wrongdoing. We should admit when we have sinned. However, instead of running from God we should lay our sin down at His feet. And as we drink from the cup of communion it will fill us with the faith that God's forgiveness is totally setting us free! So many well-meaning leaders administer communion, cautioning us to get our sins forgiven before we dare put the bread on our tongue. 1 Corinthians 11:30 teaches us that many in the Corinthian church were weak, sick and even died prematurely because they failed to *discern* (recognize) the body of Jesus. They were taking communion without understanding what His death was for. Critical to properly discerning Christ's body is to We must recognize that He was torn apart for our sin, not to make us more guilty for our sin, but to set us free from our sin. It's sad to say but *some* never come to Jesus because they have been told God doesn't accept unholy people into His presence. Rightfully discerning Jesus' body is to understand that He was crucified for all who struggle with sin issues. The truth is we all have gone astray (Isaiah 53:6). But the good news is we are made worthy through Christ the Worthy One!

It is also important in coming to the invitation for mercy that we reflect a true desire to embrace mercy. The attitude should never be, *"Well since Jesus loves me and His Grace is available, therefore I will do whatever, whenever..."* We must always approach humbly and tenderly with deep gratitude and joyful reverence. An authentic sense of brokenness and worship should always precede the communion table. We should never receive communion as a traditional ritualistic ordinance but as sincere recipients of the Grace of our Lord Jesus. Sadly, many *take part* in the communion but refuse to actually *partake.*

At this point I encourage you to get alone with God and truly partake of the communion. In your brokenness, freely receive His Grace without condemnation (damnation)! As you eat the bread and drink the cup, remember Jesus and everything He has done for you. As you do you will become extremely aware of the nearness of His presence and it will begin to break the bondage of sin over you. His shed blood is for your forgiveness (Ephesians 1:7) and His broken body is for your healing (Isaiah 53:5). Beloved, He was broken for your brokenness. Therefore, freely consume His mercy then leave the rest to Him. Where there is any sin in your life God's Grace super abounds (Romans 5:20). The potency of His love and the purity of His Grace will thoroughly scour every filthy stain.

JESUS PAID IT ALL

I hear the Savior say
Thy strength indeed is small
Child of weakness watch and pray
Find in Me thine all in all

Jesus paid it all
All to him I owe
Sin had left a crimson stain
He washed it white as snow

Lord now indeed I find
Thy power and Thine alone
Can change the leper's spots
And melt the heart of stone

Jesus paid it all
All to him I owe
Sin had left a crimson stain
He washed it white as snow

For nothing good have I
Whereby Thy Grace to claim
I'll wash my garments white
In the blood of Calvary's Lamb

Jesus paid it all
All to him I owe
Sin had left a crimson stain
He washed it white as snow

And when before the throne
I stand in Him complete
Jesus died my soul to save
My lips shall still repeat

Jesus paid it all
All to him I owe
Sin had left a crimson stain
He washed it white as snow

Lyrics by Elvina Hall & Music by John T. Grape
© 1865 Public Domain

Chapter 12

REPAINT AND THIN NO MORE

**"And Jesus said, "I do not condemn you, either.
Go. From now on sin no more." (John 8:11 NASB)**

The exterior of a small country church desperately needed to be refurbished. The pastor, who took up a collection to pay for the paint supplies, went to the local hardware store, laid the money on the counter and said, *"We figure we need 8 buckets of paint sir."* The clerk informed the pastor that he only had enough money for 4 buckets of paint, but graciously said, *"Tell you what I'll do; since you're a preacher I'll throw some paint thinner in and we'll call it even."* When the pastor returned to the eager crew waiting to paint, he informed them of the unfortunate situation... *"Folks, I hate to inform you but we didn't collect enough money to buy all the paint we need. However, I've prayed about it and I believe I have a solution. What we'll do is mix the paint thinner with the paint and hopefully it will stretch out what little bit we have. I have faith that we've got all the paint we need to finish the job. If God did it with five loaves and two fish, then I know he can do it with our paint too."* Without any hesitation, the pastor and all the church members got right to work and as they soaked up the last drop of paint, they applied it to the remaining patch of wood at the top of the gable. The congregation looked proudly upon a job *well done* as the pastor offered up a prayer of thanks. Just then, a dark cloud rolled in and hovered right over the newly painted church. A huge thunderclap preceded a heavy downpour. Shockingly all of the paint began dripping down the walls to the ground as the congregants stood watching in total disbelief and disappointment. The pastor tore his shirt, shook his fist and yelled towards Heaven, *"Why Lord?!"* Suddenly, a loud voice reverberated from Heaven and relied, *"REPAINT AND THIN NO MORE!"*

As corny as this story is, it points out a powerful truth regarding Grace. When we mix the Law with Grace it completely neutralizes the effects of Grace (Galatians 5:4) and makes more of a mess in our lives. Another implication is that many preachers preach with stern warning, *"Repent and sin no more!"* However, nowhere in the Bible (in any translation) will you find this in scripture. When we repent from our sin, it does not mean that we will never sin again. In fact, be certain; you will blow it at times. You need to know this now so you won't be disappointed when it happens. After all, no one is incapable of failing. Pride so easily deceives us into believing that we are incapable of sinning. We are at the height of arrogance and self-righteousness when we feel we have no need for Grace. Hard as it is to believe, there are people who actually believe they are sinless. However, truly humble people quickly admit that they are utterly dependent on God's Grace. Notice in our key passage that Jesus didn't tell the woman, *"Repent and sin no more."* No! He said, *"GO and sin no more."* In essence He librated her by proclaiming, *"You're free from sin and you don't have to fall prey to it any longer."* Nowhere in scripture does it say she *verbally* repented. However, because her heart was broken, Jesus simply forgave her and as she freely received His forgiveness she was able to turn and walk in a whole new direction.

We need to realize that when we sin, Jesus, our great high priest and advocate represents us before God through His finished work (1 John 2:1). An advocate is someone who pleads our case and defends us. When a Lawyer represents a client, the client is to remain silent while he is being defended. Although the evidence is completely stacked against us, Jesus in essence stands before the Father and holds out His nailed scarred hands. When the Father sees His Son, He can only pardon us based on His work on the cross. Jesus continually presents us as blameless to God in spite of our shortcomings and failures (Colossians 1:22). When we stand firm on this we will experience the power that saves us (Romans 1:16-17). Grace is more than just a free pass to eternal life. It is the very power of God that gives us victory over sin, destructive habits, sickness, confusion, and all the work of the enemy (Romans 1:16; 5:17; 6:14).

Presumptuous Repentance

At this juncture it is important to address the following question: *If Grace saves us apart from our ability to maintain or own righteousness, do we have to ask God to forgive us when we miss the mark?* To answer this we must first understand what the Bible teaches about prayer itself. Philippians 4:6 tells us, "...*In everything by prayer and supplication with thanksgiving let your requests be made known unto God.*" God is omniscient, so why or how is it ever appropriate to tell Him what we want? Though it is seemingly unnecessary because He already knows, God wants us to apply our faith by coming to Him and verbalizing our needs. Otherwise, in light of God's sovereignty, our prayer would be a futile exercise. Therefore, in view of repentance, it would be *presumptuous faith* if we didn't carry an authentic sense of remorse before the Lord when we commit sin. If God wants us to bring our confessions of *faith* before Him so also, He wants us to bring our confessions of *fault* before Him. It is critical here to understand that God has already granted forgiveness to us before we sin *(I further explain and support this with greater detail in the next chapter).* However, He wants us to recognize our error and turn from it. Humble confession helps avert us from returning to the bondage of a lifestyle of sin and also prevents us from further hurting others by our sin. We must also understand that confession isn't as much for God's ears as it is for OUR ears. God already knows we have sinned. However, when we confess our sin it has great power to release the sin we tend to bottle up inside. Sin that is not dealt with is potentially destructive to ourselves and others. Repentance by confession helps us fully admit our sin so we can deal with it. Outward confession brings to light hidden things we are prone to avoid. Repentance involves *recognizing* when we sin, *reconciling* our wrongs with others and *returning* to living the life God has called us to. When Nathan confronted David (2 Samuel 12) it would have been the height of presumptuousness for David not to have verbalized his repentance recorded in Psalms 51, but rather just "moved on" without taking time to reflect and repent. It WAS important for David to acknowledge his gross error and to ponder the consequences that it would bring upon himself and the other individuals he had involved in his twisted plot. However, no matter the depth of His sin, God was quick to forgive, set things aright in his life and restore His leadership. God is so good!

Untie God's Hands

Before we delve further into the issue of repentance we must understand that it is much more than a verbal response to our failures. For instance, suppose I were to offend my wife or cause her to be upset with me. I could verbally apologize all day long but most of the time saying, *"I'm sorry honey"* is not enough to 'seal the deal' (Can I get an amen from all the husbands out there). Although, *"I'm sorry"* helps to begin the repentance process, merely saying it doesn't mean I'm truly sorry. Likewise, the repentance process begins when we are TRULY sorry. Repentance is more a heart issue than it is a mouth issue. When we embrace Grace, we will never be at ease with our sin and will immediately feel a sense of discomfort. Repentance begins before the words *"I'm sorry"* are even formed on our lips. When earthly relationships are in tension due to unresolved conflict a *formal* apology is necessary to begin the reconciliatory process both for the offender and the offended. Likewise, although God knows our hearts, telling Him we are remorseful for our sin *reveals* our total dependency on Him and *releases* His Grace to work on our behalf. It's as if we *untie* God's hands to fix what is broken in our lives.

Confessing our faults doesn't mean that we should *focus* on our faults. Grace has already settled the issue of our failures. Rather we should focus on God's *forgiveness.* The purpose of repentance is to *recognize* our sin not *rehearse* it. When we confess our sin we are simply acknowledging our inability to "get it right" apart from God's Grace thereby allowing His love to transform us. Merely saying, *"I'm sorry"* doesn't produce real transformation. Rather, it's *coming* to the end of ourselves and *committing* to the process of change that places us back on the path to wholeness. Therefore, when we sin, we should sincerely admit our weaknesses and QUICKLY move forward trusting in God's Grace and forgiveness to restore us where we have failed. God hasn't forgiven us for HIS sake but for OUR sakes. We must understand that sin doesn't terminate our righteousness (Romans 11:29) but it can seriously jeopardize our earthly relationships, our ministries, our health, our peace of mind and our prosperity.

Get Your Mind Right

"Produce fruit in keeping with repentance." (Matthew 3:8 NIV)

John the Baptist used these words when confronting the religious Pharisees who were standing back from afar in aghast as he baptized his Jewish converts. The Greek word for 'repentance' here is *metanoia*, which means *'a change of mind.'* The Bible teaches us that Godly sorrow produces a true change of mind (2 Corinthians 7:10).

Once we change our mind we naturally change our behavior. When we are born anew in Christ our inner man truly desires to change. Repentance doesn't mean we will perform perfectly or have unflawed obedience. Rather it's the process of Christ's perfection (sanctification) at work in us. Our total salvation in Christ involves three things: justification, sanctification and glorification. Our justification is immediate, our sanctification is life long and our glorification is in the Kingdom to come. Christ is involved in all three and all three are fully promised. As believers when we struggle with sin we must remember that the Holy Spirit is still powerfully at work in us. We shouldn't worry whether or not He will be successful in that work. Know for certain that the Holy Spirit is exceedingly efficient in purifying us. He will not fail. The very notion that our inner man is struggling for freedom in the outer man is a sure sign that Godly sorrow is producing the desire to change.

So many try to change by sheer will power but eventually fail because they haven't truly changed their mind about How God truly sees them and all they are in Christ. As a result they gravitate right back to sinful and harmful behavior patterns. It reminds me of a carnival inflatable where you stand inside a lane with a heavy-duty elastic band tied around your waist. Then you see how far you can run. Try all you want to keep running but eventually the tension of the band will reach its limit and snap you back full force into the wall of the inflatable. It's the same way with trying to change your behavior without a true heart change. You can only go so far before your old mindset yanks you back into the life you've always known. The way to see real results in your life is to change your mind about the way God sees and feels about you.

Mind over Matters

"And do not be conformed to this world, but be transformed by the renewing of your mind, so that you may prove what the will of God is, that which is good and acceptable and perfect." (Romans 12:2 NASB)

Once again, there is no such thing as *spiritual growth* (see page 44). 12:2 does not tell us that we are transformed by the renewing of our *spirit,* but rather by the renewing of our mind thus proving (living out in vital display) God's good, acceptable and perfect will. This is literally how we successfully apply the mind over life's matters. Proverbs 23:7 tells us that we are a product of what we think of ourselves. Therefore, having a radically renewed mindset to all we are, all we have, and all we can do through Christ (Philippians 4:13) is vital to radical transformation. It is also absolutely essential to breaking the cycle of defeat from incessant frustration over our failures.

When we are saved our spirit is reborn in us of incorruptible seed without one single strand of sin's DNA. It never grows old and never dies. Upon the moment of salvation our spirit is Heaven-conceived and totally regenerated, wholly constituted, completely mature and fully loaded with all the make-up of Christ. We are partakers of the righteous nature of God Himself (Colossians 1:27, 2 Peter 1:4). A fully resurrected Christ lives inside of us. However, our flesh has yet to be contended with. This is the process of sanctification and rest assured it is a life long process. Our flesh has the same sinful human tendencies it had before receiving Christ. The outer man will struggle a lifetime, awaiting its glorification (the Kingdom come). However, when we *see ourselves in* Christ and *surrender ourselves to* Christ we will naturally begin to break habits and compulsions that hold us captive. Grace awakens the holiness of God inside of us! Once our mind is awakened to who we are in Christ (repentance) then the fruits of holiness and righteousness will assuredly follow (transformation). Holiness is a byproduct of a changed mind. Through the miracle of repentance (precipitated by Grace) transformation is not just possible... It is IMMINENT!

God calls us to more than just *moralism.* The worldly mind comprehends and even practices morality. But repentance leads to a true change of heart with an authentic desire to live in the fullness of God's purpose. Repentance is the powerful work of God's Grace to bring us to a place of total freedom. Repentance isn't mentally flogging ourselves for our failures until we feel some sense of penitence. Grace doesn't lead us to feel guilty. It leads us to live Godly lives in this present world (Titus 2:12). Repentance isn't *wallowing* in the sorrow of our sin. Rather it's the power to *walk away* from it.

Grace-Based Parenting

Let me make a purposeful deviation for a moment to get to the root of much of our skewed mindset. Much of the reason we often bear prolonged shame is because we have been taught throughout our childhood that we *should* be ashamed of ourselves. As parents we often unintentionally say things to our kids that can potentially cause them to bear painful lifelong insecurities, unnecessary hidden shame and the constant subliminal fear of falling into error. It's *"Shame on you"* or *"You should be ashamed of yourself."* While we want our children to be fully aware when they've sinned we should never even slightly persuade them to continue bearing their shame. One strong caution to parents; we should always point towards the love and forgiveness of God with our children. This is called *Grace-based parenting*. Children are going to make mistakes because it is in their nature to do so (as it is in all of our natures). Once while I was peeking in on my 2-year old son in the church nursery, I became frustrated as he threw a tiny temper tantrum. As I stood in the lobby fuming one of our ushers said to me, *"He's only acting his age."*

We shouldn't be surprised when our children fail to measure up to our *perfect* standards. Saying things like, *"I can't believe you would do that!"* or *"Didn't you know that was wrong?"* does absolutely nothing to change their behavior. We need to accept the fact that our kids are going to fail. Not only should we accept it about our children but we should accept it about ourselves as well. We all need Grace when it comes to our selfishness and irritable attitudes. However, it is imperative to understand that bearing shame never rectifies our conduct. Jesus came to take our shame and in return give us His forgiveness and love. Only God's mercy truly changes our sinful conduct. Reminding our children of their sin only points toward their failure. The way to solve a problem isn't to point to the problem but rather offer the solution. Likewise, when we sin, we shouldn't focus on the sin but focus on the One Who forgives and cleanses our sin. God doesn't rub our guilt in. He rubs it OUT! If we still feel guilty about past sins, we haven't truly received Grace. True repentance not only involves being aware and remorseful of our sin but also includes moving forward and completely leaving the past behind. When we feel ashamed of doing something wrong, we should immediately run into

God's arms of forgiveness. That is how to take effect steps towards effective repentance.

Actions Scream Louder

There are several Biblical examples of those who did not *repent* in the traditional sense or officially say, *"I'm sorry."* For example... The crippled man being lowered through the roof (Mark 2:1-12), The prodigal son (Luke 15:11-24), The thief on the cross (Luke 23:40-43), The woman at the well (John 4:5-30) and The woman caught in adultery (John 8:3-11). ALL of these individuals were *completely* forgiven by Jesus. However, *none* of them prayed the traditional *"sinners prayer"* or asked for forgiveness in any certain terms. The important thing was is that they *turned* to Jesus and therefore made a *turn* in their life. Repentance is an issue of *turning*. It is a 180-degree turning of our old way of life and walking after the things of God. A change of heart is accompanied by a decision to *turn* to God and leave the old way of life. Repentance is *turning* and *running* to Jesus! Now before I continue, I don't want you to misunderstand what I am saying about repentance and wholeheartedly committing your heart to Jesus. Some today preach a gospel of only ease and comfort but with no price of discipleship. There can be no true salvation without full repentance and no real sanctification without total surrender. Grace is not about a God who gives us everything but demands nothing. We cannot preach about the Grace of God and forget about the government of God. God DOES demand our repentance, surrender and obedience but not as a slave master would. As a kind Father, God showed us that He was willing to give everything for us. Therefore, He lovingly (as a shepherd) and firmly (as a Father King) draws us away from a worldly culture and it's vices in order to bring us to safety and maturity. We must surrender and submit to Jesus!

The common denominator in the stories of those who didn't verbally repent is that each person truly had a change of mind that produced heart repentance causing an active manifestation of their changed mindset. I once heard someone say, *"Your actions are screaming so loud, I can't hear what you're saying!"* Repentance is not just SAYING you're sorry; it's MAKING A CHANGE or more rightly allowing GOD HIMSELF to change us. Sorry doesn't mean anything unless a change is made. Repentance is a lifestyle. It is not merely a one-time committed act or a reciting of words. True repentance produces a life that bears the fruit of an ongoing lifestyle change (Luke 3:8).

Our key passage is from one of the stories mentioned above regarding the woman caught in adultery. In this passage Jesus isn't giving her a command not to sin. In effect He was telling her that since He had given her Grace she now had the power not to sin. Notice that He said, *"I do not condemn you."* Knowing that you are free from condemnation is key to experiencing ongoing power and victory over the oppression of sin. After such a marvelous outpouring of love and forgiveness I seriously doubt that this woman ran back to jump in bed with her lover. When we consistently learn to lean on God's Grace we will not desire to go out and sin. This is why it is critical for us to receive the love of God on a regular basis. Notice Jesus didn't say, *"You better not go out and sin any more"* (which is the way most people read this passage). When Jesus told her to *'go'* and sin no more He released her to live free from the condemnation, guilt and imputation of her sin. 'Go' here in this passage is a liberating word. When we receive God's free gift of Grace we will know the love of God that delivers us from the desire to return to the bondage and slavery of sin. We will be free to 'go' and sin no more. Oh that we would read the scriptures from the side of Grace so that it would reveal to us the loving heart of our Father God.

We will never arrive at perfection this side of Heaven in our actions or our behavior! However, there is good news that sets us free from the discouragement of failure to live up to our apology. Saying you're sorry doesn't guarantee that you won't fail again. True repentance is a *journey* of a changed mind. It's not hitting the bull's-eye perfectly. Repentance means having a determination (in spite of our shortcomings) to pursue the purposes of God and attain to the fullness of the victorious life.

"Now flee from youthful lusts and pursue righteousness, faith, love and peace, with those who call on the Lord from a pure heart."
(2 Timothy 2:22 NASB)

Repentance is a 180-degree turn from the old way of living and reaching for our new life IN CHRIST. Paul called it *"forgetting the past and pressing on to the prize."* (Philippians 3:13-14) Many Biblically misinformed people will say that you're not truly sorry if you keep making the same mistakes. This is not what the Bible teaches us. Paul himself (THE apostle of Grace) even admitted that he hadn't *arrived* at perfection. This is good news for all of us because we don't have to perform perfectly for our repentance to *'count'* before God. This should set us free to enjoy our relationship with God instead of the constant guilt that comes with not living up to His perfect standard. Remember, God's perfect standard is Jesus and you can only be perfect in Him! When it comes to the Christian life, the truth is we all will stand on the peaks of success and fall to valleys of failure at various levels for the rest of our lives. However, even though we will most certainly fall short (Romans 3:23) we don't have to *give up.* IN CHRIST we can confidently *get back up!*

A Broken Heart

"The sacrifices of God are a broken spirit; a broken and a contrite heart, O God, You will not despise." (Psalms 51:17 NASB)

God's Word teaches us that He accepts a broken and contrite spirit. Some people may periodically abstain from unholy things but yet their heart is puffed up with pride. The sacrifice that God accepts from the life of a believer is having a heart that is humble, knowing that apart from God's Grace, he is utterly hopeless and lost. When we are deeply broken by sin, God hears our heart louder than our words. It's as if God says, *"Your heart is crying so loudly I can't hear what you are saying."* The Bible teaches us that God sees into the motives us our hearts (1 Samuel 16:7). It's not important for us to get the words right when we are repentant. There's an old song that says, *"Tears are the language that God understands."* The good news is that God knows we are sorry long before the words are ever formed on our lips. When the born again believer sins, he knows it because His new and righteous nature tells him something is not right and he feels a sense of brokenness or being undone. However, when we sin, we don't need a restoration of our righteousness. We are already righteous. Rather we need a restoration of our peace of mind. When our heart is tender and humble before God we will know when we sin and will have the desire to change. This desire to change comes from our righteous nature inside of us. Be advised, new creations don't just run around looking for ways to sin. Their righteous nature yearns to do righteous things. A righteous nature produces righteous desires.

When we first come to God to be born again, we are given a whole new set of DNA (2 Corinthians 5:17) and that DNA alarms us when we sin. Allowing sin into our lives does not cut us off from our righteousness but it will sabotage our peace of mind and victory in this life. Peace with God is a by-product of living in the fullness of Grace (1 Corinthians 1:13). This assures us that we are righteous apart from our ability to *nail it* perfectly every time. When we don't *"nail it"* perfectly we need to remember that our sins were *nailed to the cross* IN CHRIST'S body! Sin separates us from enjoying relationship because of the condemnation it brings. Sin opens our lives giving in-roads to the enemy. Bear in mind that we don't lose our righteousness every time we miss the mark. Remember that God doesn't take back the gift of His righteousness (Romans 11:29). However, we can gravely jeopardize our marriages, families, finances, careers, friendships and ministries if we allow sin into in our lives. Sin is costly! Sin fascinates then it assassinates. It thrills then it kills! Sin will take you farther that you want to go, make you pay more than you want to pay and stay longer than you want to stay.

Good Grief

Sin doesn't grieve the Holy Spirit because it hurts *Him*. Sin grieves the Holy Spirit because it hurts *us* (Ephesians 4:30).[9] This is why we often feel grieved when we sin. This is a "good kind" of grief. It is not the grief we feel at funerals or the ICU at a hospital. When we sin, the Holy Spirit in us is grieving and we can feel HIS grief. However, He is not disappointed, angry or "put out" with *us*. Rather He is anguished for the *consequences* that we will face because of our sin. However, latent within His grief there is a hopefulness and confidence that we can find the deliverance for change and the peace for our unrest. Repentance is really an issue of love. When we truly love God (and encounter His love for us) we will feel deeply and authentically repentant for our offenses toward Him. It is not because we're afraid He'll stop loving us or abandon us. It's because of His astonishing, selfless love that we feel the weight of sorrow for our sin. Grace does not produce a calloused indifference to sin and holiness. Rather it produces sensitive hearts to walk in faithful and obedient love! One powerful truth we must remember regarding holy living: Although our *salvation* IN CHRIST is established by Grace; our *satisfaction* IN LIFE is experienced through obedience. To this God's commandments are no longer burdensome but rather beneficial.

One thing we must be certain of; as powerful as the grieving of the Holy Spirit is, His love for us is much more overwhelming. When we allow the love of Jesus to overwhelm us it will swallow up all grief and cause us to experience His victory in our lives. That's the power of Grace! Condemnation, on the other hand, is the hopeless feeling we get when we know we have sinned against God. Condemnation does not possess the hopeful promise that we are IN CHRIST and that His blood washes our hearts and our conscious completely clean. The effects of condemnation are crippling and ultimately paralyze us from moving forward. Remember that GOD doesn't condemn us when we sin (Romans 8:1). The devil condemns us for our failures and makes us feel there is no chance of forgiveness or reform. Thus, we end up condemning ourselves. We are never condemned in Christ. The scriptures teach us we can NEVER nullify God's Grace. This means His Grace cannot be abolished, cancelled, invalidated or reversed. If our failures could repeal God's Grace, then Christ's death would have been pointless.

"I have been crucified with Christ; and it is no longer I who live, but Christ lives in me; and the life which I now live in the flesh I live by faith in the Son of God, who loved me and gave Himself up for me. "I DO NOT NULLIFY THE GRACE OF GOD, FOR IF RIGHTEOUSNESS COMES THROUGH THE LAW, THEN CHRIST DIED NEEDLESSLY."
(Galatians 2:20 NASB)

A dead man can never be brought back to life again. He is dead forever. However, the mind still thinks like the old man and has to be renewed daily. That's why Paul said we are transformed (metamorphosis) by the retraining of the mind (Romans 12:1-2). Repentance is a retraining of the mind!

Raising the Bar

The message of radical Grace alarms religious people for fear that it will advocate *loose living* or grant people a *license to sin*. These self-appointed watchmen will say things like, *"Look out for that Grace preacher,"* or *"Preaching Grace is dangerous."* While we shouldn't think Grace authorizes our immorality; we all the more shouldn't think that Grace authorizes us to boast in our morality. Some even think that since Grace has been given, the bar has now been raised on us to live holy lives. This is as if to imply that we are without excuse to walk righteously and thus held more accountable when we sin lest we *"trample God's Grace underfoot"* which is a common misinterpretation of Hebrews 10:29 (See important endnote on page 323-324). This false mindset has a subtle fear attached to it causing people to live under paranoia and panic rather than freedom and fullness. Friend, Grace does raise the bar, but not in the way that many think. Grace lifted the heavy weight of the Law's requirements off of our lives and put it on Jesus shoulders. His sacrifice met every expectation of the Law and we are free now to receive His power to live victorious lives. Be assured, Grace doesn't permit you to live *loosely*. Rather, Grace *loosens* the hold that sin has on you and breaks every chain.

Guilt-Free Living

I truly believe we can experience guilt-free living in God's Grace. Guilt doesn't produce true transformation. Only God's Grace leads us to true repentance (Romans 2:4). This doesn't mean we won't feel a sense of remorse when we sin. However, guilt is ultimately ineffective in breaking the power of sin. It may temporarily adjust our behavior but it doesn't permanently fix the sin *nature* (which ultimately corrects our behavior). God's Grace permanently breaks the power of sin. We were once slaves to Sin, forced to submit to its oppression. Now, through righteousness, sin is no longer our slave master. The chains are broken and we are free. However, in the incredible pace of freedom's run you may trip on occasion. Yet, the slave master won't be able to put his chains back on you. You have been forever set free from the bondage of the cruel sin tyrant and you will never have to look back over your shoulder in fear again.

Fear does not produce true holiness. I don't commit adultery because I'm afraid of my wife (or even necessarily the consequences of infidelity). I remain faithful to my wife because I am madly in love with her. If I told my wife that I had to love her because God's Law told me to, she would have a hard time receiving my love if I did it out of obligation to a code of conduct or a set of rules. Rules don't produce a true love relationship. Faithfulness *to* my wife is produced by my passion *for* her. My commitment to her is supercharged because the flames of love have ignited our marriage. The same is true for our devotion to God and our commitment to live holy lives. Temptation loses its power over us when the flames of love are kindled in our relationship with God. Rules don't lead to heart felt obedience. Only the power of God's love through His Grace can do that. That's why worship is so important. It is how we re-fire the flame of devotion for God. Many think if they worship and pray that they provoke God's love for them. However, in Grace, it is just the opposite. God's love cannot be diminished or increased one single iota. It is impossible for God's love to grow cold towards us. His love is always ablaze for us. However, it is entirely possible for our love and faith to grow cold *for Him*. And so we must draw near to the flame in order to feel it's warmth and rekindle all consuming passion. The closer to the fire we are the more our hearts will burn.

Soul Rigor Mortis

Rigor Mortis is the medical term for the muscular stiffening in the body following death. *'Soul rigor mortis'* sets in when we neglect spending time with God, causing our hearts to stiffen and become insensitive to the Holy Spirit and forgetful of all His wonderful promises for our lives. Worship and prayer are the ways we allow our relationship to deepen in His presence. When we are *desperately* in love with Jesus and fuel the fire of our hearts toward Him, we won't want anything to do with sin. Although temptation to sin may present itself, if we are fully ablaze with the fires of devotion to Jesus, sin will not be able to persuade us otherwise. It is when we neglect our relationship through prayer, worship, Bible study and gathering with other believers that our love level is significantly diminished. Simply put, avoiding God creates *a void.* Run to Jesus for abundant Grace and supply. His Grace will empower you for every situation!

Prayer, worship and Bible study are gifts given by God to help prevent our hearts from spiritual fossilization. Posturing our lives in worship positions us to receive His love and helps motivate us to live holy lives. When we draw near to God we can feel His nearness and hear His secrets (James 4:8). God never shouts His secrets; He only whispers them. We must learn to trust in God's love for us *more than* our love for Him. Our love is fickle but God's love never fails (1 Corinthians 13:8). A note to preachers: if we desire to motivate our congregations to be more passionate for God, we must constantly remind them of God's love for THEM! Like the old song says, *"Oh how I love Jesus, BECAUSE He first loved me."* We cannot fulfill the greatest commandment to love the Lord with all our heart, soul, mind and strength (Mark 12:30) unless we first receive His Grace on a regular basis. We are forgetful people who need to be constantly reminded of the unfailing love of God that is greater than all our sin.

"For if our heart condemns us, God is greater than our heart, and knows all things." (1 John 3:20 NKJV)

Here the word *heart* is speaking of our mind and emotions (the seat of our thoughts and feelings). When we *feel* condemned, the truth of God's Grace is greater than our often-misperceived thoughts and deceiving feelings. The sad truth is many Christians focus on their self-love for God and become confused when they fail. After all, how could we be on-fire one minute and ice-cold the next? This is what happens when we try to live our lives for God based on *self-love*. Grace is the solution to our love dilemma. Fear does not produce true love, but rather coercion. God doesn't hold His wrath over us like a machine gun and command us to love Him. True love comes from a desire to freely surrender our hearts to God not because we are *forced* to but because we are *free* to. We love God because HE loves us.

"There is NO FEAR IN LOVE; but PERFECT LOVE CASTS OUT FEAR, because fear involves punishment, and THE ONE WHO FEARS IS NOT PERFECTED IN LOVE. WE LOVE, BECAUSE HE FIRST LOVED US." (1 John 4:18-19 NASB)

True love and obedience cannot be perfected (produced) by fear. God's perfect love drives out fear. When we no longer have a dread of being punished we are free to serve Him out of love. The wrath of God brings fear but God's love quenches ALL our fears. We don't have to be afraid of God even when we fail. Jesus said, *"Do not fear"* more times than anything else He said. Moses commanded the Israelites in Deuteronomy 6:13, *"You shall fear the LORD your God."* However, Jesus came with a new way. When Jesus was being tempted by the devil in the wilderness He firmly rebuked him by quoting this same passage from Deuteronomy. However, He gave it a totally different spin... *"You shall WORSHIP the LORD your God."*

(Matthew 4:10) Notice that Jesus didn't use the word *fear*. Rather, He restated God's original intent for man. WORSHIP! We were created for worship not for fear. True worship is birthed out of love NOT from a compulsion of fear. When we fully accept God's love for us our love for Him will flow like a mighty river and nothing can stop true love's flood. Also, love is not perfected by our *work* for God. We don't love God the more we work for Him. Love is not spelled W-O-R-K. Our labor for the Lord should never be based out of fear for Him but for passion fueled by His holy love for us. Fear and work do not empower us to live holy. True obedience is heartfelt. Obedience flows from a genuine and humble reverence for God. Psalms 111:10 says, *"The fear of the Lord is the beginning of wisdom."* The Hebrew word for "fear" is *yir'ah*, which means *possessing reverential awe.* Having an awestruck wonder for God is the seedbed of all good choices. We make wise decisions to obey God because we have a true LOVE for Him. It is impossible to trust those whom we fear. Thus, we will ultimately hate and rebel against them. However, we can totally trust God when we know He loves us and believes in us in spite of our failures. An authentic trust for God is founded on His Grace and forged in the fires of deep intimacy with Him.

A Grace Eye-view

"And we know that God causes all things to work together for good to those who love God, to those who are called according to His purpose..." (Romans 8:28 NASB)

Some treat the passage above as if it were a Law to obey. In other words, all things will work out for our good only if we love God. However, this scripture is not an *if-then* proposition; it is a *promise.* If we look at it as a promise it will cause us to be grateful for His steadfast love and respond obediently. Truth is, none of us love God perfectly. Just read 1 Corinthians 13 (affectionately known at the "love chapter") and you will discover we all fall very short of perfect love (Romans 3:23). Haven't we all kept a record of wrongs, harbored pride, envy, jealousy, selfishness, arrogance, anger, etc? We all regularly fail at the *love commandment,* which is to the Lord with all our heart, soul and strength and love others as ourselves (Deut 6:5, Matthew 27:37-39). Yet, in spite of it all God still gives us His undeserved favor.

One thing we must settle once and for all is that God's unconditional love and unconditional Grace work in complete conjunction with one another. You cannot have one without the other. We often make the mistake in believing that God's love is unconditional while His Grace is contingent upon our good behavior. Can you hear how absurd that sounds? It brings great comfort in knowing that God's love and Grace remain unconditional in spite of our imperfect ability to love Him back. God knows that our human love is flawed but His love is perfect. His love is not dependent on our *performance;* it is dependent on His *promise.* His promise is to love us without reservation, stipulation, compromise or conditions. Yet the paradox is when we focus on God's promise we will naturally grow deeper in love with Him and develop a heartfelt desire to keep His commandments! We don't keep God's commandments to get His love. God's love working in us helps us to keep His commandments.

"But whoever keeps His word, in him the love of God has truly been perfected..." (1 John 2:5 NASB)

Having a *Grace-eye-view* of the scriptures vs. a Law-based perspective produces true love and obedience. True love produces authentic awe and reverence. In other words, sin loses its luster in the light of God's Grace (1 Corinthians 15:34). The truth is we eventually become what we behold. It's a matter of focus. What are you focused on? Your sin or Jesus? Whatever dominates your imagination is a key to what's driving you. If we are preoccupied with Jesus and His finished work, we won't be sin conscious; we will be *Grace* conscious. When your life is built on the Solid Rock you will have a solid WALK! Therefore, our focus shouldn't be on what a terrible *sinners* we are but on what a wonderful *Savior* He is! After all it's not about how bad we are but how good God is. The following phrase helps me when I tend to focus on my failures instead of God's love for me: *"Look down; feel defeated. Look in; feel depressed. Look out; feel inadequate. Look UP; feel loved!"* When we stop focusing on our sin and give all our attention to God's love it will constrain us from giving into temptation and fulfilling the desire of our fleshly lusts.

"For the love of Christ constraineth us..." (2 Corinthians 5:14 KJV)

The word *"constraineth"* is also translated as *compels* or *controls* (See NLT). Therefore, this passage has a three-fold meaning. His love holds us back (constrains) when we need to be restrained, nudges us forward (compels) when we need to be released and steers (controls) us in the right direction for our lives. The love of Jesus is both protective and proactive. It prohibits and it projects. The love of Christ keeps us from falling into sin when all of hell is pulling on us and props us up when we've lost the strength to stand.

Condemnation clouds the love of Jesus in our lives causing us often to feel paralyzed in our spiritual growth. Therefore, in order for Grace to work the way God intended, we must retrain our minds to be constantly aware of Jesus' unfailing love and abiding presence in our lives. This releases the power of God to continually transform us into the image of Christ! (Romans 8:29) We may fail but God's love NEVER fails. That is we must rely on His love.

"Love never fails…" (1 Corinthians 13:8 NASB)

Chapter 13

FAILURE COMES FIRST

"For a righteous man falls seven times, and rises again..."
(Proverbs 24:16 NASB)

Read the above verse very carefully. Did you notice anything significant? Ironic? Paradoxical? Look closely again. It says it in black and white... A RIGHTEOUS man falls. Not only does it say righteous people fall but it says they fall *"seven times."* This isn't a number of how many times a righteous person is going to fail. Rather it's symbolic of HOW a person will fall. The number '7' is God's number of perfection or completeness. In other words, when (not if) a righteous man falls, he will fall *perfectly and completely flat* on his face. Some say, *"Well I made a tiny mistake" or "God didn't count that one."* No friend! When you fall you might as well call it what it is. It's sin. The bottom line is that it's an inescapable fact that saved people are going to sin sometimes. You may ask, *"Is it actually possible for righteous people to sin?"* Absolutely! Notice this verse doesn't say that a sinner falls. A sinner is already in a state of *falleness.* Nor does it imply a righteous man *might* fall. The context of this passage denotes that It's emphatic! A righteous man WILL fall. This is not just a possibility. It is one of the over three thousand promises in the Bible. However, people who truly know they are righteous are able to brush themselves off, deal head-on with their sin and move forward. In Philippians 3:13, Paul called it *"forgetting those things which are behind"* (which is so difficult for most of us to do). However, forgetting the past is the key to *'rise again'* and shake off the condemnation that will only keep us from all God has for us. Failure is the prevailing mentality to those who live under the Law. The Law is oppressive and demanding and it is never satisfied. Therefore, if we refuse God's Grace and continue in our self-strivings to be perfect, we will constantly feel trapped under condemnation for failing to live up to the standard of the Law. The Law never sets us free. Anytime we allow ourselves to feel condemned we immediately come under the

Law. A person who lives like this will always be disappointed and discouraged. That's why Paul had to constantly encourage those who had converted from Judaism to Christianity they were triumphant and more than conquerors THROUGH CHRIST...

"But in all these things we overwhelmingly conquer THROUGH HIM who loved us." (Romans 8:37 NASB)

"But thanks be to God, who always leads us in triumph IN CHRIST, and manifests through us the sweet aroma of the knowledge of Him in every place." (2 Corinthians 2:14 NASB

Did you catch the last part of 2 Corinthians 2:14? It says that God's sweet aroma is always around us in EVERY PLACE. Many times we have been told that God's presence withdraws from us when we fail. This is not the message of Grace. When we 'miss the mark' it is then that God's presence envelops us to confirm His everlasting love with us. "In EVERY PLACE" implies that in the high times and the low times, God is with us. One of the lyrics in one of my songs entitled "Loving You Loving Me" says, *"Your Grace is holding on to me... When I fall and when I fly."* Grace is holding on to us especially in our times of failure and even though righteous people fail they are not *failures*! Failure is not a dead-end street. Its only a *detour* towards victory! Failure is never final unless you make the choice to stop moving forward. *Failing forward* is the mentality of a champion!

A dear friend of mine lost his marriage six-years ago due to moral failure. He had two small boys and felt like he would never be the father they needed, totally convinced that he had lost everything (including a successful ministry). He had tried everything in his power to work towards restoration but his wife had been too hurt and was not willing to reconcile. It was truly over. On several occasions he would visit my wife and I and at some point would breakdown and weep from the pain he was going through. I remember telling him that He may have lost his marriage for now but that by the Grace of God he would still be an awesome father to his two boys.

Recently my friend and I spoke on the phone and reminisced the past few years. Today he is remarried to a wonderful wife (having two beautiful girls of their own). His ministry is thriving more than ever, his relationship with God is strong and there is great anticipation for the marvelous things God is unfolding before him. He has actively stayed involved in the lives of his two sons and even recently had the opportunity to have them stay with him for the entire summer. As well, he and his ex-wife consistently communicate and work toward mutual agreement for the children's best interests. As we reminisced we praised God together for all He had brought him through. Never in a million years would he have thought that he'd be looking back with joy at those very painful days. Not only has my friend experienced God's unfailing love and faithfulness first hand, but he has also been able to help many others through difficult times because of His own Grace journey.

There are thousands of stories out there just like this that show we all regularly fail and come miserably short of God's perfect standard (Romans 3:23). Yet God's perfect love restores even the worst of failures. Thank God that he doesn't grade us on the curve. He grades us through Grace. We all deserve a big fat 'F' on our spiritual report card, but through Grace, we have all been given what we don't deserve: an A+. When we believe we are righteous through Jesus, in-spite of our shortcomings (2 Corinthians 5:21) we won't look at our failures the same way. Rather than feel like we are falling backward we will see ourselves as falling forward. It's simply a matter of perspective. People who are trapped in self-efforts to please God will have a difficult time getting back up on the horse. This is because they feel that they have lost ranks with God and have been demoted to lower status. They are the type of people who cash it all in and return to a life of sin (this is especially true of 'all-or-nothing' type personalities). But when we believe that our righteousness is not dependent upon our works and regularly lean heavily on God's Grace, we will have power to get back up and go on with confidence knowing that God loves and accepts us and still has an awesome plan for our life.

The Righteous WILL fall

According to our key passage, righteous people will fall. It is one of the three thousand promises in the Bible. This is a truth you have to grasp. Righteous people have more potential to fall. Think about it... Fallen people can't fall. They've already fallen. It is simple common sense that those who stand are the ones who are most probable to fall. However, as believers we are in right STANDING with God regardless of our present state of struggle. The reason we are in right standing with God is because of what Christ has done, not what we have done. We must be careful not to believe just because we're saved that we can avoid falling. That's why Paul emphasized...

"Therefore let him who thinks he stands take heed lest he fall."
(1 Corinthians 10:12 NKJV)

Ask yourself if you failed this week and you will find some point of the Law you broke. Quit worrying about what other people will do when Grace is radically preached. Put down your rock and consider this... We ALL need radical Grace! Think about that the next time YOU sin. So many times we feel that people will have license to sin if extreme Grace is taught. That may be true, but our focus shouldn't be on what other people are doing. That's why the apostle Paul said...

"Work out your own salvation with fear and trembling..."
(Philippians 2:12 NKJV)

Paul wasn't saying we should work AT our salvation. To have said this would have contradicted everything he believed in. What he meant was that we should reckon with OUR OWN issues and quit meddling in other people's affairs. Besides, we have enough *stuff* of our own that needs *ironing out*, let alone trying to straighten the wrinkles in everyone else. This is why Jesus taught us to deal with the log-sized fault in our own lives before trying to remove the toothpick-sized faults of others.

"Why do you look at the speck that is in your brother's eye, but do not notice the log that is in your own eye? "Or how can you say to your brother, 'Brother, let me take out the speck that is in your eye,' when you yourself do not see the log that is in your own eye? You hypocrite, first take the log out of your own eye, and then you will see clearly to take out the speck that is in your brother's eye." (Luke 6:41-42 NASB)

Failure Comes First

We've heard the phrase for years, *"If at first you don't succeed, try again."* There's a key here that I want you to see. In order to succeed you will always fail FIRST. Every time you fail you get another opportunity to get it right. When you fail think of it as starting over again. Actually, when you fail God considers it the first *and last* time you fail. How is this? It is because God forgets your past failures. So the moment you fail and start over, God forgets it, puts it behind you, and empowers you to move forward. (Mull it over a bit. It'll come to you). And the good news is, failure may come first but it doesn't have to be final. Remember this... Only those who succeed greatly are the one who dare risk failing greatly. The only true lessons we learn in life are from the tests that we fail. Failure teaches us what no success can. In fact all of the great lessons I've ever learned in my life didn't come from succeeding but rather failing (even miserably).

Did you know that a pro baseball player, on average, fails at the plate 700 out of 1000 times at bat (i.e. ground out, pop out or strike out)? That means if a professional player hits a 300% average he is still considered a successful pro-level hitter. Think of all the money pro hitters make to fail nearly two-thirds of the time (unbelievable). Next time you see one of your favorite players up to bat, look at their average and subtract that from 1000. That will show you how many times they have failed at the plate.[7] When a child learns how to walk he may fall on every piece of furniture in the room. However, eventually he will understand that falling hurts too bad and will *naturally* learn how to walk in order not to feel the pain of falling. When we sin it hurts US. God doesn't get angry because sin hurts HIM. He has a merciful anger *at the pain sin causes us*. God hates sin, not the sinner. We too can naturally overcome sin when we rely on God's Grace instead of our own ability to master perfect behavior.

Many times we picture God like an angry old man or a cosmic cop ready to hit us with his billyclub every time we jaywalk. Sometimes we feel as if God is so concerned about being offended when we sin that He will cut us out of His inheritance. If my young daughter burns her hand on the stove, my anger will not help ease the pain. In fact it will make it worse the more I scold her. My immediate concern will be to rush to her aid and help soothe the pain by applying cold water, burn cream or even rushing her to the emergency room. Even if she purposely puts her hand on the burner I am not going to disown her. God doesn't turn His back on us when we sin; He runs to our rescue. When asked about his many successes and failures to create the electric light bulb, Thomas Edison once said, *"I have not failed 10,000 times. I have successfully found 10,000 ways that will not work."*[17]

When we fail we learn a great deal more we never would have learned had we succeeded. Failure doesn't have to be fatal. In fact, every failure has the potential to teach us how not to do something. When we fail (and we will) we simply learn the many ways we did it *wrong* and from that learn to do it *right*. Failure is always turned to success when we learn from it! We can always choose to *grow* as we *go* through our tragedies, not be *stumped* and *stopped* by them! Learning from our failures also helps to show others the path to victory. Remember this the next time you fail... You may have failed, but YOU are not a failure. No matter how many times you fail, you cannot ever make God stop loving you. Why? Because His love for you is not based on who you are or what you have done but on who HE is and what HE has done!

It is utterly stupefying to imagine that God may not have chosen us merely in spite of our failures, but BECAUSE of them. The reason for this is because it is God alone who qualifies us for His service and not our own natural abilities or even our spirituality (Colossians 1:12 NASB). God always chooses us based on our ineptness so that our successes may be of His glory and not ours! When the world looks at us they should say, *"If not for God..."* We should also say this of ourselves. In this way even our trouble can be turned into triumph, our problems become the platform for our promotion and our disasters be used to make our dreams reality!

Forgiven Forever

Prolonged remorse causes spiritual paralysis. Therefore, to help break the crippling effects of failure, we must understand the power of God's forgiveness. I re-introduce the story of the woman caught in adultery in order to further illustrate God's heart of forgiveness.

"The scribes and the Pharisees brought a woman caught in adultery, and having set her in the center of the court, they said to Him, Teacher, this woman has been caught in adultery, in the very act. Now in the Law Moses commanded us to stone such women; what then do You say? They were saying this, testing Him, so that they might have grounds for accusing Him. But Jesus stooped down and with His finger wrote on the ground. But when they persisted in asking Him, He straightened up, and said to them, 'He who is without sin among you, let him be the first to throw a stone at her.' Again He stooped down and wrote on the

ground. When they heard it, they began to go out one by one, beginning with the older ones, and He was left alone, and the woman, where she was, in the center of the court. Straightening up, Jesus said to her, 'Woman, where are they? Did no one condemn you?' She said, 'No one, Lord.' And Jesus said, 'I DO NOT CONDEMN YOU, EITHER. GO. FROM NOW ON SIN NO MORE.' (John 8:3-11 NASB)

Notice that the woman caught in adultery did not *ask* for forgiveness. She just stood there humiliated in her sin, totally exposed for Jesus and all to see. The Bible doesn't verbally indicate that she was sorry. However, Jesus knew her heart and was privy to her brokenness and shame. Pay close attention to what Jesus says to her... *"I do not condemn you, either. Go. From now on sin no more."* Jesus wasn't telling her that if she sinned again she would lose her forgiveness. He said, *"From now on sin no more"* because He didn't want to see her get in the same trouble again. In the literal sense, Jesus was saving her from certain death. Simply put, He wanted her to live. Under the legal ramifications of the Old Covenant Law, this woman was to be stoned to death for the sin of adultery. Yet when Jesus said, *"He who has no sin let him cast the first stone"* they all walked away cut to the core. Could it be that Jesus was scribbling (in plain sight for everyone to see) the individual commandments that each of the religious accusers had broken? Jesus knew their hearts and He knew the Laws they had disobeyed. After all, He's the one who engraved the Law with His own finger on the tablets of stone at Mt. Sinai (Exodus 31:18). Upon hearing Jesus' words and reading what he had stooped to write in the dirt, they ALL walked away in shame. Sometimes I wonder how many of us today would have been in the crowd with a stone in our hand. After carefully looking at this passage, I truly believe this woman was set up by the religious leaders in order to trick Jesus. After all, how could they have just *discovered* her in the very act of adultery? Instead of falling prey to their conspiracy, look at How Jesus handles her accusers. Instead of condemning her, He immediately forgives her. This woman was so broken BEYOND WORDS that she couldn't even mutter, *"I'm sorry."* Yet Jesus forgives her before she even asks. Oh how awesome is the forgiveness of God.

"In Him we have redemption through His blood, the forgiveness of sins, in accordance with the riches of God's Grace that He lavished on us with all wisdom and understanding." (Ephesians 1:7-8 NIV)

"For he has rescued us from the dominion of darkness and brought us into the kingdom of the Son He loves, IN WHOM WE HAVE REDEMPTION, THE FORGIVENESS OF SINS."
(Colossians 1:13-14 NIV)

The scriptures here tell us that if we are IN CHRIST, forgiveness is something we have already been given. For instance, if I were to give you $10,000 and you asked me for $10, I would respond, *"You already have it! Why are you asking me for it?"* God has already given you forgiveness of sins. Therefore, when you fail, you should fall hard upon the forgiveness that is *already* yours! When we think of forgiveness in these terms we will experience greater levels of victory in our lives than we could have possibly imagined. Why? Because when God forgives us, it's forever! The more we enjoy the freedom of God's forgiveness we will not want to sin. John Piper says it like this, *"Grace is the enabling gift of God not to sin. Grace is power, not just pardon."* God's overwhelming forgiveness empowers us to *"go and sin no more."* When Jesus told the woman to *"go and sin no more,"* He was also empowering her by those words. In essence He was saying, *"My forgiveness has completely broken the power of sin over your life."* Not only will focusing on God's forgiveness decrease the tendency to sin, it will also increase the desire to live for God in extraordinary ways. It is interesting to note according to Bible tradition, the woman who anointed Jesus feet with the costly alabaster oil and displayed such an extravagant act of worship in Matthew 26:7-13 was the same adulterous woman whom He forgave and rescued in the streets. God's Grace makes us more extravagant worshippers.

"For this reason I say to you, HER SINS, WHICH ARE MANY, HAVE BEEN FORGIVEN, FOR SHE LOVED MUCH; but he who is forgiven little, loves little." (Luke 7:47 NASB)

Can you see it? God forgives us before we even ask. His forgiveness is a free gift. Therefore, we must simply receive it. The root word of forgiveness is GIVE. When we believe on the name of Jesus, renounce our past and accept His free gift of forgiveness, we can stand firm in our righteousness knowing that our sins are forgiven forever.

"The righteous stand firm forever." (Proverbs 10:25 NIV)

A Prodigal Pause

On top of all of this, there is a significant nugget of truth found in the story of the prodigal son (Luke 15:11-32). The story indicates that the real reason the son came to himself and went home is because he was starving and knew there was food at His father's house.

"But when he came to his senses, he said, 'How many of my father's hired men have more than enough bread, but I am dying here with hunger!' " (Luke 15:17 NASB)

No matter the motivation, the son returned home nevertheless. Notice as the father catches a glimpse of his son *"a long way off"* ashamedly making his way back up the road, the Father *all-out* RUNS TO HIM, falls upon him, embracing and kissing him! Likewise our Heavenly Father is suspended in forgiveness towards us and is faster to forgive us than we are to ask for it. Also notice the son didn't ask for forgiveness. Rather, he said, *"I have sinned and am no longer worthy to be called your son."* This indicates that the son didn't even think there was a chance for his sonship to be restored. However, according to the father's actions it is evident that the son never really lost his sonship. Admitting failure is what most of us do when we fail. But we shouldn't stop there. God's forgiveness is reaching out and all we must do is accept it. God doesn't forgive part of the time. He forgives ALL of the time. No matter where we've been, what we've done or whom we've done it to, God always forgives (Psalms 100:5).

Forgiveness God's Way

"Then Peter came and said to Him, "Lord, how often shall my brother sin against me and I forgive him? Up to seven times? Jesus said to him, "I do not say to you, up to seven times, but up to SEVENTY TIMES SEVEN." (Matthew 18:21-22 NASB)

There is a very profound secret in this passage regarding God's forgiveness. Jesus taught the disciples that when someone trespasses against us (violates, maligns or hurts us in someway) that we are to forgive them the *same way* He forgives us. He told His disciples that if it was necessary they were to forgive those who had wronged them 70 x 7 (490 times). Now to be sure, it is highly unlikely that someone will actually ask us for forgiveness that many times. The

490 times Jesus was referring to wasn't a specific number of times we are to forgive. It was an illustration of the Father's forgiveness for us. Through this model prayer Jesus was teaching us that we will always need forgiveness and that we will always need to forgive others. We are to have forgiveness towards others *before* they sin against us because THAT IS HOW THE FATHER HAS FORGIVEN US. That's what it means to *"walk in forgiveness"* with one another. We are to release forgiveness just like God releases His forgiveness (before anyone has need of asking). Now can you see how God's forgiveness works? We need to accept God's eternal forgiveness. God's mercy never wanes thin. In fact when we became born again, God's mercy not only took into account all our past and present sins, but also ALL the sins we would ever commit. His mercy forgave us in advance. Friend, God's mercy is EVERLASTING! When we fail we must believe that there is far more mercy in God than there is sin in us![32]

"The mercy of the LORD is from everlasting to everlasting..."
(Psalms 103:17 KJV)

To more deeply understand the forgiveness of God in this context we must also look at the powerful statement Jesus made regarding his murders while stretched out, bludgeoned and hemorrhaging on the cross.

"But Jesus was saying, "Father, forgive them; for they do not know what they are doing." And they cast lots, dividing up His garments among themselves." (Luke 23:24 NASB)

This presents an overwhelmingly compelling case for the forgiveness of God. You see, if Jesus could plead with God to forgive those who were killing Him without them even asking for it, how much more is His forgiveness extended to us as His own beloved. Oh the love of God that goes beyond all description!

A Model Prayer

Considering all of this some may ask, *"Doesn't the Lord's Prayer teach us to ask for forgiveness?"* To answer this question we must remember that the prayer Jesus uses in Matthew 6:9-13 is a MODEL prayer to teach us how to understand the Father's heart when we pray. It is not an outline to follow nor is it given to teach us how to be good *pray-ers*. In other words, it isn't so much as *what* to pray as *how* to pray. Some treat this prayer as a religious creed to recite or an intercessory guideline that covers every possible area of our prayer life. There's nothing wrong with utilizing The Lord's Prayer in this way. For some it really helps to aid in the process of prayer. I have used it similarly myself and have experienced powerful results in my life. However, I believe the *real purpose* of this *model* prayer is to show us that we can fully expect our prayers to be answered because God is our Heavenly *Father*. This is why Jesus teaches us to start our prayers with *"Our Father."* Not in a religious way, but rather to understand that our prayers are based on relationship, not religion. God is not some formidable force peering down from the Heavens to check in on us from time to time making sure we've repented enough to qualify for His forgiveness. He is our loving Heavenly Father! When we are confident in the Father's love we will *relate* with Him rightly and as a result we will *believe* and *pray* rightly! We won't pray from a distance as if God isn't listening but rather we will know that His eyes are always upon us and that He is ready to bring His purposes to pass in our lives (Jeremiah 1:12 NKJV). If we were truly honest with ourselves, at best, we are all stumbling along trying to find our *rhythm in life* anyway. The good news is that our Heavenly Father is always forgiving us because He loves us and remembers that we are frail human beings clothed in flesh. When Jesus instructs us to say, *"forgive us our sins as we forgive those who sin against us"* He is teaching us that we should forgive others IN THE SAME WAY that God forgives us; to forgive others *before* or *as often* as they offend us.

Another important implication to consider is this... What if we don't feel we have sinned? Should we still say, *"Forgive us our sins?"* Again, if we treat prayer as a religious exercise we will be always approach God with head bowed, ashamed, fearful, hoping He will forgive us. It's as if we would ask Him to forgive us for being human. However, if we know He is our loving Heavenly Father we will know we are already forgiven and run into His arms to enjoy intimacy and friendship. Besides, whether we know it or not, there is usually some hidden inconsistency and character flaw in our lives anyway. However, if we constantly focus on the flaws we will fall into constant patterns of insecurity instead of resting in the confidence in who we are IN CHRIST!

Everything we think, do and say flows from our relationships (Heavenward and Earthen). Resting in God's Grace is how we develop an unmovable security in His steadfast, unwavering love and is the only way we can establish the proper perspective in every area that governs our relationships. All of our relationships can be summed up in the following six areas:

What we think about God

What we think about ourselves

What we think God thinks about us

What we think of others

What we think others think about us

What we think God thinks about others

Possessing a healthy concept (in these key areas) builds a healthy *self-image.* This in turn causes us to be more drawn to God's opinion of us and not pressured to give into people's estimations of us. Grace empowers us to make a stronger contribution towards healthy *relationships* in every area of our lives, which results in healthy *living.* When Grace is flowing through our lives, it creates a powerful sense of our core identity IN CHRIST resulting in a solid Christ-like esteem. In other words, when we submit to God's Grace we allow His power to control us verses the power of others. When Grace rules all of our perceptions, how can we not live victoriously? This is why we must let Grace rule!

Don't Take the Stairs

The reason why we often fail is because we try to serve God in our own strength. There are two ways to get to the top of the Empire State Building. We can tackle the 102 floors by way of the stairs or we can simply step into the elevator and allow it to lift us effortlessly to the top. Failure is inevitable when you *take the stairs* (try to earn God's acceptance) By stepping into a relationship with Jesus we allow His Grace to carry us upward. Being in a vital and loving relationship with Jesus enables us to operate in His power.

"I have been crucified with Christ; and it is no longer I who live, BUT CHRIST LIVES IN ME; and the life which I now live in the flesh I live by

faith IN THE SON OF GOD, who loved me and GAVE HIMSELF up for me. (Galatians 2:20 NASB)

Onward and Upward

The forgiveness of God is the power that sets us free to move forward when we fail, or more rightly, AS WE FAIL. God's unending pardon in our lives enables us to forget the past and compels us to grab hold of our awesome future. As we make the choice to move forward we must trust God to work out all the complexities and perplexities of our failures. Focusing on God's mercy is the key.

"O remember not against us former iniquities: let Thy tender mercies speedily (effectively) prevent us (from falling into sin): for we are brought very low." (Psalms 79:8 KJV)[37]

Turning Failure Around

If you're facing failure it is most likely because you are *facing* your failures! To live in God's Grace is to face forward! Here are 7 ways to turn failure around (I use the acronym F.A.I.L.U.R.E.)...

FORGET the Past. Release all regret. It is the final chain to be broken. To be strong is to let go of yesterday. Therefore, take one last look over your shoulder and say to your past, *"I'm letting you go forever. You cannot follow me into my future!"* (Philippians 3:13-14)

ACCEPT the Consequences. You cannot re-write the past but you can start a whole new book. Your yesterday does not have to determine your tomorrow. Remember, no matter what happened, God is working everything out for your TOTAL good. (Romans 8:28)

INVITE Correction. Only fools despise instruction but honor belongs to those who embrace correction. Every mistake you've made serves as a stepping-stone for your success. And remember: to use a stepping-stone it has to be firmly *under your feet.* (Proverbs 13:18)

LEARN the Lesson. As we grow in Grace, we often take the test first then learn the lesson afterwards. Truth is, God knew you were going

147

to fail. But no matter what the failure, the number one lesson Jesus wants you to learn is to rest in His love for you. (Matthew 11:29)

UNDERSTAND the Process. Accept that failure happens. In fact, failure is as vital a part of the growing process as succeeding. Our failures remind us of our total dependence on God's Grace and give us courage to keep moving forward at a steady pace. (Proverbs 24:16)

RECEIVE Total Forgiveness. God has already forgiven you. It does you no good to punish yourself. Often, the problem isn't that God hasn't forgiven you but that you haven't forgiven yourself. You'll just have to accept that God loves you no matter what! (Ephesians 1:7-8)

EXPECT to Succeed. No matter how many times you may have lost you are not a loser. God sees you as a complete and TOTAL SUCCESS story. Your failures don't define you; they refine you into the image of Jesus. Facts are, IN CHRIST You are undefeatable! (Romans 8:37)

Chapter 14

MARKED FOR DELETION

**"He who overcomes will thus be clothed in white garments and I will not erase his name from the book of life, and I will confess his name before My Father and before His angels."
(Revelation 3:5 NASB)**

My favorite movie of all time is the Matrix. I have probably watched the trilogy 100 times. I'm addicted and yes, I am thankful for Grace. Now, you have to be a fan to understand the premise. Basically, the movie is set far into the future where machines rule the world. In the machine world, fields of humans are harvested to provide power for the machines to survive. A cable is plugged into every brain connecting them to the Matrix (a complex computer program). While humans sleep in individuals pods filled with cryonic fluid, their minds are still very much alive and active in the Matrix. However, they are totally unaware that they are in this deceptive computer program and simply go on living their mundane lives. The machines use the Matrix as form of mind control so they can continue to draw sustainable energy from human body heat. There is a line in the move where one of the characters tells Neo (the main character) that when a program (person living in the matrix) fails to serve his purpose he is *"marked for deletion"* and thus dies in the real world because the body cannot survive without the mind.

Many Christians believe if they fail to achieve their purpose and fully live up to God's expectations, they are marked for deletion. For years, I too thought if I failed to live a spotless, holy life and overcome in every area that God would blot me out of His book of life. Praise God the truth of the Gospel has completely rebooted my skewed mindset. This is NOT the Good News of the Gospel nor what our key passage above means at all. The Bible teaches us that the moment we are *born again* we're given the title "Overcomer."

"For EVERYONE born of God overcomes the world. This is the victory that has overcome the world, even our faith." (1 John 5:4 NIV)

God calls us 'overcomers' ahead of time because of our right-standing with Him. Notice it says, *"EVERYONE born of God overcomes the world."* All truly born-again believers are overcomers. It is not sensible to give someone a title he does not earn. For instance, if someone doesn't go to college to become a doctor, he won't get to wear the white coat. In order to be given a title we must earn that title. However, in the economy of Grace we don't earn our righteousness. We are made righteous by *believing* not by *doing.*

"And may be found in Him, not having a righteousness of my own derived from the Law, but that which is through faith IN CHRIST, THE RIGHTEOUSNESS WHICH COMES FROM GOD ON THE BASIS OF FAITH." (Philippians 3:19 NASB)

Being a 'Christian' isn't something we *earn*, it's something we *receive.* Our key passage says we are made overcomers by faith, not by working hard. We don't overcome to get righteousness. We get righteousness to overcome! In other words, works don't produce results. Only Grace does! Now that's *good news!* Just because we struggle with sin in certain areas of our lives doesn't mean we aren't overcomers. Paul puts it this way...

"Yet in all these things WE ARE MORE THAN CONQUERORS THROUGH HIM who loved us. For I am persuaded that neither death nor life, nor angels nor principalities nor powers, nor things present nor things to come, nor height nor depth, nor any other created thing, shall be able to separate us from the love of God which is IN CHRIST Jesus our Lord." (Romans 8:37-39 NKJV)

Paul was making a *faith statement* to the Roman Church. He made it clear that they were already overcomers because they had simply accepted their righteousness *by faith.* We know through historical and Biblical accounts that the Roman church hadn't *worked out* all their issues nor had they mastered perfect behavior. Yet, Paul told them that in spite of their shortcomings, they were still conquerors. This is the champion's mentality. Developing a deep-seated confidence in who You are IN CHRIST is the key to winning in life. You can overcome if you believe you are an overcomer. Not only are we conquerors; we are MORE than conquerors. You see, in God's righteousness, we don't believe *for* the victory. We believe *from* the victory. In other words, the victory that overcomes the world (as our key passage tells us) is our *faith.* It is scripturally accurate to say (from the side of Grace) that we are already victorious whether or not we have gained mastery in every area of our life. We don't reign in life by being perfect. We reign in life through *Christ's* perfection and *His* perfect work. When we abide in the Perfect One we reign in HIS authority.

"And Jesus came up and spoke to them, saying, 'ALL AUTHORITY HAS BEEN GIVEN TO ME in Heaven and on earth.'" (Matthew 28:18 NASB)

Christ has never been nor will ever be defeated and because we are in Him we are NEVER on the losing side! This is the faith that overcomes the world. Faith says we have victory BEFORE we see it manifested. Paul said absolutely NOTHING can separate us from the Love of Christ. The word *'nothing'* means *nothing.* We are His beloved forever! Remember, in *ourselves*, we are not conquerors. It is only through Jesus that we are made overcomers. We don't make ourselves righteous. The scriptures tell us that we *have been made* the righteousness of God *through Him* and are already complete IN CHRIST.

"He made Him who knew no sin to be sin on our behalf, so that we might become the righteousness of God in Him."
(2 Corinthians 5:21 NASB)

"In Him you have been made complete..." (Colossians 2:10 NASB)

Beloved, we are as righteous as God. God doesn't give us part of His righteousness. He imparts His full righteousness to us when we believe in the work of His Son and surrender to His Lordship. Note the scripture doesn't say, *"We are BECOMING the righteousness of God."* No beloved! We have BECOME God's righteousness through Jesus. Some say, *"I'm working on being righteous."* That's the problem! Many are still trying to work on their righteousness because they don't believe they ARE fully righteous IN CHRIST. While hanging on the cross Jesus said, *"It is finished."* (John 19:30) The Greek word for *finished* is *teleo* which means, *PAID IN FULL!* All our sins were punished once and for all on Jesus body on the cross and the payment for our salvation was complete. There is nothing left for us to pay. We are not indebted to God for any of our sins! According to Colossians 2:10 above, being complete means we have NOTHING lacking in our lives pertaining to life and holiness (1 Corinthians 1:4-8).

Although this is hard to grasp we must believe it nevertheless or we will never enjoy rest and intimacy with God which will result in bearing abundant fruit in our lives.

You may ask, *"How can I be complete when I have so many 'issues' and inconsistencies in my life?"* That's what's so amazing about God's Grace. In Grace we can rest in CHRIST'S completeness. God makes us righteous through Jesus' perfection, not in our own ability to be perfect (Romans 4:6). Therefore, it is right to say we are already overcomers whether or not we are presently reflecting tangible evidence. However, be strongly advised, if we truly believe we are overcomers, it won't be long until we start reflecting it in our lifestyle. Paul said that faith is the *evidence* of things NOT SEEN (Hebrews 11:1). Eventually we have to start learning how to believe what we can't see. We aren't overcomers because we overcome. We are overcomers because Christ overcame. Either you believe what the Bible says about you or you don't. We are victorious period! Christ doesn't lead us to the victory; He leads us IN the victory!

"But thanks be to God, who always leads us in triumph IN CHRIST."
(2 Corinthians 2:14 NASB)

The picture here is of a parade or a processional of victory, not of a battle *towards* victory. Not only does God lead us IN a victorious processional of victory, He ALWAYS leads us in victory. Therefore, we are *always* overcomers. Grace makes us overcomers. This is the awesome paradox of God's Grace. Although we may be failing in certain areas in our lives, we can still call ourselves *victorious* because we stand IN CHRIST'S victory. And when we surrender *inwardly* to Christ's victory we will begin to experience the reality of His victory *outwardly.*

Filthy Rags

Our key passage tells us that we are clothed in white garments. This is a perfect visual of our righteousness. Beloved, we stand before God as righteous clothed in HIS righteousness. Our self-effort to become righteous only resembles *filthy rags*.

"But we are all like an unclean thing, and all our righteousnesses are like FILTHY RAGS..." (Isaiah 64:6 NKJV)

The words *"filthy rags"* come from two Hebrew words: *'ed* and *beged'* (Strongs #899 & #5708). These two words combined connote a cloth used to shield a woman's menstruation cycle. This may seem crude. Yet we should seriously ponder what Isaiah is saying! Isaiah used the analogy of the most *unclean thing* according to Hebraic Law concerning regulations on personal hygiene to vividly illustrate the worth of our self-righteousness. Trying to earn righteous through works is like trying to clean yourself with a filthy rag. The more you try the dirtier you become. We cannot cleanse ourselves. Therefore, we must receive the free gift of righteousness by faith and trust in the Grace of God thereby allowing the precious blood of to cleanse us and continue cleansing us from all our unrighteousness (1 John 1:7).

We don't stay clean by attempting to keep our behavior aligned to God's standard. ONLY THE BLOOD cleanses us from our sin. In order for us live in the freedom that Grace offers we must understand the power of God's eternal love towards us. To be certain sin is indeed costly and we can pay dearly if we allow it to influence our lives. Think of this in earthly paternal relationships. I dearly love my children and have set certain boundaries for their safety. For instance, when they were very little I warned them not to tamper with the bottles underneath the kitchen sink. If they had disregarded my precautions they would have placed themselves at risk for serious injury, even death. However, even if they had swallowed any of the prohibited poisonous substances, I would not have stopped loving nor disavowed them, no matter how fatal the outcome. My blood runs through their veins. We have a paternal bond that cannot be broken. If the earthly bond I have to my children is that strong, how much stronger the bond you and I have to our Heavenly Father (Psalms 103:12-13). Rest assured, giving in to sin is like sipping poison. It has the potential to destroy us. Yet, because our names have been signed in the book of life by Jesus own blood, it is impossible for them to be erased. God cannot undo the work of His Son in our lives. We are His forever.

"All that the Father gives Me will come to Me, and the one who comes to Me I will certainly not cast out." (John 6:37 NASB)

Grace Against the Clock

From the giving of the Law to the time just before Christ, the children of Israel failed to satisfy the standard of God's Law. This was because God planned it that way (Galatians 3:24). God created the Law in order to drive us to fall dead to our own works and receive His free gift of Grace! And that Grace came precisely in the nick of time to rescue us from futility. God's timing is perfect.

> "But when the fullness of the time came, God sent forth His Son, born of a woman, born under the Law, so that He might redeem those who were under the Law, that we might receive the adoption as sons." (Galatians 4:4-5 NASB)

False Perceptions of God

Some people see God as an angry dictator ruling with an iron fist: a perfectionist with no tolerance for failure. Some picture Him as a policeman passing out citations if they as much as jay walk. Others see Him as the *party-pooper* telling them to turn their music down or the grumpy old man barking at trespassers to stay out of his yard. False perceptions like these, and many more are often formulated from negative experiences with authority figures (i.e. abusive parents, overbearing bosses, crooked politicians, etc.). As well, much of organized religiosity (i.e. toxic churches, corrupt pastors, betrayal of church people, etc.) is a major contributing factor to our flawed perceptions of God. When our expectations are skewed to those in spiritual authority it is easy to transfer our feelings of suspicion onto God. In psychology this is known as *transference.* Friend, God is nothing like any of these unpleasant examples. The Bible does not teach us that God is *so angry* with us. It teaches us that He SO LOVES us.

> "For God SO LOVED the world, that HE GAVE HIS ONLY BEGOTTEN SON, that whoever believes in Him shall not perish, but have eternal life." (John 3:16 NASB)

Many feel that God is a God of wrath. This warped mentality mainly stems from an Old Covenant concept of God. It is easy to read through the Old Testament writings of the Major Prophets (Isaiah, Jeremiah, Ezekiel, Etc.) and arrive at this conclusion. However, although God can be *provoked* to wrath (as vividly displayed in the Old Covenant), His mercy, Grace and LOVE (as marvelously revealed in the New Covenant) completely overshadows His wrath. God's great mercy has extinguished the infernos of His jealous rage through His sacrificial love. In His justice, God had to chastise sinners but He loved us so much that He chose Jesus (His own Son) to be the whipping boy in our place. Jesus was the scapegoat for our grave disobedience. His finished work totally mollified God's anger. This is God's love in all its magnificence. God is not a God of wrath. Nowhere in scripture does it say, *"God is wrath."* It is not His nature. He can display wrath but it is not at the core of His character. Although God is perfectly righteous in His nature He is not indignant in His character. In fact, His righteousness prohibited Him from carrying out the severity of this wrath. In other words, His nature caused Him to do the *right* thing. The *just* thing would have been to punish mankind for their rebellion. A gracious God would have been just, right and correct in holding us accountable for sin – foregoing Grace. His justice demands penalty. However, God's righteous, loving character required Him to provide a way of escape for those whom He created and loved. The Bible clearly tells us, *"God is LOVE."* God not only loves, He IS love and all He does flows from loving nature.

"Beloved, let us love one another, for LOVE IS FROM GOD; and everyone who loves is born of God and knows God. The one who does not love does not know God, for GOD IS LOVE." (1 John 4:7-8 NASB)

"Behold what manner of love the Father has bestowed on us, that we should be called children of God!" (1 John 3:1 NKJV)

Now be certain that without a real sense of God's wrath we wouldn't feel the need for His mercy. This explains why we feel a sense of God's disapproval when we sin *before* we become believers. His anger is real and is kindled like a raging fire against iniquity. Yet, God knew that unquenched wrath would not save us. Therefore it was His great love that compelled Him to offer His full mercy. It is incomprehensible that God would offer His own mercy in lieu of His own wrath. God's Grace rescued us from the wrath that would have surely destroyed us. Nothing (including any amount of self-effort) can save us from God's great wrath except His own great mercy. In fact it was when we were the worst of sinners that Christ saved us.

"But God demonstrates HIS OWN LOVE for us in this: while we were still sinners, Christ died for us." (Romans 5:8 NIV)

Cross-Stitched by Grace

John 3:16 is one of the most familiar verses in the Bible. We learned to memorize it when we were kids in Sunday school. It is recited it at funerals, cross-stitched it on pillows and engraved it on plaques. We can even mumble it in our sleep, yet we really don't know the gravity of it's meaning. No matter how well we think we know this verse, there are still multitudes that haven't the slightest inkling what this verse or especially what the following two verses say.

"For GOD DID NOT SEND HIS SON INTO THE WORLD TO CONDEMN THE WORLD, BUT THAT THE WORLD THROUGH HIM MIGHT BE SAVED. HE WHO BELIEVES IN HIM IS NOT CONDEMNED; but he who does not believe is condemned already, because he has not believed in the name of the only begotten Son of God." (John 3:17-18 NKJV)

We have been *cross*-stitched into God's heart by Grace. We're woven so tightly by His love that no force in Heaven, hell or earth could ever tear us apart. Now we must get this truth cross-stitched in our mind. Many *God-fearing* people believe that Jesus came to save, but after saving them He judges their behavior on a more stringent standard. The mindset is, *"Since God made such a great sacrifice, how dare we sin lest we be subject to a greater punishment."* Friend, Jesus' sacrifice doesn't *subject us to* punishment; His sacrifice saves us from punishment. Look at the scripture above closely... *"He who BELIEVES in Him is NOT condemned!"* It doesn't say, *"He who OBEYS is not condemned."* Our righteousness isn't a righteousness of *doing;* it's a righteousness of BELIEVING! And we must believe that Jesus didn't come to judge us; He came to SAVE us. Jesus is not the condemner. He is the REDEEMER! Through Christ we escape the judgment for our sin (Hebrews 2:3). In fact, God has already JUDGED JESUS on our behalf and there is no more judgment left for us AT ALL.

"Herein is love, not that we loved God, but that he loved us, and sent his Son to be the propitiation for our sins. (1 John 4:10 KJV)

The Greek word for *'propitiation'* is *hilasmos,* which means *something that appeases.* Religion says that we must appease God by our goodness. But only Jesus' sacrifice appeases God's wrath. God freely offered His only Son so we could freely receive His righteousness. God judged Jesus in our place so we would never have to be judged. Once we are born again, God never judges us according to what we deserve. He only judges us based on the work of Jesus. God never condemns the believer. Besides, if God is such an angry, merciless God, then why did He send His OWN Son to die for a corrupt world full of thieves, murders, rapists and adulterers? If God were a God of retribution then He would seek to punish those who have sinned against Him. Yet, instead of purposing to enact vengeance on us, He provided a way of escape for us.

"For the Son of Man has come to seek and to save that which was lost."
(Luke 19:10 NASB)

God's vengeance was completely satisfied by Jesus. Does God hate sin? Absolutely! God hates sin because of the destructive things it does to us. God doesn't want ANYONE to go to Hell (2 Peter 3:9). The place God is preparing for us makes the most beautiful place on Earth look like a condemned building. But Hell wasn't created for us. It was created for the devil and his demons (Matthew 25:41 NASB). It makes no sense that people would want to side with the concept of an angry God. No wonder so much of the world wants nothing to do with Him. It is because religion is always pointing to an angry God and our need to appease His wrath. But through Grace, God's wrath is fully appeased. God's full wrath is now aimed at satan.

"I will love You, O LORD, my strength. The LORD is my rock and my
fortress and my deliverer; my God, my strength, in Whom I will trust;
my shield and the horn of my salvation, my stronghold. I will call upon
the LORD, Who is worthy to be praised; so shall I be saved from my
enemies. The pangs of death surrounded me, and the floods of
unGodliness made me afraid. "The sorrows of Sheol surrounded me;
the snares of death confronted me. In my distress I called upon the
LORD, and cried out to my God; He heard my voice from His temple,
and my cry came before Him, even to His ears. Then the earth shook
and trembled; the foundations of the hills also quaked and were
shaken, because He was angry. Smoke went up from His nostrils, and
devouring fire from His mouth; coals were kindled by it. He bowed the
heavens also, and came down with darkness under His feet. And He

rode upon a cherub, and flew; He flew upon the wings of the wind. He made darkness His secret place; His canopy around Him was dark waters and thick clouds of the skies. From the brightness before Him, His thick clouds passed with hailstones and coals of fire. The LORD thundered from heaven, and the Most High uttered His voice, hailstones and coals of fire. He sent out His arrows and scattered the foe, lightnings in abundance, and He vanquished them. Then the channels of the sea were seen, the foundations of the world were uncovered at Your rebuke, O LORD, at the blast of the breath of Your nostrils. He sent from above, He took me; He drew me out of many waters. He delivered me from my strong enemy, from those who hated me, for they were too strong for me. They confronted me in the day of my calamity, but the LORD was my support. He also brought me out into a broad place; He delivered me because He delighted in me."
(Psalms 18:1-19 NKJV)

This is one of my favorite Psalms. I included this lengthy passage so you could picture what is happening here. God is stomping mad and rushing to our defense with earthquakes under His feet, smoke blowing from His nostrils, tumultuous clouds enveloping Him, hailstones spewing out of His mouth and lightning bolts thrashing from His fists of fury. God is seriously 'ticked off' and kicking up a storm. Why? Because He saw that we were in trouble! Our distress aroused our Heavenly Father's outrage and He came running to our rescue. God gave everything to save us, even His own Son's life. God's *desire* for us *drove* Him to *deliver* us. Ultimate wrath met ultimate mercy. Beloved, His wrath isn't kindled against *us*. It is ignited against *our enemy*. And because God is for us, nothing in Hell or Earth can come against us or separate us from His love. Who would dare tangle with the God of Heaven and earth or presume to think they could mess with one of His children.

"So what do you think? With God on our side like this, how can we lose? If God didn't hesitate to put everything on the line for us, embracing our condition and exposing himself to the worst by sending his own Son, is there anything else he wouldn't gladly and freely do for us? And who would dare tangle with God by messing with one of God's chosen? Who would dare even to point a finger? The One who died for us—who was raised to life for us! — is in the presence of God at this very moment sticking up for us. Do you think anyone is going to be able to drive a wedge between us and Christ's love for us? There is no way! Not trouble, not hard times, not hatred, not hunger, not homelessness, not

bullying threats, not backstabbing, not even the worst sins
listed in Scripture (Romans 8:31-39 THE MESSAGE)

Out of Sight, Out of Mind

When God forgives, He forgets (Psalms 103:12). He purposely puts our sins out of His thoughts. He does not keep a record of our wrongs and does not give us a limit on how many times we can fail. So often we keep our *own secret record* of the times we fail and feel as if we have exceeded our quota. Sin has a way of making us paranoid. However, we don't have to fear when we fail. All we need to do is acknowledge our sin and turn to Jesus for His unending forgiveness. The good news of the gospel is that God will never blot our name from His book of life. God promises us that the only thing He will blot out is our sin. He is faithful to uphold His name and reputation as the One Who forgives and forgets our sins. And once those sins are erased from our heart they are forever erased from His memory.

"I, even I, am He who blots out your transgressions for My own sake;
and I will not remember your sins." (Isaiah 43:25 KJV)

Chapter 15

IT'S ALL IN YOUR HEAD

"Blessings are on the head of the righteous."
(Proverbs 10:6 NASB)

O ur key passage states that God's blessings are on our HEAD. This is vital for us to understand because our head is where we struggle with almost every issue of life. Behind the boney wall of our skull we deal with every circumstance, problem, sin, fear, anxiety, worry, dread, doubt, confusion, depression, insecurity and the most dreaded of all... *Condemnation!* The primary battlefield is our mind.

"For the weapons of our warfare are not carnal but mighty in God for pulling down strongholds, CASTING DOWN ARGUMENTS and every high thing that exalts itself against the knowledge of God, BRINGING EVERY THOUGHT INTO CAPTIVITY to the obedience of Christ,"
(2 Corinthians 10:4-5 NKJV)

Grace Under Pressure

Fear, worry, doubt, stress, depression, confusion, strife, envy, disappointment and condemnation seem to hit full force on the bull's-eye of your forehead right in the area between your eyes (take your pointer finger and touch that spot). That pinpoint spot is where all the tension of life seems to land and make the deepest impact. Many times we suffer from tension headaches and even deep-seated migraines from life's struggles. No matter how much medication some of us take, the mounting pressure remains unbearable. (I had originally titled this chapter *"No More Headaches"*).

In our key passage the author could have said, *"Blessings are in the HEART of the righteous."* Yet, instead, he chose to use the word *"HEAD."* I believe the men who wrote the Word of God didn't randomly select words out of the air. They were inspired by the Holy

Spirit to accurately address every issue we face with intelligence and deep insight (2 Peter 1:21; 2 Timothy 3:16).

The writer of the proverbs hit the nail right on the *head* (pun intended). Why? Because, for the believer, we have the promise that God's blessing is on our *head.* God's Grace not only cushions us; it is the impenetrable barrier that keeps every pressure and weight from bearing down to the point of crushing us. Now that's true Grace under pressure! Notice that in 2 Corinthians 10:4-5 it says, *"casting down imaginations."* I don't know about you but sometimes if feels as if the enemy is arguing with God inside my brain. It feels like an ultimate fighting championship. That's what Paul meant when he said...

"For we do not wrestle against flesh and blood, but against principalities, against powers, against the rulers of the darkness of this age, against spiritual hosts of wickedness in the heavenly places." (Ephesians 6:12 NASB)

In Paul's day they didn't have the WWF (I hate to break it to you but that stuff is totally fake). The type of fighting he was referring to was Roman gladiator fighting in the Coliseum. (our modern day equivalent of UFC). For those men it meant fighting *to the death.* The arena we fight in is for our peace and the enemy holds no bars. It's a bear knuckle brawl for our lives. However, the Holy Spirit constantly reminds us that we HAVE peace with God and that the fight isn't ours but it's the Lord's (2 Chronicles 20:15). Anytime the devil comes to you and says, *"C'mon, let's fight,"* Your response should calmly be, *"What for? You're already defeated!"* However, the enemy will try everything he can to convince us otherwise and draw us into needless skirmishes. In order to be at peace with God we must settle the *'righteousness issue'* once and for all! Being righteous doesn't mean we're performing perfectly to the standard of the Law. Being righteous means that we are positioned IN CHRIST and that we qualify for the blessings of God apart from our performance. The moment we receive salvation, God's Grace qualifies us to receive all the blessings and benefits that come with our righteous status.

"Giving thanks to THE FATHER, WHO HAS QUALIFIED US to share in the inheritance of the saints in Light." (Colossians 1:12 NASB)

Blessings Belong to the Righteous

"Do not fear, little flock, for it is your Father's good pleasure to give you the kingdom." (Luke 12:32 NKJV)

Our key chapter verse (Proverbs 10:6) means that God's blessings *come along* with His righteousness. Now look at the verse above and notice the word *"give."* When God *gives* us something it isn't contingent upon our earning it. It's a gift: the gift of His Kingdom, which is RIGHTEOUSNESS, PEACE and JOY (Matthew 6:33). Peace and joy are a part of our righteous standing. Notice, it doesn't say in the passage above that it pleases God when we work really hard to EARN the blessings of the Kingdom. No Beloved! God, our Father, is pleased when we RECEIVE the GIFT of His Kingdom. Many times we fear that we've lost our Kingdom blessings when we fail God. This passage puts us at rest. We have NOTHING to fear. We shouldn't be trying to change ourselves in order to receive His promises. Rather, we should receive His promises in order that those promises may change us.

Sadly, there are ministers actually teaching people that although God's love is unconditional, His blessings come by hard work. As a result of this erroneous teaching many work hard to please God by *straining* to believe in His promises and earn points with Him by perfect behavior and diligent Christian service. Many well-meaning ministers will even tell you that if your faith isn't *"strong enough"* then God isn't pleased and therefore you won't receive His blessings. My friend, faith is not a work; rather faith *produces* good works. The truth is if you're straining and striving to believe God, then faith is not truly active. There is something about real faith, that when activated by the Spirit, it is *easy* to believe. You just know that you know that you know. This is because real faith is a byproduct of the Spirit. Faith is the fruit that naturally flows from a believer who is connected to God's Grace (Galatians 5:20). Please understand that I am not saying that we shouldn't do good works. However, it isn't OUR good works that please God. It is God's Grace WORKING IN US that pleases Him and produces good works through us.

"So that you walk worthy of the Lord (know you are worthy by Christ's work and walk with your head held high not bowed down in shame) to please Him in all respects, bearing fruit in every good work and

increasing in the knowledge of God (we please Him in all respects when we bear fruit from being rooted in His Grace)."
(Colossians 1:10 NASB)[37]

Faith in God's promises pleases Him. Hebrews 11:6 says, *"Without faith it is impossible to please God."* This doesn't mean we earn His favor by *exercising* our faith. It means He is pleased when we increase in the knowledge of His Grace thereby allowing the full force of HIS POWER to work in us! When we bear fruit from being rooted in Grace, God in essence says, *"Yes! You're finally getting it! You're resting in Me and My Grace is producing authentic fruit through your submitted life! I am overjoyed to see you living this way."*

God loves us and sees when we try hard to *please* Him. However, He doesn't want us to mentally and physically burn ourselves out to please Him being motivated by condemnation. He simply wants us to learn to allow His Grace to exert His limitless power through us. God did not intend for you to run out of *you!* In the equation of works we must remember that works are not necessarily fruit. We can be working out of our own strength and producing *dead works* (James 2:20). Dead faith produces dead fruit. There is an obvious difference between plastic fruit and real fruit. At first, from a distance, there is a striking resemblance. However, at closer view the dissimilarity becomes evident (not to mention after tasting it. This is the difference between self-based works and Grace-based works. If we are naturally producing good works by God's Grace, then it qualifies as REAL fruit! What really pleases God is that you have *already received* all the blessings available to you. You must simply believe that they are *already* yours.

"Christ redeemed us from the curse of the Law, having become a curse for us--for it is written, "Cursed is everyone who hangs on a tree" in order that in Christ Jesus the blessing of Abraham might come to the Gentiles, so that we would receive the promise of the Spirit through faith."
(Galatians 3:13-14 NASB)

Being redeemed from the curse of the Law means that we don't prove anything to God in order to receive His favor. This relieves the mind. The scripture above tells us that Jesus became sin for us so that we might receive His righteousness. The imputation and punishment of sin was our curse; but Jesus took our curse and gave us His righteousness. He became sin so we could become righteous. Only by *faith* (not by strict observance of the rules) do we receive the same blessings that Abraham enjoyed: FULL RIGHTEOUSNESS! Abraham simply believed God and he was given righteous standing and all the benefits that come with it. When we try to behave and mind all our P's & Q's to get the blessings we go about things backwards and end up frustrated. But when we relax and receive the blessings of God, those blessings will transform us into the fruitful people God intended us to be. The problem with many people is that they don't feel worthy enough to qualify for God's blessings and therefore can't enjoy them. For example... In order to enjoy an apple you have to eat it. Holding it your hand isn't enough. You actually have to take a bite out of it. You can actually have the blessings of God right in front of you, and still not receive them because you feel like you haven't been good enough for them. In order to enjoy God's blessings you must first taste of them.

"O taste and see that the LORD is good; how blessed is the man who takes refuge in Him!" (Psalms 34:8 NASB)

Being at peace with your righteousness is God's will for you. When you actually believe that you are saved apart from your own efforts, you will be able to taste the fruit your salvation (i.e. joy, peace, strong self-image, confidence, contentment, etc). However, the enemy opposes everything God says *(remember that argument I was talking about earlier that goes on in our heads)*. If God says you are saved, the enemy says, *"You're not because you failed today."* If God says you are His *'beloved,'* the devil tells you, *"God is disappointed with you."* If The Holy Spirit says, *"You don't have to feel condemned,"* the devil will try to scream louder and say, *"You're doing everything wrong! You call yourself a Christian?"* The devil loves to do this especially when you come into prayer, praise and worship. As soon as you start to worship the enemy proceeds to scream out his arguments in your mind against the truth of your righteousness. He does this by pointing at your poor performance and what you have failed to do or not do for God. When you feel that you've performed lousy then you'll feel liable for judgment. Eventually you will begin to believe in that lie and say things like, *"I have made such terrible decisions with my life that I don't deserve God's blessings."* Receiving God's blessings isn't a matter of whether or not you deserve them. It is God's good pleasure to give you His blessings! Truth is, saint or sinner, none of us deserve God's blessings anyway!

It is vital to have a proper perspective of righteousness. When we are secure in our righteous then we will know we already qualify for the blessings. This results in TOTAL PEACE of mind. We need to understand that the fight has been *fixed*. We have already won! Who wouldn't want to live for and wholeheartedly serve a God that loves them enough to bless them even when they don't deserve it? This is liberating and empowering!

Everything Starts in the Mind

Everything we do starts in our mind. We *are* what we *think.* If we see our selves as grasshoppers in a world of giants then we will hop around in constant fear of being squashed (Numbers 13:33). Every single thought is a product of our belief system. What we believe about God and the way He relates to us directly affects the way we see ourselves (and treat others) and ultimately defines the quality of our lives.

"For as he thinks within himself, so he is" (Proverbs 23:7 NASB)

This is why the Bible warns us above EVERYTHING ELSE to guard our heart, which includes our mind, will and emotions. God never said to guard our finances, career, health or our relationships. He said to guard our thought life. The reason this is so important is because our perception of God and how He relates to us is the source of every *issue* (positive or negative) in our lives.

"Above all else, guard your heart, for it is the wellspring of life."
(Proverbs 4:23 NIV)

For years I interpreted our theme passage (Proverbs 10:6) to say, *"Blessings are on the head of those who **live righteously**."* However, as we have been studying, our righteousness isn't based upon the way be *behave* but is based on what we *believe*. Righteous Position = Righteous Provision. *Who* you are determines *what* you have access to. This is important when understanding our position IN CHRIST. For instance, look at the following passage...

166

The steps of a GOOD MAN are ordered by the LORD: and He delights in his way." (Psalms 37:23 NKJV)

THE word *"good"* can also be translated as *righteous*. This scripture has two entirely different meanings depending on your concept of righteousness. If you feel that you have to maintain your righteousness by your own works then you will be afraid of being abandoned, lost and without direction whenever you fail. However, if you believe that you are fully righteous based on Christ's finished work alone then you will always feel a sense of belongingness and never feel 'off track' even if you 'miss the mark.' Just because you fail doesn't mean you've been thrown off course. Having a proper understanding of righteousness makes us confident that we are never out of the Lord's watchful care.

"Because God has said, 'NEVER WILL I LEAVE YOU; NEVER WILL I FORSAKE YOU.'" (Hebrews 13:5 NIV)

"I am with you always, even to the end of the age.' Amen." (Matthew 28:20 NKJV)

Beloved, none of us deserves God's abiding presence, abundant favor and constant, overwhelming and overflowing kindness. Yet, He gives it to us anyway because He wants to keeps us close to His heart. God knows that the best way to keep us running after Him is to lay down a trail of Grace for us to follow. God's goodness keeps us in hot pursuit of Him (Romans 2:4). God doesn't cut us off when we disobey. Our hearts know full well when we've fallen short. Yet, when we fail, God throws His arms wide open and welcomes us to come and receive of His goodness. In His arms is the love that saves us, and the power that delivers us.

Blood, Sweat and Tears[4]

Jesus suffering (particularly having to do with the head and the mind) and His agonizing death contain astonishing revelations of God's remarkable Grace. His death speaks loudly of the price that was paid to bestow upon us the free gift of His righteousness. Within in the story of the Passion of Christ, there are three powerful ways that Jesus redeemed our peace of mind.

Sweating Great Drops of Blood

"And being in agony He was praying very fervently; and His sweat became like drops of blood, falling down upon the ground."
(Luke 22:44 NASB)

On the night Jesus was betrayed, just before His trial, flogging and crucifixion, Jesus entered into the garden of Gethsemane to pray. His prayer was so deeply agonizing it caused the vessels in his head to dilate to the point of rupturing causing the blood to flow into the sweat glands. As the sweat glands produced sweat it pushed the blood to the surface pouring out as drops of blood mixed with sweat. The medical term for this is called *hemtohidrosis*[5] (medical evidence supports this). This is so important for us to grasp. You see, the first mention of Jesus shedding blood isn't from the beating at His trial, the Roman scourging or His crucifixion. The first instance where we see Jesus spilling His blood was when He was praying in the Garden in John 17. Do you know what He was praying for? Jesus was praying for those who were *yet to believe in Him.* That's you and me!

"I do not ask on behalf of these alone, BUT FOR THOSE ALSO WHO BELIEVE IN ME THROUGH THEIR (THE DISCIPLES) WORD..."
(John 17:20 NASB)[37]

Sweat represents self-effort. As Jesus' intercession intensified, His sweat became as great drops of blood! Think about this when you exercise at the gym or when you work in the hot sun. Sweat is produced by self-effort. While Jesus' blood and sweat poured out, God's Grace was overpowering our fears and redeeming our peace. This was Jesus' first act of redemption. Sweat also represents the curse. In Genesis 3:19 God tells Adam and Eve that they would work the ground and eat bread by the sweat of their brow. In Ezekiel 44:17-18 the priests were to wear turbans to absorb the sweat from their head in the Holy Place. In fact according to the Law they weren't allowed to wear anything that caused them to sweat. The turban is a type and shadow of God's covering of Grace around our minds. When we come before Him we don't have to "sweat it." We are fully covered by His Grace!

The Crown of Thorns

"And the soldiers twisted together a crown of thorns and put it on His head..." (John 19:2 NASB)

Thorns represent the *"cares"* or worries of this life (Luke 8:14). Whenever we worry about our salvation it's like we're wearing a crown of thorns around our head. Thorns are usually produced in arid and dry places. Did you know that cactuses are actually flowering plants? The thorns are actually *leaves* that haven't budded in order to retain any remaining moisture. When we are in the dry seasons, we tend to produce "thorny" areas in our lives. But the Word of truth about God's Grace word is like water to us.

"So that He might sanctify her, having cleansed her by the washing of water with the word. "(Ephesians 5:26 NASB)

The truth about God's Grace is water to our dry souls that will produce flowers of righteousness where once thorns of condemnation grew. When Jesus bore the crown of thorns for us, He was redeeming us from the fear of condemnation and judgment. Jesus took our worries upon His own head so you and I would not have to endure the anxiety that condemnation brings. That is why we need to keep running to the Word of God. When we are saturated in the water of God's Word we won't produce thorns. Jesus took our crown of thorns and gave us His crown of glory and honor.

"What is man that You are mindful of him, and the son of man that You visit him? For You have made him a little lower than the angels, and You have crowned him with glory and honor." (Psalms 8:4-5 NKJV)

By the way, the Hebrew word for *'angels'* is *Elohim,* which is one of the names of God. It means *"The Mighty God"* or *"Divine One."* The NASB version of this passage even translates the word as *"God."* This verse is telling us that we are right beneath God and ABOVE the angels. The scriptures tell us that we are seated with Christ in Heavenly places (Ephesians 2:6). That means we've been promoted above the angels. The angels are God's servants to His people (Psalms 104:4). Oh if we only knew how we were positioned IN CHRIST. It would revolutionize our lives forever!

A Hill Called Skull

"They took Jesus, therefore, and He went out, bearing His own cross, to the place called the Place of a Skull, which is called in Hebrew, Golgotha." (John 19:17 NASB)

Jesus was crucified on a hill called Golgotha. The Hebrew word for Golgatha is *the Skull*. Likewise, the Greek work for Calvary is *kranion*, which is where we get our English word *"cranium."* Are you beginning to get a clearer picture of why the proverbs say, *"Blessings are on the HEAD of the righteous?"* The reason we have so many head *battles* is because of Satan's massive head *wound.* That's right! When the cross of Christ was jammed into the top of Mount Calvary and that first drop of precious blood splattered on the ground, it violently cracked the devil's skull and gave him permanent head trauma. Thus, fulfilling the prophecy given to Adam and Eve that Jesus would crush the head of satan.

"And I will put enmity between you and the woman, And between your seed and her seed; He (Jesus) shall bruise you on the head, and you shall bruise him on the heel." (Genesis 3:15 NASB)[37]

When Jesus hung on the cross, satan's skull was crushed. It wasn't just bruised or bumped. It was smashed with a deafening blow. The cross gave satan a fatal concussion and he's been suffering from brain damage ever since. Every time we trust in Jesus and receive the free gift of God's Grace, we are set at peace and that peace gives the enemy another concussion. He's been banged in the head so many times you'd think he'd learn by now to quit coming around God's people.

"The GOD OF PEACE will soon CRUSH SATAN under YOUR FEET. The GRACE of our Lord Jesus be with You." (Romans 16:20 NASB)

As previously mentioned, the word *Golgotha* (cranium – from which we get the word Calvary) is a combination of two Hebrew words: *Goliath* and *Gath*. Goliath was the giant from Gath (1 Samuel 17:4). Notice also that David had five stones (five being the number that is symbolic for Grace).[33] After David slew Goliath with a stone (directly into his skull) he cut his head off and brought it to Jerusalem and buried it there. Tradition says that Goliath's head is buried in the road that runs right by Golgotha. Thus it's name. When Jesus was crucified he crushed the skull and severed the head of condemnation.

Be Head Strong

The story of Samson (Judges 13-16) is significant in relation to the war for our wits. Samson's strength and divine empowerment to perform mighty miracle feats came from the Holy Spirit. This may sound humorous, but I don't imagine Samson looked like someone straight out of the WWF. However, I think he must've looked more like Barney Fife from Mayberry. Why do I believe this? Well if he had the muscles of a bodybuilder, the skills of a ninja warrior or the weapons of an action hero, the people would have thought his power came from natural abilities. However, the Bible says that the Philistines couldn't figure out where Samson's strength came from (Judges 16:5-6). It's simple really! God put His *super* on Samson's *natural* and that made him SUPERNATURAL! However, most of Sampson's trouble began when he relied upon and operated in His flesh (self-effort). This eventually led to him losing his hair (the equivalent to our war in the mind). Why is all of this important to understand? The scriptures teach us that Samson tragically divulged the secret of his strength to a deceiving Delilah. What was that secret? The secret of his strength was in his hair.

> "So he told her all that was in his heart and said to her, "A razor has never come on MY HEAD, for I have been a Nazirite to God from my mother's womb. IF I AM SHAVED, THEN MY STRENGTH WILL LEAVE ME AND I WILL BECOME WEAK AND BE LIKE ANY OTHER MAN."
> (Judges 16:17 NASB)

Did you see it? If Samson's *head* was shaved then he would became as any ordinary man. When the Philistines snipped away his locks, he immediately lost his strength and they were able to overpower him and gouge his eyes out (Judges 16:21). We are no ordinary people. God has created us for greatness. However, when we are defeated in our minds, we lose our vision and the ability to see who we are IN CHRIST. But look at what happens when Samson's hair began to grow back...

> "However, THE HAIR OF HIS HEAD BEGAN TO GROW AGAIN... Then Samson called to the LORD and said, "O Lord GOD, please remember

me and please strengthen me just this time, O God, that I may at once be avenged of the Philistines for my two eyes... And he bent with all his might so that the house fell on the lords and all the people who were in it. So the dead whom he killed at his death were more than those whom he killed in his life..." (Judges 16:28-29)

Our faith in God's Grace and His awesome future for us starts in our head. If we can get it into our thick skulls that God's Grace is greater than any failure, that's the very moment our strength starts to come back. Samson was chained to a corn-mill trudging in circles, getting no-where, trapped by his failures. However, the moment his hair started to grow, his hope revived. When this happens to us, our *"milling around in circles"* comes to an end as God's Grace fills us with fresh faith to believe and new power to live!

Chapter 16

STRESSED TO IMPRESS

**"Lord, do You not care that my sister has left me
to do all the serving alone? Then tell her to help me."
(Luke 10:40 NASB)**

When Jesus came to visit at Martha's house she was scurrying about in the kitchen, slaving over the hot brick oven trying to impress Jesus, most likely hoping to win His attention and affection (as so many do). On the other side of the room, Mary was simply sitting at Jesus' feet listening to His words and receiving or His love. She had discovered the powerful secret of Grace.

**"Now as they were traveling along, He entered a village; and a woman named Martha welcomed Him into her home. She had a sister called Mary, who was seated at the Lord's feet, listening to His word. But Martha was distracted with all her preparations; and she came up to Him and said, 'Lord, do You not care that my sister has left me to do all the serving alone? Then tell her to help me.' But the Lord answered and said to her, 'Martha, Martha, you are worried and bothered about so many things; but only one thing is necessary, for Mary has chosen the good part, which shall not be taken away from her.'"
(Luke 10:38-42 NASB)**

Martha, in sheer aggravation, barges in imploring Jesus that He command Mary to get off of her *dairy-aire* and help her with the work in the kitchen. Jesus lovingly responds by telling her that after all her serving she is still *"worried and bothered"* about so many insignificant things. Out of continued frustration Martha tries to get Jesus to listen to her. In other words, Martha tries to manipulate Jesus. You see Martha wasn't dressed to impress... She was *stressed* to impress! That is precisely the results of trying to earn God's favor: We wind up more frustrated than ever! Martha's irritation vividly illustrates what happens when we get caught up in the self-defeating cycle of works

The Heart Attitudes of Self-Effort

Our key passage suggests four different attitudes of the heart that surface when our relationship with God is based on self-effort to earn right standing with God:

The Heart Attitude of *Disappointment*

The Heart Attitude of *Abandonment*

The Heart Attitude of *Self Sufficiency*

The Heart Attitude of *Manipulation*

1. Disappointment *("do you not care")*

Trying to *please* God through self-effort stems from the false perception that God doesn't *really* care about us. We feel He smiles on us when we succeed and frowns on us when we fail. Subconsciously we hope our hard work and diligent service earns God's approval. This is what has been referred to as the *orphan spirit*. Many children growing up without fathers tend to live very driven and performance based lifestyles. Geared towards success, they scrape and cLaw their way to the top, meanwhile hurting themselves and even causing irreparable damage to their relationships. There is an old proverb that says, *"Be careful who you hurt on your way to the top. You might meet them on the way back down."*

Many Christians relate to their Heavenly Father and to others in the same way. The skewed mindset that we must earn God's favor causes us to become extremely disappointed in ourselves when we fail. Disappointment makes us feel *'dis' appointed.* Sadly, the longer we allow disappointment to settle in the more we eventually start to believe that we have missed our opportunity with destiny. However, God adopted us because He loved us not because we fit the mold of what we think His children should look like. God loves us for who we are (Romans 8:15; Ephesians 1:5). After all, He saved us while we were sinners. And although we may come to God as the song says; *"Just as I am"* God won't let us stay that way. When God is finished with us, by His Grace, we will be transformed into the glorious people He has purposed us to be. Rest assured, a changed *source* will produce a changed *stream* (James 3:11-12).

2. Abandonment *("my sister has left me")*

The 'good-works' mentality will always cause us to feel as if we are alone in our endeavors to please God. It causes us to become watchful of other people's behavior leading toward *judgmentalism.* Paul said that he was persuaded that NOTHING could separate Him from the love of God (Romans 8:35-39). This is what living on the side of Grace feels like! We are inseparable from God no matter what.

3. Self-Sufficiency *("do all the serving alone")*

Self-sufficiency is a form of pride. The mentality is, *"It's all up to ME!"* Failing God feels like the end of the world for self-sufficient people. Paul finally realized his religious fervor and self-reliant efforts were no longer sufficient. His only sufficiency was God's Grace (2 Corinthians 12:9). We can do NOTHING of ourselves. Paul made it abundantly clear, *"Not that we are sufficient of ourselves to think any thing as of ourselves; but our sufficiency is of God." (2 Corinthians 3:5 KJV)*

4. Manipulation *("Then tell her to Help Me")*

When self-effort to please God rules our lives we try to steer God in the direction we think best. At this we usually wind up more frustrated. This is because we don't get results by trying to prove to God that He should do things the way we think He should. Martha was only more frustrated after much serving. Her self-effort to please Jesus put her in a position as if to tell Him what to do. But Mary positioned herself to listen to Jesus and prepare her heart to do what HE wanted her to do. This is the quintessential illustration of the opposing forces of Law and Grace and how they cause us to operate. It is also interesting to note that in this whole story Mary is silent. She is simply content in the Lord's presence. Our words lose their importance when we hear the voice of Jesus (Ecclesiastes 5:2). Mary realized that being with Jesus was all that mattered and that every desire she could ever have was to be captivated by His love. The story of Mary and Martha teaches us that it's not about *achieving* God's love; it's about RECEIVING His love. Besides, if Jesus would have wanted something all He had to do was simply ask and I'm sure Mary would have bounded off to serve His request. When we receive from Jesus and all that His Grace offers, our service will have the necessary zeal and motivation to fully accomplish God's purposes. Grace doesn't make us lazy. In fact Grace makes us *more effectual doers* (James 1:25). When we live on the side of Grace we become much more efficient, effective, creative, proficient, productive and harder working than ever the average person.

> "But BY THE GRACE OF GOD I am what I am, and His Grace toward me was not in vain; but I LABORED MORE AUNDANTLY THAN THEY ALL, yet not I, but the Grace of God which was with me."
> (1 Corinthians 15:10 NKJV)

> "But one who looks intently at the perfect Law, the Law of liberty (the revelation of Grace), and abides by it (rests in it), not having become a forgetful hearer but an effectual doer (more productive, efficient and effective) this man will be blessed in what he does.
> (James 1:25 NASB)[37]

No one with an *encounter* with God is at the mercy of someone with an *ideology* from God. In other words, those in a vital relationship with God will never be the victims of religious opinion. An ongoing encounter with God's Grace produces a profound conviction that cannot be shaken. Once you encounter the truth of God's radical Grace you cannot return to the religious grind! Mary had a steadfast confidence in Jesus love for her and nothing anyone said or did could convince her otherwise.

> "But only one thing is necessary, for Mary has chosen the good part, WHICH SHALL NOT BE TAKEN AWAY FROM HER." (Luke 10:42 NASB)

David's Sweet Secret

Another person in the Bible who had learned the secret of God's Grace and the blessing of waiting in His presence was David. David knew that God was a good Judge and that, even in his worst sins, he was welcome into intimacy with God.

> "The Law of the LORD is perfect, restoring the soul; the precepts of the LORD are right, rejoicing the heart; the commandment of the LORD is pure, enlightening the eyes. the testimony of the LORD is sure, making wise the simple. the judgments of the LORD are true; they are righteous altogether. They are more desirable than gold, yes, than much fine

gold; sweeter also than honey and the drippings of the honeycomb."
(Psalms 19:8-10 NASB)

Although David recognized God's Law was perfect, unyielding, unbending, he also knew that God's Grace was greater than His sin. How could David say God's judgment was sweet? After all, the Old Covenant Law exacted heavy expectations and consequences for not living up to it's perfect standard. Yet, David knew something that many in the Old Covenant hadn't discovered. David encountered God's presence like no one else. He touched something in God's heart to such an extent that he was able to even touch the ark of the covenant and place it directly outside in his back yard without dying (2 Samuel 6:17). You see, David discovered God's Grace and realized that God was a GOOD judge and that His judgments are good. God's justice is IN OUR FAVOR and if God is for us who or what can be against us? No one who knows a harsh judge can testify that his judgment is good. When you read the Old Covenant your first impression is that God is a harsh judge. Remember though that God gave the Children of Israel a harsh *Law* in order to eventually cause them to run to Him and surrender to His Grace. The Law is harsh but God is not! That was sweet music to David's ears. David knew He wasn't exempt among the disobedient and rebellious. Yet, he knew by God's Grace, his sins wouldn't be held against him and that he wouldn't be cut off from the promises of God.

"How blessed is he whose transgression is forgiven, whose sin is covered! How blessed is the man to whom THE LORD DOES NOT IMPUTE INIQUITY, and in whose spirit there is no deceit! When I kept silent about my sin, my body wasted away through my groaning all day long. (Psalms 32:1 NASB)

David knew he didn't have to hide his sin from God and was quick to repent (Psalms 51). It was when he tried to hide his sin that it felt like his bones were wasting away (Psalms 31:10). Those who believe God will a harsh judge purposely avoid intimacy with Him for fear that their failures will always come up at some point. Therefore they continue to hide their sin and thus fall deeper into it. This explains why many people choose to stay busy (like Martha). They feel their flurry of activity will drown out the call for intimacy. They are afraid that if they stop long enough to hear God that He will remind them of their failures and so they scurry about with much business. Friend, God does not woo us into intimacy to remind us of our sin but to overshadow us with His love and mercy (Songs 2:4). People who know the Grace of God are quick to turn from their sin and fall into the arms of Jesus. God's presence is the complete remedy for sin, condemnation and fear. Martha hustled franticly to make preparations for the One who had already made preparations for her. Could it be that Martha didn't feel welcome into the presence of Jesus until she had DONE something for Him? Many of God's people feel like they aren't welcome into His presence until they deal with their sin. Therefore, there is no rest until they have performed their duty for Him. Yet, God sees everything in our lives (the good, bad and the ugly) but wants us to run into His arms, baggage and all, so He can love away our sin.

Mary's prolonged silence at Jesus' feet indicates she felt comfortable in His presence. Some ministers say that when we come into God's presence, He lays everything bare making us feel unworthy and undone. Friend, God doesn't want to belittle us but rather enlarge our vision of who we are in Christ. True, all pride is crushed at the revelation of Jesus but His Grace never leaves us empty. When Mary gazed into the eyes of the Person of pure Grace, all her inadequacies vanished in His love. Christian tradition suggests that Mary of Bethany was the woman caught in the act of adultery that Jesus forgave in the city square (John 8:3-11). This could explain why Mary was so captivated with Jesus. Those who regularly experience God's forgiveness best know Him and cling to His every word. As we gaze upon the tender loving-kindness of Christ we will experience the acceptance that empowers and liberates us.

In Old Testament times, sin made us unacceptable to approach God (Psalms 66:18). However, David came before the Ark of the Covenant with *known* sin in his life and yet God allowed him to enter. It was David's faith in God's Grace that pleased Him. This is why God said of David that he was a man after His heart (Acts 13:22) not after His Laws. David's boldness to approach the throne of Grace so deeply moved God's heart to the extent that this is the kind of worship He wants to restore in the Church (Acts 15:16). When we gaze into the eyes of Grace (like David and Mary) it causes us to abandon all else and surrender to His purposes (Matthew 26:7-13). God desires the kind of worship that is not birthed out of fear, compulsion or guilt, but rather out of sincere gratitude, pure love and abandoned devotion.

To truly worship God we must understand His love for us. And if we want to know God's love we must look closely at Jesus. Hebrews 1:3 tells us that Jesus is the EXACT REPRESENTATION of God. In fact, He IS GOD! John 1:14 says that Jesus is full of Grace. Therefore if Jesus is full of Grace then God also is full of Grace. So when we see Jesus, we see God and His enormous heart of love for us. Why is it so critical to understand God's love? Galatians 5:6 tells us that our *faith works by love.* For years I believed this to mean that if I labored diligently to love God and love others then my faith would work. This would be an endless cycle (and legalism in rare form). Why? Because our operable faith would ultimately be dependent upon how well we serve, give and love. This was Martha's dilemma. She was *caught up* in her efforts for Jesus instead of getting *caught way* in Jesus love for her. However, Jesus told Martha that Mary had chosen the ONLY THING that was necessary: to receive God's love for her. The Greek word for *love* in Galatians 5:6 is *agape* (God's unconditional love). Faith works by agape. When we truly believe God loves us UNCONDITIONALLY our faith will work UNINHIBITEDLY because it's based on God's perfect love for us not on our imperfect love for Him!

The Good, the Bad and the Ugly

God wants us to bring the good, the bad and the ugly to Him and fully embrace intimacy with Him, trusting that He will perfect all that concerns us (Psalms 138:8). This is the worship God desires.

> **"But an hour is coming, and now is, when the true worshipers will worship the Father in spirit and truth; for such people the Father seeks to be His worshipers." (John 4:23 NASB)**

There are 13 different words for *worship* in the Bible. The word in this passage is the most colorful usage found in all of scripture. The Greek word is *proskeneu*, which is derived from two Greek words: *pros* (to lean in the direction of) and *kuneu* (to kiss). It is a word that illustrates total intimacy with God. In this context it is a Middle Eastern word-picture of warm affection describing a puppy nuzzling his master's hand or snuggled peacefully on his lap. Dogs are known as 'man's best friend.' This is the kind of worshippers God is looking for. He is not looking for slaves; He is looking for best friends.

"No longer do I call you slaves, for the slave does not know what his master is doing; but I have called you friends, for all things that I have heard from My Father I have made known to you." (John 15:15 NASB)

God's Grace sets our hearts at peace from condemnation, fear and anxiety. Thus, He is calling us to come and rest in His presence so that He might minister *to us* and that His Grace may transform us. God is not looking for great worship. He is looking for *worshippers* and longs to share His intimacy with us. God wants us to *rest* in His presence not *stress* in His presence. Mary learned how to rest from stress because in the presence of Jesus there is NO STRESS! Through Grace we get all we need from God while resting for it! Quietly resting in God's Grace produces a steady confidence and strength in our lives.

"For thus saith the Lord GOD, the Holy One of Israel; IN RETURNING AND REST SHALL YE BE SAVED; IN QUIETNESS AND IN CONFIDENCE SHALL BE YOUR STRENGTH..." (Isaiah 30:15 KJV)

Martha was too busy to notice what Mary had discovered. As Mary quietly sat and listened at the feet of Jesus, she could hear the love and sense the attractive fragrance of His peace filling the entire room. Jesus is calling us to lay down our efforts to earn His approval or impress Him with religious performance. He is bidding us to simply come rest and allow His Grace to transform us from the inside out.

Chapter 17

GET A GRACE LIFT

"Every branch in Me that does not bear fruit, He takes away; and every branch that bears fruit, He prunes it so that it may bear more fruit." (John 15:2 NASB)

Many today are turning to the scalpel for all kinds of cosmetic surgery to improve their looks and their self-image. It is even happening among teenage girls as young as 12 and 13 years old. Young girls at this age are having their lips and their hips altered under the blade of the cosmetic couturier. Tragic! The reality is that no matter how much you change on the outside eventually the perception of your ideal self image with catch up with you. Having a concept of who you are IN CHRIST will change everything about you. Yes, you may still choose to change certain things on the outside and that's OK to a certain degree. But getting a *face-lift* is not going to change the permanency of your happiness on the inside. What you really need to get is a *Grace-Lift*.

Grace Lifts

The verse above does not refer to a tree like we know it. Rather it is speaking of a vine. Our traditional concept of trees is not the same as the picture of the vine that Jesus talks about in John 15. Vines are completely different from trees. Jesus did not say that He is the trunk and we are the branches. The right way to picture this is that Jesus is the vine and we are the extension of that vine. A grapevine is one continuous, contorted, twisted, interwoven branch that wraps itself in a hundred different directions. This so vividly illustrates the body of Christ. Notice that Jesus says, *"Every branch in me..."* All believers make up the body of Christ: the True Vine. Being IN CHRIST means we are completely wrapped up in Grace.

If you read further into John 15, Jesus says of those who don't abide in Him that they will be cast out like dry branches to be burned in the fire (John 15:6). Many Christians shudder in fear when they read this scripture. However, be at peace! This passage primarily refers to the contrast of the condemning religious legalists of Jesus' day and those who were joyfully coming into the Kingdom. In a New Testament sense it also draws a distinction between those who are IN CHRIST and those who aren't (the unsaved). This passage does not infer (as some believe) to those believers who struggle with sin resulting in being cast into Hell. Rather, it is our DEAD WORKS of self-effort (not the individual) that will be burned in the fire (considered worthless). Paul supports this truth...

"Now if any man builds on the foundation with gold, silver, precious stones, wood, hay, straw (worthless works of self-effort) each man's work will become evident; for the day will show it because it is to be revealed with fire, AND THE FIRE ITSELF WILL TEST THE QUALITY OF EACH MAN'S WORK (whether it is of self effort or Christ's sufficiency). If any man's work which he has built on it remains, he will receive a reward. If any man's work is burned up, he will suffer loss; BUT HE HIMSELF WILL BE SAVED, yet so as through fire."
(1 Corinthians 3:12-15 NASB)[37]

All our self-efforts are like wood, hay and straw that will be burned up in the fire. No self-works will remain. Only Christ will get the glory for our righteousness! When we lay down our ego and refuse to live by our own strength we in effect throw our dead branches into the fire. When we do this, we stop trusting in ourselves and allow Christ to become our sufficiency. The question remains then: How is it that believers IN CHRIST struggle to bear fruit? The reason it is difficult for many to receive Grace is because it just seems too easy. My friend, God made it easy to receive Grace through the finished work of His Son (Matthew 11:30). Jesus did the work so we could simply receive the reward for HIS labor. We must remember the *way of Grace* isn't hard. Rather it's the *way of the transgressor* that is hard (Proverbs 13:15). We live defeated lives from being sin and *self-consciousness* instead of being *Christ-conscious*. When we put the burning spotlight on Christ's goodness and holiness, our goodness and holiness fades into His incomparable light. It's when we obsess over our failures that we tend to reject Grace, which eventually leads toward depression.

"I am BENT OVER and GREATLY BOWED DOWN; I go mourning all day long." (Psalms 38:6 NASB)

When part of a grapevine drags the ground it will wither and will not be able to produce grapes. Likewise, when we come under condemnation we cannot experience God's favor nor bear spiritual fruit. Our key passage (v.2) says that Jesus *"takes away"* the branch that doesn't bear fruit. The NIV translation says *"cut-off."* This specific wording causes many Christians to fear that they will be cut off from their salvation or that God will use tragedy to teach them a lesson. Not so! The Greek word for *"takes away"* is *'egeiro'* meaning *to lift up, elevate and call the dead to life.* When a vineyard owner sees a vine branch dragging the ground, he immediately lifts it up and gently wraps it back *into* the vine (Jesus). This is what Jesus did for us. No wonder the Psalmist exclaimed...

"But You, O LORD, are a shield about me, my glory, and the One who lifts my head." (Psalms 3:3 NASB)

Another instance where the Greek word *'egeiro'* is used is in (Mark 2:1-12). This is the story of the man who was lowered through the roof and was miraculously healed.[4] In verses 9-10 Jesus indicates that condemnation was preventing him from being healed.

"Which is easier, to say to the paralytic, 'Your sins are forgiven.' or to say, 'Get up, and pick up your pallet and walk?' But so that you may know that the Son of Man has authority on earth to forgive sins'--He said to the paralytic..." (Mark 2:9-10 NASB)

Jesus tells the religious leaders standing by that through the power of the forgiveness of sins, salvation and healing are available. However, condemnation prevents us from accepting them. Look at what happens when Jesus forgives the paralytic...

"I say to you, ARISE (egeiro), take up your bed, and go to your house.' Immediately he arose, took up the bed, and went out in the presence of them all, so that all were amazed and glorified God, saying, 'We never saw anything like this!' " (Mark 2:11-12 NKJV)[37]

When writing to the Roman Church, Paul used the same analogy that Jesus used of broken and withered branches (specifically the gentile nations, including you and me) that we are brought back into the family of God by way of faith in Jesus Christ. IN CHRIST we are grafted into a loving relationship with God without fear of the imputation and punishment of sin.

"If some of the branches have been broken off, and you, though a wild olive shoot, have been grafted in among the others and now share in the nourishing sap from the olive root." Romans 11:17 NIV)

The Hunchback of the Sabbath Day[4]

Another powerful story illustrating the restoration of Grace is where Jesus is teaching in the synagogue (on the Sabbath) and uses the illustration of a vineyard. While He is expounding on the scriptures, He sees a woman hunched over with crippling scoliosis.

"On a Sabbath Jesus was teaching in one of the synagogues, and a woman was there who had been crippled by a spirit for eighteen years. She was bent over and could not straighten up at all. When Jesus saw her, He called her forward and said to her, 'Woman, you are set free from your infirmity.' Then He put his hands on her, and immediately she straightened up and praised God. Indignant because Jesus had healed on the Sabbath, the synagogue ruler said to the people, 'There are six days for work. So come and be healed on those days, not on the Sabbath.' The Lord answered him, 'You hypocrites! Doesn't each of you on the Sabbath untie his ox or donkey from the stall and lead it out to give it water? Then should not this woman, a DAUGHTER OF ABRAHAM, whom Satan has kept bound for eighteen long years, be set free on the Sabbath day from what bound her?' When He said this, all His opponents were humiliated, but the people were delighted with all the wonderful things He was doing." (Luke 13:10-17 NIV)

For 18-years this hunched-back woman could only identify people by their feet. This so powerfully illustrates how we are when we are *hunched* over underneath the weight of condemnation and unworthiness. In verse 13 when Jesus looses her from her condition she immediately stands up straight. This is what happens to us when Jesus *lifts us* (egeiro). We no longer have to look at the ground in shame. We can look up and see the light of God's Grace shining upon us. (Reading the scriptures from the side of Grace always inspires confidence). Notice in Luke 13:16 Jesus calls this woman a *"daughter of Abraham."* Abraham believed God and was considered righteous (Romans 4:3). Notice He didn't call her a daughter of Moses because Moses was considered the *father* of the Mosaic Law. Jesus rightly called her a *daughter of Abraham* implying that she was righteous by her faith (not her works) and was qualified to receive her healing.

All those who believe that they are the righteousness of God IN CHRIST are considered sons and daughters of Abraham. Therefore, when we come before God, we must believe and receive His righteousness through faith in spite of our shortcomings. Our righteousness isn't based on our good performance; it is based on Christ's performance. His performance is a finished work. Often, when we fail, we feel a sense of unworthiness; but it's Christ's worthiness we stand on and not our own. Condemnation causes us to feel unworthy of God's blessings. But through the finished work of Jesus we can feel confident, qualified and worthy to receive *all* of His blessings. In order to pick up Grace we must release our failures.

Pruned to Produce

The word *"prunes"* in our key passage means *"to clean"* (*KJV 'purge'*). Jesus told His disciples that they were *already clean by the word,* which He had spoken to them. The truth of the gospel (good news) is that we are forgiven, loved, accepted, well pleasing to God and free from the condemnation of sin forever. When we believe otherwise we become polluted and therefore the sap of God's love cannot flow freely through us. This is a totally different concept than the traditional interpretation of *pruning* (God painfully cutting on us to remove dead branches). When we believe and receive the truth of God's Grace we are cleansed from all unrighteousness (1 John 1:7) and thus begin to mature. A branch does not have to struggle to grow. It grows *naturally* because the life-sap is flowing through it. Also notice that John 15:2 doesn't say that God prunes the branches that *don't* bear fruit. Rather, He prunes the branches that *are* bearing fruit. God cleanses us with the truth of His Grace so we will produce MORE fruit. In John 15:1 God is called the *vinedresser* (KJV *Husbandman*). Our loving *Father* doesn't prune (cleanse) us with cancer, disease, poverty, sickness, disaster or any such thing. He cleanses us through the shed blood of Jesus and His Word (Revelation 12:11). Notice also when a vine-branch is dragging on the ground it lies among the stones. Stones represent the tablets of the Law (the ten commandments). When God sees us lying in the dirt, not producing fruit for being under the burden of condemnation, He doesn't resort to punishing, destroying, burning or cutting us off. We are members of Christ's body.

"For no man ever yet hated his own flesh; but nourisheth and cherisheth it, even as the Lord the church: For we are members of His body, of His flesh, and of His bones." (Ephesians 5:30 KJV)

Do you think Jesus would torture His own body after He has already been punished for us? No! Rather, He lovingly restores us like His own body and *lifts us up* into Himself (The Vine) so we can reach our maximum potential in Him.

Chapter 18

SINGING IS BELIEVING

"Come before His presence with singing"
(Psalms 100:2 NKJV)

When I was a young and less mature worship leader, I used this passage of scripture to legalize or enforce singing in worship. This is what happens when leaders don't understand God's Grace. Out of their insecurity they will they use their gifts and ministry platform to manipulate or coerce people to respond to them rather than lead them *'beside still waters'* (Psalms 23:2). That's why it is so important for leaders to know who they are IN CHRIST and not identify themselves with what they do. As leaders we must remember that our identity is IN CHRIST! This will help us lead from a place of confidence no matter how people do or do not respond. There will always be those who choose not participate in corporate worship. They'll purse their lips as if to say, *"I am not a good singer," "I don't want to embarrass myself" or "I won't sing because you are telling me to sing."* However, as worship leaders we must never become frustrated to the point of pressuring people to respond to our enforcement of a corporate response. Only the Holy Spirit can convince people to enter God's presence. The more we try to coerce people to worship the more they will oppose our efforts. God's Grace is the true remedy for a silent heart. Therefore, we must still our striving to make others worship and let Grace lead the way. When we do this, people will respond out of genuine desire to connect with God. Grace inspires hearts and releases true spiritual joy causing songs of authentic praise!

Have you ever noticed that most people sing when they are in a good mood or feeling carefree? Singing is the response of *worry-free* living. Many times we sing when we are doing simple household chores, shopping, cruising, taking a shower or other menial, non-stressful activities. My son likes to whistle all day long. We've nicknamed him 'Whistling Pete.' I was chuckling under my breath the other day while he was whistling in the car (completely out of tune immersed into his headphones) and he told me not to laugh because he is the *'best whistler in the world.'* God wants us to come into His presence with singing because we have absolutely nothing to worry about.

"BE ANXIOUS FOR NOTHING, but in everything by prayer and supplication with thanksgiving let your requests be made known to God. And the peace of God, which surpasses all comprehension, will guard your hearts and your minds IN CHRIST Jesus." (Philippians 4:6 NASB)

"Casting all your anxiety on Him, because He cares for you." (1 Peter 5:7 NASB)

God's approval rating doesn't go up when we sing but the level of our peace does. He isn't concerned about being *appeased* with our gift of song. Rather, He is more concerned about our *peace* of mind. One of God's remedies for depression is singing. He invites us to come believing that He has everything under control and that we are free to let Him deal with life's issues. Singing isn't a prerequisite to come before the Lord nor does He charge us a *gate fee* to come into His presence. His free gifts of love, joy, peace and righteousness already belong to us as children of God. Our response is to rest in His Grace and sing to our heart's content. Singing is *believing!* Have you ever noticed when you are singing in worship you begin to slip out of thinking mode and suddenly faith starts to explode within you? When we sing we cease to intellectualize things and enter the realm of imagination and possibilities. Faith is not birthed when we *think* about it. Faith is birthed when we *sing* about it. When we look at singing in this way we don't have to be concerned about the tone quality of our voice or how we sound to others. We should simply enjoy God's presence and sing to Him as the melody of Heaven fills our lives. Is it any wonder why Paul told the believers at Ephesus...

"Speaking to one another in psalms and hymns and spiritual songs, SINGING AND MAKING MELODY IN YOUR HEART TO THE LORD." (Ephesians 5:19 NKJV)

God loves to hear His children sing (I know I love to hear my kids sing). I used to ask my kids when they were toddlers to make up a song about me and they would immediately burst into full volume making up a song with my name in every phrase (I truly miss those days). When we sing to God we reinforce our confidence in His great love and that He is working everything out for our good.

"And we know that God causes all things to work together for good to those who love God, to those who are called according to His purpose." (Romans 8:28 NASB)

Grace causes our hearts to sing thereby releasing faith. Nothing but good things can come from our singing. We don't sing to get into God's presence; we sing FROM A PLACE OF HIS PRESENCE! Oh if you could only get a revelation of this it would set your heart free to sing in the midst of every trial and test. The enemy is baffled when we respond to life's cares by singing!

Open the Eyes of my Heart

Scientific studies have shown that music stimulates the imagination and increases the brain's capacity to concentrate. This is because the right side of our brain produces creativity, imagination, artistry and dreams while the left side of our brain is the center of logic, statistics, theories and formulas. When we sing we literally open the door to our imagination (where faith is born). Paul puts it this way…

"I pray that the EYES OF YOUR HEART MAY BE ENLIGHTENED, so that you will know what is the hope of His calling, what are the riches of the glory of His inheritance in the saints, and what is the surpassing greatness of His power toward us who believe…"
(Ephesians 1:18-19 NASB)

The words 'eyes of your heart' in this passage can be translated as 'understanding' or 'imagination' or more accurately "eyes of the brain." The Greek word for 'eyes' is opthalamos from which our word hypothalamus is derived. In psychology and neurology, the hypothalamus has been referred to as the 'brain of the brain' (the central hub or command control of all the brain's activity). It is about the size of an almond and controls most all of the body's activities such as: pituitary gland regulation, blood pressure, hunger, reflexes, thirst, body temperature, heart rate, bladder function, hormones regulation, ovarian and testicular function, mood and behavioral functions, metabolism, sleep cycles and energy levels.[10] The hypothalamus is the control center of the entire body and the hub for all five senses. It is responsible for managing temperature, hormone levels, stress, metabolism and digestion. The hypothalamus literally links our mind to our body. It governs and organizes our emotions, feelings and moods. It controls our appetite and everything to do with stimulation, pleasure, satisfaction, comfort and creativity. Conversely, when the hypothalamus is not working correctly, the *wrong* signals are generated making us feel empty, deprived and emotionally *unsatisfied.* This often leads to depression, sickness, disease, learning disability, abnormal responses to stress, bitterness, worry, fear, panic attacks, fatigue, co-dependency, sleep and eating disorders and obesity to name a few.[11] Why do I say all of this about the hypothalamus? Because when our eyes are open to God's grace, we literally cause the *'eyes of our understanding'* (eyes of our brain/hypothalamus) to come alive with the power of God. This gives a whole new meaning to the song *"Open the Eyes of My Heart."* When we live under fear and condemnation (which is the opposite of faith in God's Grace) we lose our song and fall victim to the enemy's lies about who we are IN CHRIST. When our minds become alive to the power of God's grace, it literally changes everything in our lives (body soul and Spirit). Look at what happens when we lose our song...

"Upon the willows in the midst of it we hung our harps. For there our captors demanded of us songs, and our tormentors mirth, saying, 'Sing us one of the songs of Zion.'" (Psalms 137:2-3 NASB)

The Children of Israel hung up their harps and stopped singing the praises of Zion and as a result they settled for the gloom and despair of their captivity. Just because you are going through difficult times doesn't mean that you still can't experience the freedom you have in God's Grace. You see; Grace doesn't help us *barely* make it through difficult times. Grace gives us the power to bear under, bear up and BEAR THROUGH every situation in life! If we hold on to our song it will be just a matter of time before we find ourselves singing our way right into the wide-open spaces of freedom. Hallelujah!

Condemnation kills your worship, preventing spiritual songs to arise in your heart. When condemnation is out of the picture, your mind and body begin to perfectly harmonize together resulting in health, healing and abundance of joy (Psalms 16:11). I can't tell you the importance of worshipping God like you truly believe in His Grace. When you lift your voice to sing in faith you actually stimulate the *'eyes of your understanding'* and nothing but good things can help but follow.

Grace-Based Worship Therapy

"God, who made the world and everything in it, since He is Lord of heaven and earth, does not dwell in temples made with hands; Nor is He worshiped with men's hands, as though He needed anything, since He gives to all life, breath, and all things." (Acts 17:24-25 NKJV)

When you fully embrace God's grace and the free gift of your righteousness in Christ, it changes the way you worship. You will no longer try to pry open the heavens by your worship. You will worship as if under a constant open Heaven. This kind of worship is therapeutic? In the above passage, the Greek word for *worshipped* is *therapeuo*, which means, *to heal, cure or restore to health.* It is where we get our English word *therapy.* When we worship without the limitations of condemnation, it's as if we enter the *spa* of Heaven and receive therapy for our minds (which control every other function in our lives including our spirit, emotions and our physical bodies). God's Grace is better than aromatherapy. When we worship in this way, the fragrance of God's presence powerfully affects our bodies and our emotions. Can you see the importance of holding on to your worship and your song? This is especially encouraging for those who have entered into middle age and beyond. Hypothalamic function becomes impaired with age. So as we grow older the hypothalamus needs even greater support to maintain optimum performance.[11] You don't have to let the effects of *long-term gravity* take over. Of course exercise, diet and a healthy lifestyle are important but that's not what's going to keep you young at *heart.* You can literally renew your youth as you embrace God's free gift of Grace, lift your hands to God in faith and worship and declare His marvelous works and promises over your life. Refuse to just lie down and let life's circumstances or your age defeat you. Hold onto the promise that God's Grace will keep you strong healthy, mentally alert, creative and on the cutting edge for many more years to come.

"Yet those who wait for the LORD will gain new strength; they will mount up with wings like eagles, they will run and not get tired, They will walk and not become weary." (Isaiah 40:31 NASB)

The Apostle Paul prayed that the believers in Ephesus would get a revelation of the hope of their calling in order to experience the riches of their inheritance IN CHRIST and the SURPASSING GREATNESS of His mighty power (Ephesians 1:18-19). The theme of our life should be of God's surpassing *faithfulness* not our surpassing *failures.* It is because of God's faithfulness that we are not consumed (Lamentations 3:22). Sometimes it feels like the circumstances of life consume us. Yet when we embrace a Grace-based lifestyle of worship we arise from the sledging swamps of self-effort. Worship is all about perspective. The way you believe God relates to you will ultimately determine the overall quality of your emotions and outlook in life. That's why it's so important to worship God from a joy filled, Grace-based perspective. Believing and receiving God's Grace causes our hearts to rejoice! And when our heart is happy we abound with soundness of mind and good health.

"A joyful heart is good medicine, but a broken spirit dries up the bones." (Proverbs 17:22 NASB)

Chapter 19

THE 'S' WORD

"For the Grace of God has appeared, bringing salvation to all men, instructing us to deny unGodliness and worldly desires and to live sensibly, righteously and Godly in the present age." (Titus 2:11-12)

The liberating message of Grace has been attacked for centuries. History proves that many who have preached the gospel of Grace have been accused of heresy and even maliciously martyred for their convictions (See page 228). Likewise, many today are accused of the same heresy as not presenting the *doctrine* of Grace in proper *balance.* Although, not physically martyred, they are often misunderstood and their reputations are maligned.

Grace must be taught in compliance with balance. However, by balance I don't mean preaching Grace and also a strict adherence to the Law. That is the wrong perception of *balance.* Balance isn't teaching a little Grace and a little Law at the same time. The passage above doesn't say we are saved through the Law. Rather, the gospel of GRACE properly instructs and empowers us in the matters of our salvation in how to deny unGodliness, shun worldly desires, behave prudently and live righteous, Godly lives in a presently unGodly generation. Grace doesn't turn us into wimps but transforms us into Spiritual brutes. Know for certain; I believe in firmly confronting sin and warning people to immediately pull out from vices that hold them captive. However, in my own ministry experience I have been much more successful in helping people get free from sin when I was motivated out of love and a position of Grace vs. an attitude of self-righteousness. One leads others to freedom while the other drives people into bondage. Having a religious *spirit* causes us to be angry and irritated with people for sinning rather than being hurt at what their sin is doing to them. Before we know it, that self-righteous, *holier-than-thou* attitude can creep up on any of us (including myself). The problem with many of us preachers is we often preach with great conviction but not enough compassion. The tool of choice to nail home the truth of the gospel is humility not a hammer. The reason we tend to scoff at people's sin is because we have much too high of a regard for ourselves. We must watch out for this *spirit* and give it no quarter in order to minster from heart of love for the broken. We need to be broken for the broken. Grace flows down to the lowest of the low, so we should be careful not to take too high a position. Therefore, if we want people to experience God's unconditional love then we must love them unconditionally. The best way to help people *veer* from sin is to *steer* them head-on in the direction of Grace.

Escorted by Grace

Many think teaching Grace creates lax, lazy and lascivious Christians. Nonsense! Actually the GRACE of God is THE motivating factor towards holiness. Paul wrote to Titus about the issue of Grace and living Godly.

"For the Grace of God has appeared bringing salvation to all men. Instructing (bringing) us to deny unGodliness and worldly desires and to live sensibly (in moderation) righteously and Godly (live like God) in the present age (this sinful, rebellious, Godless culture)."
(Titus 2:11-12)[37]

The center reference of my Bible (NASB) renders the word "instructing" as *"bringing."* It's as if Grace lays its strong right arm around our shoulder and firmly *brings* us towards the heights of holy living. Our ingrained concept has been that because we've been *taught* to do right therefore we *should* do right. However, merely reinforcing the Law only causes us to fall deeper into sin because the Law gives strength or fuel to our sin (1 Corinthians 15:56). That's why God's Grace appeared. He knew we couldn't do it so He sent His Son (the wonderful person of Grace) to save us from self-effort and to redeem us from Lawless deeds.

"...To redeem us from every Lawless deed, and to purify for Himself (He Himself purify us) a people for his own possession, zealous for good deeds (God's Grace makes us zealous, excited and pumped up about living holy)." (1 Titus 2:13)[37]

Along with Grace comes God's powerful mercy. When God saw us compassion filled His heart and He knew that there was no way we could free ourselves. Therefore, God gave us His own Son in spite of our evil, our rebellion and our sin. God's mercy always triumphed over sin (Ephesians 2:4) and pardoned us from destruction. Remembering God's mercy inspires our hearts and fills us with overwhelming gratitude that helps us veer from sin. Our focus determines our direction. If we're looking to our own shortcomings then we will always come up short. That is why we must remember God's mercy. It is HIS GOODNESS that makes us good. Focusing on God's mercy instead of His wrath keeps our hearts in tune with His love and firmly establishes us.

"Keep yourselves in the love of God, LOOKING FOR THE MERCY of our Lord Jesus Christ unto eternal life." (Jude 1:21 KJV)

Although we should possess a reverential respect, humble adoration, sincere admiration and a sense of awestruck wonder for God, we shouldn't be afraid of Him when we fail to live up to His standard. Our God is full of mercy and forgiveness. When we focus on His mercy and forgiveness, it heightens our awareness of His power and presence in our lives and produces genuine holy living. Grace gives us power over and above sin (Romans 6:14). However, we are not to live fatalistic lives as if Grace permits us to live like *hell*. Grace enables us to experience more of *Heaven* on earth. For example: Just because I know my wife loves me unconditionally even when I'm being a jerk doesn't make me want to continue being a jerk.[36] Rather, her unconditional, selfless love for me makes me want to show her the love and genuine respect she deserves. Likewise, because Grace has set us free from sin, it naturally affects our desires and serves to motivate us towards holiness. Grace ignites the flames of love and devotion to serve God. Grace doesn't condone a sinful lifestyle! No way! God's Grace does not free us *to* sin; it frees us *from* sin.

"Well then, should we keep on sinning so that God can show us more and more of His wonderful Grace? OF COURSE NOT! Since we have died to sin, how can we continue to live in it Or have you forgotten that when we were joined with Christ Jesus in baptism we joined Him in His death? For we died and were buried with Christ by baptism. And just as Christ was raised from the dead by the glorious power of the Father, now we also may live new lives." (Romans 6:1-4 NLT)

Big 'S' Little 's'

To live victoriously on the side of Grace, it is vitally important to understand the difference between the state of Sin (Captial 'S') and the acts of sin (lower case 's'). The Bible tells us that when sin entered the world through Adam and Eve's disobedience that death and Lawlessness emerged.

"Therefore, just as through one man sin entered into the world, and death through sin, and so death spread to all men, because all sinned..." (Romans 5:12 NASB)

When Adam and Eve disobeyed God (and God knew it would happen) *Sin* (capital 'S') was born in the heart of man. Sin can also be defined as the state of being separated from God. This *root* of Sin caused man to continually practice and live in the *fruit* of a lifestyle of sin (lower case 's'). Before we were born again we had no consciousness of our separation from God (Sin) and therefore freely practiced (indulged) in the lifestyle of sin (small 's'). However, when Grace came, Sin was dealt its final blow! When we were born again and converted from sinner to saint through the shed blood of Jesus, our *Sin* nature died. As we continue to grow in the confidence of our new righteous, God-like nature, we daily gain fresh strength over *sinning.* In other words we decreasingly *sin* as we become more formed in the image of Christ. As long as we live, the ongoing work of sanctification never ends. We are constantly being changed from glory to glory (2 Corinthians 3:18). Know that even the most mature Christians sin from time to time. The Apostle Paul even admitted that he was the chief of sinners.

"This is a faithful saying and worthy of all acceptance, that Christ Jesus came into the world to save sinners, OF WHOM I AM CHIEF." (1 Timothy 1:15 NKJV)

Not only did Paul call himself the *"foremost"* of all sinners (NASB); he said that it was a *"faithful saying."* In other words, he emphatically refused to deny his desire to sin. That's why he said it was *"worthy of acceptance."* He just accepted the fact that He would sin. The problem with many of us is that we cannot accept our inclination to sin and therefore become disillusioned when we do. Paul didn't say that He used to be a sinner. He said, *"of whom I AM chief."* The words, *"I* am" denote present tense. If Paul admitted he had a huge propensity to sin, how much more do we have that same propensity? Think of it this way... When WWII ended many of our U.S. troops and American allied forces were unaware that the war had ended (and visa-versa). Thus for a brief time our soldiers were drawn into needless skirmishes by their enemies. This is the way the enemy of our souls schemes against us. Although the war for our righteousness is over, the devil will continue to pull us back into the battle for holiness. We will lose some battles, sometimes. However, when this happens, we must stand our ground believing that through Christ we have won the war over sin and march onward in HIS victory. The truth is many try to aim for the holiness part before they get the believing part right. When we believe and stand firm on the truth that we are the righteousness of God IN CHRIST, we will eventually find ourselves living in the fullness of Christ's victory.

"In this way stand firm in the Lord..." (Philippians 4:1 NASB)

Practicing Sin

Before we were born again we lived a lifestyle of sin and took no thought of God nor wanted anything to do with Him. We freely crossed those *lines* at will. Those who sin without consciousness of their sinful behavior have never accepted Jesus as Lord.

"Everyone who practices sin also practices Lawlessness... NO ONE WHO IS BORN OF GOD PRACTICES SIN, because His seed abides in him; and he cannot sin, because he is born of God."
(1 John 3:7-9 NASB)

John isn't advocating that Christians never sin. He is saying that *born again* believers have been sensitized to their proclivity of *practicing* sin. Practicing sin means to be caught in the habitual vice of sin or to freely and deliberately indulge in sinful behavior. Look again at what John says again: *"No one who is BORN OF GOD practices sin."* Once you are born again, God engraves His Laws on your heart (Hebrews 10:16). Now you are fully aware when you sin. However, just because you may *sin* from time to time doesn't mean you are a *sinner*. When you were born again your old sin nature was crucified with Christ. Before, you sinned without consciousness of it. Now that you have been made alive IN CHRIST sin isn't comfortable to you. Your new nature doesn't want to sin; it wants to live for Jesus. Truly born again, devoted followers of Christ are quick to acknowledge their sin and turn to Jesus for His abundant Grace! Living under God's Grace doesn't guarantee that you won't occasionally fall short (or *long* as is the case). However, God's Grace has liberated you from the bondage of a Lawless and habitually sinful lifestyle. Trying to live *"by the book"* is a miserable way to live. Through God's Grace, His Book lives in you and empowers you to have victory over living a lifestyle of sin.

So the question remains: Why do some born again believers return to a lifestyle of sin? It is because they somehow lost sight of what saved them in the first place.

> **"Let me put this question to you: How did your new life begin? Was it by working your heads off to please God? Or was it by responding to God's Message to you? Are you going to continue this craziness? For only crazy people would think they could complete by their own efforts what was begun by God. If you weren't smart enough or strong enough to begin it, how do you suppose you could perfect it? Did you go through this whole painful learning process for nothing? It is not yet a total loss, but it certainly will be if you keep this up!"**
> **(Galatians 3:3 THE MESSAGE)**

Here Paul was writing to the Church at Galatia and told them that they started out so well falling hard on the Grace of God and were experiencing amazing results in their lives. Holiness was blooming! However, because of pressure from the Judaisers, they began to return to strict observance of the Law. The outcome was worse than before they believed in Jesus. They returned to a system that could not empower them to obey God. The same is so true of many of us. Somewhere in the process of sanctification we are deceived into believing that we must maintain our righteousness good behavior. However, trying to live holy under the system of the Law is the same as attempting to throw a ball into outer space. Impossible! When you toss the ball up it will always come back down. Why? It is because the Law of gravity governs it. However, if the natural Law of gravity were cancelled by some metaphysical phenomenon, the ball would continue to rise effortlessly into outer space. See where I'm going here? Grace is the supernatural phenomenon in our lives that cancelled out the system of the Law that now makes it impossible for us to rise to new levels of holiness. What the Law once required,

Grace now empowers. Under Grace, we are no longer subject to the system of the Law. The Law drags us down but God's Grace lifts us up. The moment we attempt to live holy outside of God's Grace, we will inevitably gravitate back to a habitual lifestyle of sin.

God Forbid

Paul emphatically told the believers at Rome that Grace did not give them license to sin.

"Well then, should we keep on sinning so that God can show us more and more of his wonderful Grace? OF COURSE NOT..."
(Romans 6:1 NLT)

The KJV translation for *"of course not"* is *GOD FORBID!* God forbids us to Sin! Why then do we sin? The answer is pride. Pride goes before every fall (Proverbs 16:18). Self has always been the root and perpetuator of every sin. Sin results when we substitute ourselves for God. Therefore, in order to save us, God had to substitute Himself for us. I find it difficult to believe that those who habitually live in a lifestyle of sin yet claim to be righteous and display no consciousness of sin are embracing Grace. In God's Grace, righteousness is the *root* and right living is the *fruit!* When we wholly rely on God's unconditional love for us, His Grace will eventually manifest in our lives. Some may say they believe in Grace but they only believe in the concept and not the person. Big difference! When you gaze into the eyes of Grace and let it penetrate your heart it will change you. Faith comes by hearing but change comes from beholding. Many people are hearers but not beholders. People who *profess* to accept Grace and yet deliberately continue to display rebellious and abject behavior aren't fooling anyone, especially God. Living a *lifestyle* of sin is a sure indicator that you haven't grasped the truth of the gospel of Grace! Conceptualizing and believing are two totally different things. If you know you belong to God forever and that He will never let you go, it will profoundly affect the way you relate to Him and result in a dramatic lifestyle change! You won't ask, *"Since Grace has come, can I continue in my sin?"* Rather you'll ask, *"Since Grace has come, how can I give God GREATER GLORY!"* The Grace of God produces authentic and noticeable change even in the most difficult areas of your life where legalism and religion failed to do it! It was never God's purpose to send Grace to remove boundaries of safety and blur the lines of sin. Please understand that we CAN dishonor God by our sinful decisions and actions. However, it doesn't change God's unconditional love and acceptance of us. We can DISHONOR God but He never DISOWNS us. It's difficult to fathom it but that's the love of Christ! However, in saying that, it is important to add that when we reduce the Grace of to mere 'fire insurance' we produce 'me-centered' Christians: Christians nevertheless, but selfish and self-serving. This was never God's intent. When our hearts are genuinely grasped by Grace, it will stimulate an irreversible love for God and a stubborn tenacity to walk in loyal obedience to Him. Surrendering at the altar of Grace forever *alters* your life!

Dead to Sin – Alive in Christ

Lawless people are those who have no recognition of their sin and don't care. These people mostly consist of non-believers who have had no regeneration of Spirit. They are alive to the world and dead to Christ. However, born again believers who struggle with sin (even often) are aware that they sin and possess a deep desire to change. No born again believer ever freely runs out to sin without consciousness of it. When you are born again, your spirit man is dead to sin and alive IN CHRIST. Although you may struggle in the flesh with certain sin issues your spirit is fully alive and righteous.

"Even so consider yourselves to be dead to sin, BUT ALIVE TO GOD IN CHRIST JESUS." (Romans 6:11 NASB)

**"If Christ is in you, though the body is dead because of sin, yet THE SPIRIT IS ALIVE BECAUSE OF RIGHTEOUSNESS."
(Romans 8:10 NASB)**

**"For as in Adam all die, so also IN CHRIST ALL WILL BE MADE ALIVE."
(1 Corinthians 15:22 NASB)**

**"Even when we were dead in our transgressions, MADE US ALIVE TOGETHER WITH CHRIST (by Grace you have been saved)."
(Ephesians 2:5 NASB)**

Being alive IN CHRIST makes us sensitive to foreign invasion of spiritual contamination. Our *born again spirit* does not want to sin!

However, our mind still operates under the same old patterns and practices. This is why Paul said we must be transformed by the *renewing of our minds* (Romans 12:1-2). Although our *Spirit man* is alive IN CHRIST, our mind needs to learn a whole new way of living. Many well meaning people lack the patience with themselves and other believers (new or mature) when it comes to their spiritual growth. However, when our mind is constantly reinforced and retrained by the revelation of Grace we grow stronger with each passing day. Eventually our desire for sin weakens and we find ourselves struggling less with vices that once gripped us!

Don't Be a Yoyo!

We've heard the statement for years that *"Cleanliness is next to Godliness."* This meaning in order to maintain our righteousness we must stay clean. However in Grace, it actually works in the converse. When we believe that we are already fully clean and perfectly righteous (John 15:7) then the fruit of our lives will more and more reflect that belief. Conversely, if we *strive* to live holy and to *achieve* righteousness we will constantly *yoyo* up and down between sinful and holy behavior. Therefore, in order to experience greater consistency in our Christian walk we must be regularly conscious of our position of victory IN CHRIST to reign over sin (Ephesians 2:6; 1 John 4:17). However, we must also realize that even doing our very best for God is still not good enough because the Law is never satisfied by our attempts at perfect behavior. The Law always demands something better from us. That's why God sent His Son. Only Jesus completely satisfies the demands of the Law. And remember: Being good doesn't make us righteous; being righteous makes us good!

Why Weight?

"Let us lay aside every weight, and the sin which so easily ensnares us, and let us run with endurance the race that is set before us." (Hebrews 12:1 NASB)

The born again believer has been delivered from Sin (capital 'S'). However, there are *things* that pre-empt certain *acts* of sin (lower case 's') in our lives. Paul called these things *"weights."* These *weights* may not necessarily be sin in and of themselves. However, they might be things that allure us to an unholy attraction to sin. Therefore, Paul recommends (when necessary) that we should avoid certain things (such as people, places, media, etc.) that would incite any further temptation relative to the particular sins we struggle with. In short, we must do everything we can to avoid whatever pulls us down into sin (weight). By God's Grace we are not only free but we can stay that way. We must ask for God's help to remove anything that is causing us to stumble (Psalms 101:3). When we give one inch to the enemy he won't be satisfied until he gets a whole football field on us. Therefore, we need to be sure not to give sin any room in our lives.

"Neither give place to the devil." (Ephesians 4:27 KJV)

The NASB translation says, *"Do not give the devil an opportunity."* We should never make provision for sin in our lives (Romans 13:14). In other words, don't see how close to the fence you can get. If you keep riding *on a fence* you'll eventually fall into *offense!* I like to keep the milk jug on the refrigerator shelf where it stays ice cold instead of hanging it on the door. There's nothing more disgusting than lukewarm milk. That's the way many Christians are. They would rather hang out at the door *of the* world and be lukewarm than remain where they will be the most refreshing *to a* world looking for restoration and hope. The bottom line is sin never wants to be our friend. Therefore, we should never flirt with anything that could potentially spoil our influence and sabotage our destiny and assignment here on earth.

"...Watch out! Sin is waiting to attack and destroy you..."
(Genesis 4:7 NLT)

Passive or Passionate

Passivity is the thief of passion. Sinful living and unholy temperaments give inroads to the enemy to drain our passion and rob us of our influence. There's nothing worse in the Christian life than our passion to slowly seep out through the puncture wound of indifference.

Therefore we must be careful not to allow anything into our lives that desensitizes us to the leading of the Holy Spirit. God can powerfully use us when we surrender and commit to purity in our thoughts and actions. In this way, God's anointing will freely flow unhindered through us and strongly impact others. Living holy lives empowers our leadership and increases our effectiveness when confronting a sinful culture. *Christians* go to heaven but *disciples* change the world! In order to make a lasting *impression* on the world, the world needs to see God's *imprint* on us! To make true disciples we must also be true disciples! The gospel of Grace is not only a gospel of words but a gospel of power.

"For the kingdom of God is not in word, but in power."
(1 Corinthians 4:20 KJV)

When we walk in the power of God's Grace, we will have a deeper commitment to purity and a stronger desire to live consecrated lives that reflect our love and devotion to Jesus. Living on the side of Grace will cause us to be more receptive and wholeheartedly responsive to the Holy Spirit's warnings to veer away from the pitfalls and snares that sin puts in our path. Grace does not make us indifferent or tolerant to sin. Rather it sharpens our sensitivity to sin and diverts us from the devastating effects it can have upon our future. The gospel of Grace accompanied by a lifestyle of purity is a surefire combination that will powerfully impact our culture... Guaranteed! Why is this? In order to radically transform a generation, the world needs to witness the power of God's Grace at work in our lives. When we authentically demonstrate a dramatic and distinctive change in our words and actions it convinces them that Grace truly gives us lives of significance!

Chapter 20

GRACE BASED WORSHIP

"Even as the Son of man came not to be ministered unto, but to minister, and to give His life a ransom for many." (Matthew 20:28 KJV)

This statement may be difficult to comprehend but the vast implications must be seriously contemplated nevertheless: *Jesus did not come to be worshipped!* In fact the scripture above tells us that Jesus came to GIVE HIMSELF to us, to serve us, to minister to our every need. Even in our best we are spiritually bankrupt. We have nothing to give Him anyway. He alone has everything to give TO US! Therefore, our best worship posture is to RECEIVE all He is and all He has! In fact, Jesus desires to minister to us more than He desires us to minister to Him. And remember this: we don't achieve God's love through worship. We RECEIVE His love through worship. From this position we are empowered to change our generation and be the hands and feet of Christ to a desperate world!

We've previously covered this but there are 13 different words for 'worship' throughout the Bible. The most colorful of all the words for *'worship'* is found in the New Testament.

"God is Spirit; and those that worship Him must worship in spirit and in truth." (John 4:24 NASB)

In this passage the Greek word for worship is *proskeneu,* which is a term of intimacy, contentment, love, peace and rest. The Middle Eastern concept of the word is that of a puppy laying contently on the lap of his master in total contentment. This word differs from all of the other words for worship throughout the Bible. The Old Testament word for worship conjures images of bowing, serving, slavery, homage, indebtedness, etc. However, the new covenant idea of worship in this passage is that we can come close without fear, obligation, debt or penalty. It is what I call *Grace-Based Worship.*

Friend, we are not indebted to Jesus nor do we *owe* Him our worship, service, loyalty or homage. Jesus paid our debt in full and cancelled any obligation we have to Him forever. Worship is not a payment for any debt we owe. If we truly realize how much we have been forgiven we will love God much in return (Luke 7:47). We will more effectively ignite our congregations to worship and serve God when we point to what Christ has already done, not what we should be doing. Grace inspires extravagant love and extreme obedience.

"We love Him, because He first loved us." (1 John 4:19 KJV)

So many worship leaders and ministers attempt to heap guilt on people to worship Jesus because of the great debt He paid for us declaring that we "owe" Him our worship. Friend, I can never pay Jesus back for what He has done for me. NEVER! Even my best gift to God would never be enough. However, God's great love for me produces a genuine desire to bring Him my *first fruits* (the best of all I have) in my worship, service, attitude and behavior (Exodus 22:29).

The Frequencies of Grace

So often as worship leaders our first method of preparing songlists is to cram as many of the "Top 10" worship songs into our services in attempts to please the *relevancy palate* of our people. However, as GRACE-BASED worship leaders, we must have a healthy and correct revelation of Grace or we will tend to insert songs that have everything to do with us, our failures and what we must do for God instead of songs that declare Christ's finished work, our total salvation and His perfection freely extended to us. These kinds of songs will inspire us toward more extravagant acts of worship. Therefore, in our worship setlists we should seek to replace songs of self-striving to please God, and *"make him smile"* (as it were). Songs containing the constant, frustrating, repetitious cadence of trying to *"get to God"* becomes wearisome. His presence is always with us (Isaiah 41:10). We need to constantly reaffirm this truth in our music. After all the song says *"Amazing Grace HOW SWEET THE SOUND!"* Grace has a sound that goes beyond just the notes and the music. In fact, I believe that the frequencies of Grace literally have the spiritual power, and quite literally, the physical elements to dissipate the power of sin over our lives (Romans 6:14). The sound waves of Grace wash over us as we sing filling us with overwhelming joy and peaceful satisfaction. Isn't this what we want our people to experience? Consequently, this type of planning in our worship times will have a profound effect on our congregations. When we are consumed with ourselves, our failures, our inabilities, etc., we all the more plummet to the depths of condemnation, defeat, and discouragement and even despair (the total opposite of what worship is supposed to do). We don't want people worshiping out of obligation and fear of the command. Songs of Grace inspire authentic heartfelt worship!

An Empty Platter

The gospel truth is God not offended by our inability to worship Him *perfectly*. Besides, we really don't have anything to give God anyway. It's like being a waiter with an empty platter. The best we can do is sit at His feet and receive from Him. He is the bread of life and it delights Jesus for us to receive from Him (John 6:51). The story of Jesus visiting Martha and Mary so vividly illustrates this (Luke 10:38-42). When it's time to serve Him He'll let us know and give us the plan and the energy to accomplish the task. Instead of running out of ourselves, we'll have His divine nature and power as our reserve.

God sent His Son to steal our hearts with His love. His Grace is a *gift* not a *bribe* to win our allegiance, loyalty and service. He came to bring us to Himself, to heal, deliver and set us free out of pure love and devotion to us. His genuine act of mercy COMPELS me to give my abandoned loyalty and service to Him. His amazing Grace is not a lure or bait to trick me into a yoke of bondage to His will. It is a strand of love that forever binds my soul to follow Him wherever He may lead, not out of obligation but out of authentic love. The gospel of Grace powerfully leads people to encounter Jesus.

Unfiltered Grace

When we declare the Grace of God in worship, people are drawn into His presence. It is His goodness that leads us to Him (Romans 2:4). In fact I believe that the more we allow God to shower us with the goodness of His Grace, we will gain a distaste for the old life we once knew before we met Jesus and die to it all together. This is the theme of the songs we should be singing. No one in his or her right mind wants to trade a life of slavery for more labor. Therefore we must emphasize the REST that our new life in Grace brings. If we want to attract a world of sinners to follow Jesus and a church full of saints to more passionately serve Him, we must present the goodness of the gospel of Grace UNFILTERED through songs about laboring, toil and obligatory service! A pastor once told me that he was having a hard time growing his church. He had tried everything (i.e. programs, creative sermon series, outreaches, potluck dinners, carnivals, circuses, door prizes, etc.) and his church still wasn't growing. I told him if he preached the pure gospel of Grace he wouldn't be able to keep people away from church.

"And as God's Grace brings more and more people to Christ, there will be great thanksgiving and God will receive more and more glory."
(2 Corinthians 4:15 NLT)

Grace is the drawing factor. The world is attracted to the message of the love and Grace of Jesus. Coercing messages of condemnation and guilt may scare people to respond to the call to worship but ultimately it will push them away. God's Grace is love demonstrated. This is why we must sing songs and preach sermons that are full of the Grace of God so that a lost and dying world will run into the arms of a loving Savior. We must be sure our lyrics and the content of our messages are latent with the good news of the gospel of Grace.

Grace Songs

Pastor Brian Houston of the great Hillsong Church in Sydney, Australia is a powerful example of the principle of ministering in the theme of the Grace-based gospel. Many of us have heard and sung their world-renown songs over the years. Did you know that Pastor Houston will not allow any songs to be sung in his church that do not declare the finished work of Christ and His awesome Grace? I work alongside a few young worship leaders who have graduated from the *Hillsong International Leadership College* and can attest to this fact. In fact the theology teachers of Hillsong College meticulously review and critique songs from their writers to be sure that their lyrics are Biblically sound and reflect the true nature of God's Grace. Is it any wonder why God has allowed this church to have such an enormous platform for these amazing songs of worship? A special note to all worship songwriters... We must carefully scrutinize our song lyrics and also the lyrics of others for theological content and correctness before we use them lead other in worship. After all, we are not only causing people to sing our words, but more importantly, adopt our views of God. God has entrusted us with the great responsibility of writing songs based upon the delivering truths of His Grace. Songs profoundly impact and even define a generation. When people sing songs they not only sing them but they eventually believe and live by them. For instance why as believers would we sing, *"Come and live inside our hearts"* or *"Lord, we come before You"* as if to say He isn't already living in our hearts or that He has temporarily left us. It would be scripturally accurate to sing, *"God You live in our hearts"* or *"Lord, You will never leave us."* We must pay close attention to semantics never taking for granted the need to make even the tiniest edits! Singing even one small phrase of untruth reinforces an Old Covenant mentality that God is still at a distance or that He's with us one minute and gone the next. Singing songs from a Law-based perspective will always make us feel as if we have to struggle to get into God's presence. My friend, there are so many scripture references declaring God's constant presence and promises to never leave us (Isaiah 41:10; Jeremiah 22:23, Matthew 28:20; Hebrews 13:5-6 to name a few). Proclaiming this truth in our worship produces an unshakable confidence in His everlasting faithfulness and love.

In lieu of this our songs and the way we minister them must help to remove anything that brings judgment upon believers. As worship leaders, we must also be careful not to use our exhortations as a means to manipulate or coerce people into a response. As New Covenant ministers, it is our high calling to help *roll away the stone* of the Law from the cold, dark tomb of people's hearts so they can see the resurrected Savior and that the work for their salvation (initial and ongoing) has been made complete. One of Satan's main strategies is to use condemnation to drive us away from God thereby making us believe the lie that we are not righteous enough to enter His presence. He tries to make us feel unqualified by our lack of prayer or previous failures. Apply this to your own situation. When you worship, have you noticed times when you begin to feel unworthy because you haven't measured up to God's standard in some way? As soon as the invitation is given to worship the enemy pulls out the inventory of everything we've done wrong pointing to our inconsistencies and shortcomings. That is why our worship songs must be based on God's liberating Grace and the finished work of Christ. So often, we feel separated from God due to our failures. Beloved we don't worship God from afar. In fact, we are closer to God than we realize. We are not failures trying to get God. He has already removed the wall that separated us and brought us to Himself.

"Remember that at that time you were separate from Christ, excluded from citizenship in Israel and foreigners to the covenants of the promise, without hope and without God in the world. BUT NOW IN CHRIST JESUS YOU WHO ONCE WERE FAR AWAY HAVE BEEN BROUGHT NEAR THROUGH THE BLOOD OF CHRIST. For He Himself is our peace, who has made the two one and HAS DESTROYED THE BARRIER, THE DIVIDING WALL OF HOSTILITY, BY ABOLISHING IN HIS FLESH THE LAW WITH ITS COMMANDMENTS AND REGULATIONS... thus making peace." (Ephesians 2:13-14 NIV)

The foundation for all true worship is Grace!

Chapter 21

THE ENCHNANTED KINGDOM

"He brought me forth also into a large place; He delivered me, because He delighted in me." (Psalms 18:19 KJV)

When God created Adam and Eve and placed them in the Garden of Eden, He put them in the perfect environment to prosper and flourish. God gave them everything they needed to not only survive but to thrive. However, when they sinned against God the first thing they did was try to hide from God…

"They heard the sound of the LORD God walking in the garden in the cool of the day, and the man and his wife hid themselves from the presence of the LORD God among the trees of the garden."
(Genesis 3:8 NASB)

Adam and Eve must have thought God was sorely disappointed with them so they tried to run from God. This is what condemnation does. When we sin it's as if we feel like God is coming with retribution in His right hand and when He finds us we are in a *heap o' trouble.* Our fear of God causes us to conceal our sin and reject Him. Did you notice that God was walking in the garden in the *"cool of the day?"* The Hebrew word for *'cool'* is *'ruwach,'* which means the *wind of Heaven* or *breath of God.* It refers to the Spirit of God, which made man become a living soul (Genesis 2:7). This passage has for so long been interpreted to mean that it was the cool *part* of the day or a specific *time* of the day when God came looking for Adam & Eve. This is not what this means. It means that the very Spirit of God came blowing through the garden the moment that Adam and Eve sinned. The Holy Spirit did not withdraw Himself from them; rather He came rushing *toward* them. Could it be the very same rushing sound of wind that the disciples heard on the Day of Pentecost (Acts 2:2)?

When God finally *found* Adam and Eve (knowing all the while where they were) they were frightful and started passing off blame, as so many of us do when we are 'caught in the act.' Have you noticed that nowhere in this passage does it say that God came storming into the garden with anger and retribution, kicking up dirt and fuming at the nostrils? This is actually the first instance where we see God responding to sin and it isn't in a fitful rage. There's a theological term called the Law of First Mention. It tells us that when something is first mentioned in the Bible that it sets the precedence of God's pattern and that we should take special notice of it. Interesting! God's response by rushing toward Adam and Eve when they sinned shows us His amazing heart. God doesn't vanish when we sin. He rushes to us with love and compassion!

Yet, what did Adam and Eve do when they sinned? Like most of us, they ran and hid, pitifully trying to cover themselves with leaves. The leaves represent self-righteousness: using our efforts to try and cover our sin. Yet only God's Grace truly covers us. God HIMSELF provided them with coats of skin to cover their unrighteousness. God had to sacrifice an animal of HIS choosing to atone for their sin. This was the pattern of things to come. From now on it would have to be by blood that people's sins were covered. However, Jesus would ultimately become the perfect sacrifice for us. Why? For so long the people of God sacrificed animals on their own and by their own efforts they would attempt to earn right standing with God. But eventually the requirements of the Law would only wear them out driving them to fall hopelessly dependent in need of a Savior (Galatians 3:24). All their self-effort accomplished nothing. God finally sacrificed His own Son to wash away our sin. When we sin we are often just like Adam and Eve. We try to run and hide and all the while God is saying, *"Where are you going? Come back. Please don't run. I'm not mad atyou?"* Did you notice that the first person that God was angry with was satan?

The LORD God said TO THE SERPENT, "Because you have done this, cursed are you more than all cattle, and more than everybeast of the field; on your belly you will go, and dust you will eat all the days of your life." (Genesis 3:14 NASB)

God was angry with the serpent for deceiving Adam and Eve into thinking that God did not have their best interests at heart. Satan planted seeds of doubt in their minds to think that God did not truly love them and in so doing caused them to fail. When we doubt in God's love for us, we will ultimately fail. When we know that God believes in us and is pulling for our success, it will empower us in our obedience walk. It's when we think that God *'has it out for us,'* that we fail, run away and hide from Him. Notice also that satan implied to Eve that God had deceived them (Genesis 3:1-6). Neither Adam nor Eve had any reason to question God's love until the moment Satan began to deceive them. It was only when Satan planted seeds of doubt about God's love in Eve's heart that she began to question God. The enemy tried to convince them that God was not being totally honest and 'holding out' on them. Being assured of God's unfailing love for us will cause us to have strong confidence in how He relates to us. The false information that satan fed Adam and Eve about God is what ultimately caused them to fail in the first place. However, from the moment they sinned (and God knew it would happen) God was already making plans to put His own Son's life on the line for them.

When God banished Adam and Eve from the Garden, He did it to protect them. God wasn't finished with them nor was He finished with us for that matter. In fact, God had something much better for mankind. The Garden of Eden could not compare to the place of joy and liberty that we would eventually find IN CHRIST! You see; the Tree of Life was still in the midst of the Garden. If Adam and Eve had eaten from that tree they would have lived eternally separated from God. Even though God would still love them, they would never gain access to His presence. The implications of this are terrifying. Therefore, God lovingly led them away from this demise by providing a covering of Grace and sending them out of the Garden. He did this in order that He might initiate His plan to permanently redeem man from his sin and bring him back to the tree of life to be fully restored.

In the Land of 'Fake' Believe

By "enchanted" I don't mean that the Kingdom of God is a fairy tale. Although it's hard to believe that God's Grace alone makes you righteous, there could be nothing more real. Many cannot accept that it is possible to be fully righteous. Although we've heard all our lives that God's Grace is enough, we don't sincerely comprehend it. Therefore, whenever we fail, we feel we have fallen out of righteousness with God. Many Christians think they believe that they are righteous and yet subconsciously don't feel they 'do' good enough to get God's 100% approval rating. Many feel as if God is 75% happy with them and 25% displeased in their progress. In other words, many fake like they believe but deep down they are not convinced that they are truly righteous. To leave the land of *Fake Believe,* you must rest IN CHRIST'S righteous perfection. Some of you are having a hard time with this because you think it's prideful to say you are perfectly righteous. However, if you can't say it then most likely you don't believe it about yourself. If you have received Jesus by trusting in His finished work, then you are perfectly righteous IN HIM! And the truth is, that's the way God sees you, whether you believe it or not!

Never 'Dis' Appointed

Child of God, did you know that God is not disappointed in You? Whenever you feel that God is disappointed with you, you will not rightly discern His heart. You will literally become *dis*–appointed (separated from your destiny). If you feel that God has *rejected* you when you sin, then you will never feel worthy enough to *receive* from Him and it will drive you into hiding. We can't do *anything* to earn deliverance from God. The truth is most of the time when we're in trouble we are utterly helpless (Psalms 1:17). It is God's sheer *delight* in us that arouses Him to move on our behalf. Our key passage tells us that God DELIGHTS in us. You see, to the world you might be just one person. But to one person, you are the world. In God's eyes, you are His world. Oh how we desperately need to get a revelation of God's utter delight in us! And because He delights in us He has prepared awesome things for us (Numbers 14:8 NKJV). Some very colorful synonyms for *'delight'* are: to enjoy, to take pleasure in, to have total satisfaction, to be captivated or fascinated, to be overwhelmed, overjoyed and enchanted. Therefore...

God takes pleasure in us!

God is totally satisfied with us!

God is captivated and fascinated with us!

God is overwhelmed and overjoyed in us!

God is enchanted with us!

The *'large place'* (Hebrew = *merchab*) spoken of in our key passage is a metaphor describing a broad place of freedom and liberty much like that of setting a wild horse free to sprint on the wide open plain. Because God is enchanted with us, He rescues us and sets us free to experience the vast possibilities of living in the freedom and fullness of the blessings of His Kingdom (Galatians 5:1). His Kingdom is indeed an Enchanted Kingdom. (Psalms 8:4-5 NASB)

Much of modern worship declares that we are captivated and fascinated with God. All the while the concept that God is captivated with us is simply outlandish. We try so hard to impress God with our praise yet never stop to consider the possibility that God might actually want to praise US. That's right! God is waiting for us to give Him the opportunity to show us admiration and honor. Most of the time we subconsciously believe that we must spend most of our time trying to applaud and appease God. This is not the message of Grace (Matthew 20:28). We must be introduced to a new mind-set that God is not disgusted with us because of our struggles with temptation and sin. The truth is we will never be adequate enough to approach God. Grace, allows us to approach Him in our inadequacy in order that we might serve Him in His sufficiency. The scriptures clearly tell us that we can boldly approach His throne of Grace IN TIME OF NEED (Hebrews 4:16)! We try so hard to avoid our weaknesses and yet they are the very doorways to God's Grace in our lives. In fact I believe our greatest encounters with God are often when we experience our deepest failures. These are the times we are most broken and humble and God promises that He gives Grace to the humble (1 Peter 5:5) and the more humbled we are the more of His presence we experience. It is when we are at our worse that we can approach His throne to find greater Grace. When we fall we find Grace. And the beauty of it all is that God's delight *in us* ultimately inspires us to delight *in Him.*

God's Favorite Child

God's favorite child is Jesus (Matthew 3:17) and He alone is the only acceptable sacrifice on behalf of our sins. Yet since we are IN CHRIST we are also His favorite sons and daughters. Not only does His Word declare that we are acceptable in His sight but experience has also taught me He gives great favor to His favorites! God's favor cannot be earned or merited. It must simply be received. Truth of the matter is His happiness is just to be near you (Songs 2:10). God loves *your* presence, more than you love *His* presence. His greatest delight is to be with you. God is the most real friend you will ever have. He doesn't abandon you when you are at your worst; He draws closer to you when you're at your worst because He wants to show His strength through you in your weakness…

"And He has said to me, 'My Grace is sufficient for you, for power is perfected in weakness.' Most gladly, therefore, I will rather boast about my weaknesses, SO THAT THE POWER OF CHRIST MAY DWELL IN ME." (2 Corinthians 12:9 NASB)

The power of Christ dwells in our human weakness. God comes quickly to our aid when we are weak. God isn't just favorable to us when we are performing well. His favor surrounds us all the time. The reason we need God's undeserved favor is because we are nothing without it. God's strength is for the struggle: the struggle with sin, self and the flesh. Even when we *make our bed in Hell,* God is with us (Psalms 139:8). He's there through the good times and the bad times. He is good to us all the time. When we don't "measure up" to God's perfect standard for our lives, He comes closer to us to help us reach our fullest potential. What kind of God would He be if *turned us over to the dogs* every time we failed Him? The Bible truth is that God can't take His eyes off of you (Psalms 32:8 NLT). Know for sure that He never left nor took His eyes off of Adam and Even. He was always watching over them. Satan did not sneak past God nor was He caught by surprise when Adam and Eve failed. God had a perfect plan from the beginning and satan couldn't spoil it. If the devil knew everything he did worked in perfect conjunction with the plan of God, he would stop doing things that always backfire on Him (1 Corinthians 2:8).

God isn't disappointed in you! He loves watching you sleep when you are incapable of doing anything (Proverbs 3:24). God not only loves you; He LIKES you! It's not about who you are; it's about WHOSE you are. God is certainly not blind to your faults and failures, but His great love for you doesn't change when you fail. God isn't insecure or *thrown off* when you make a mess of things. In fact it's His *Grace* that swallows up your *DISGrace!* Many feel God packs up and pulls out when we fail. On the contrary, His presence draws closer to us when we are in NEED of His Grace (not the other way around). He is a *present help* in the TIME OF TROUBLE (Psalms 46:1). When we have a deep abiding confidence that God is with us in our successes and our failures; condemnation loses its power over us. The Holy Spirit doesn't abandon us when we are weak. In fact when we are weak the Holy Spirit takes over and envelops us with His strength.

"In the same way the Spirit also helps our weakness..."
(Romans 8:26 NASB)

On my 40th birthday, one of my best friends gave me a card that said, *"Tony, God delights in you!"* Often when I feel like a big disappointment to God, the Grace in those words drowns out the voices of condemnation and regret *(Thank God for people who move in the power of His Grace).* Many think God is frowning on them. This is only because they are gawking into the mirror of regret rather than gazing upon God's dazzling face of approval. A couple of years ago God began to deposit this revelation deep inside my heart that His eyes dazzle with delight over me. Not only has this healthy concept of God help develop stronger bonds of love for Him, it has also helped me to rightly point others towards the Heavenly Father's love for them.

The following is a song I wrote for those who struggle with defeat and disappointment. The lyrics reinforce the theme of God's utter delight and undeserved favor toward us.

HOW YOU LOVE ME

I can see the cross rising for me
The mercy in Your eyes reaching toward me
I can hear You say I'm forgiven
Precious Son of God
Precious Son of God

You love me deeper than the ocean
You love me bigger than the sky
Jesus, crucified for all the world to see
How You love me

I can see Your face shining on me
The flame that's in Your eyes burning for me
I'm forever Yours I surrender
I give my life to You
I give my life to You

You love me deeper than the ocean
You love me bigger than the sky
Jesus, crucified for all the world to see
How You love me

Your great love for me makes me love You more
Your great love for me is what I'm living for
You're all I'm living for

You love me deeper than the ocean
You love me bigger than the sky
Jesus, crucified for all the world to see...

You love me stronger than the mountains
You lift me higher than the stars
Risen, You're alive for all the world to see
How You love me

Tony Sutherland
© 2010 Praisetown Publishing/ASCAP
(Admin by Fun Attic Music)

Chapter 22

THE GRACE AWAKENING

"Awake to righteousness, and do not sin..."
(1 Corinthians 15:34 NKJV)

To tell the truth I had been *asleep* for so long in my Christian life. Somehow I had the idea (in the shrouded recesses of my mind) that God loved me but was always disappointed in me. My extreme self-will to perform and my hard work ethic were in constant overdrive and I found myself subtly trying to prove to myself, others and God that I was worthy of my calling. Ever since I have been awakened by the revelation of God's Grace, my whole perspective has dramatically changed to the point where I feel the presence of God moving more powerfully in my life than ever before. For example... I used to struggle to wake up in the morning to have that special 1 to 2 hours with God in order to have a successful day. Now GOD wakes me up and starts speaking to me.

I am not demeaning the importance of having special moments of intimacy and fellowship with God. However, I don't make time with God in order to please Him and maintain my righteousness with Him. Rather, I am *drawn* to prayer because I *long* to be with Him and to hear His voice. Most of the time I am clueless as to what to do and I need to hear from God in order to have direction in my life. I don't want to make *decisions* without clarity of *vision*. That's why I spend time with God. However, there are many days when my schedule is packed with activities involving my young children, ministry responsibilities, travel itinerary, etc. and it is extremely challenging to carve out that prolonged time for personal reflection, prayer and extended Bible study. However, rather than feel guilty about not having *time* with God, I simply enjoy Him ALL THE TIME. He is with me all day long.

"DO NOT FEAR, FOR I AM WITH YOU; DO NOT ANXIOUSLY LOOK ABOUT YOU, for I am your God. I will strengthen you, surely I will help you, surely I will uphold you with My righteous right hand."
(Isaiah 41:10 NASB)

Dumped in the Weeds

When I was growing up, my grandmother used to tell my younger brother when he was *acting up* or throwing tantrums in the car that she would pull over and leave him in the weeds if he didn't' settle down and mind his manners. Once she even stopped the car and walked him out into the sagebrush. Of course being the supportive brother that I was I would sit in quiet laughter as I watched the horror on my brother's face. The thoughts of Grandma leaving him in the weeds was more than his terrified, little heart could bear. Soon he got the idea that Grandma was serious about him changing his behavior. Of course she never really intended on abandoning him out on the Wyoming prairie with the wolves and the crickets, but I assure you he got the picture loud and clear that the car was not the place for *showing himself.* Now in my Grandmother's defense, she was the kindest, most amazing woman of God and probably the single greatest influence in my life this side of Heaven. However, I'll assure you of one thing... I made sure never to *cross her* in the car... EVER!

This illustration may be humorous to some while disturbing to others. However, the point I'm trying to make is that many of God's Children suffer from the same spiritual and emotional separation anxiety. We often fear that our Heavenly Father abandons us to teach us a lesson or to scare us back into holy living and committed service. It's as if we believe that God loves us when we are good and leaves us when we're bad. Beloved, God's word tells us we don't have to fear because He IS ALWAYS with us. He will never dump us on the side of the road. What a relief to know that that we don't have to anxiously wear ourselves out to maintain His nearness in our lives. We can simply rest in His constant abiding presence. What an amazing comfort to know that the peace of Christ is our dwelling place. As the old song says, we are *"safe and secure from all alarm."*

Loud & Clear

Since this awesome Grace awakening I am hearing God's voice clearer and more frequently than ever before. Contrary to times past, I don't find myself struggling to pull information out of Him. It's true! His Grace has turned everything around. Now, I don't just have a prayer *time*; I have a prayer LIFE! My spiritual sensitivity is heightened to the voice of the Holy Spirit and I am daily learning the powerful secret that Paul spoke of when he said that it is possible to praise and pray without ceasing (1 Thessalonians 5:16-17).

In other words Paul was saying that we don't have to be like the religious folk who beat their chests, scream into the Heavens making a religious amuck of worship and prayer.

"When you pray, you are not to be like the hypocrites; for they love to stand and pray in the synagogues and on the street corners so that they may be seen by men. But you, when you pray, go into your inner room, close your door and pray to your Father who is in secret, and your Father who sees {what is done} in secret will reward you. 'And when you are praying, do not use meaningless repetition as the Gentiles do, for they suppose that they will be heard for their many words. So do not be like them; for your Father knows what you need before you ask Him.'" (Matthew 6:5-8 NASB)

It's not 'Hip' to be a Hypocrite

The Greek work for "hypocrites" is *hypocrites*, which means *actor or stage player.* Greek dramatists of Jesus' day used masks that had the ability to project their voices to large audiences so they could be heard in the amphitheaters where they performed. Now to be sure, Jesus wasn't saying that we are never to be public with our praise. There is definitely a time and place where it is necessary to make a *much-ado* about God. That's what the word *Hallelujah* means. It means that we are to boast, rave about and make a ruckus and foolish clamor about our God. However, in Matthew 6, Jesus is saying that it is possible to regularly experience God's nearness without feeling the need to make a religious commotion. Religion loves to make a big *show* of everything!

My Grandmother so demonstrated this quiet power and strong confidence in God's presence around our family. Whenever she would open her mouth to pray, you could instantly feel the tangible presence of God fill the room. This is because she learned the secret of prayer. The secret of praying is *praying in secret.* I learned from her that cultivating the *secret place* is learning to commune in intimate fellowship WITH A PERSON. We can worship Jesus and draw power from His nearness anytime anywhere. Prayer is not a duty; it's a delight! Worshipping God is enjoying a relationship with a real person who is ever with us at all times.

Now to be sure, I highly value the gifts of personal worship, dedicated prayer and Bible study. These gifts aren't what keep us out of Hell but they certainly will keep the Hell out of us. However, when there is an overemphasis on the assiduous observance of 'disciplined' prayer it eventually causes us to focus on our much *praying* rather than the one we are *praying to*. I am not devoted to disciplines. I am devoted to Jesus! When I was growing up, I was taught to believe that our short prayers aren't truly effective and don't really *count* unless they are preceded by longer and more laborious ones. I've even heard it said that prayer is *hard work*. Why should fellowship with our best friend be a labor? It should NOT be so. Intimacy with God is rest! We rest with God in Grace so we can run with Him in the race.

I used to regularly drag myself out of bed at 5am and proceed to enter the 'quiet place.' Yet, once I got to the 'place' of prayer I found myself often drifting into a deep sleep and feeling shamefaced for not persisting through the early morning hours. At the end of the day I still wasn't experiencing the freedom that so many said would come from this practice. I yet found myself full of anger, wrestling with envy, jealousy and insecurity, choking back irritability, holding grudges, displaying greed, giving into impulsivity and compulsivity, making irrational decisions and struggling with doubt, fear and unbelief. Many times I experienced these emotional and spiritual setbacks even more when I would pray and fast. How could such a *holy man of God* who prayed two hours a day and fasted for long periods of time exhibit such unGodly temperaments and selfish tendencies? Inconceivable!

In days gone by, I felt like I had to beat the Heavens down in prayer for God to respond to me. I even dogmatically preached that people's lives would be a total wreck if they failed to have that "secret place" with God everyday. Preaching prayer from this vantage point gave me the smug feeling of self-righteousness. Without being fully aware of it, I was subtly conveying to others that my life was bliss because I had successfully cornered the prayer life. Through all of this I have realized that prayer doesn't make me righteous. In fact when I practice prayer as a religious exercise to try and improve my self worth, increase my anointing and become a better person it actually works against me. Now, through this marvelous Grace awakening, prayer is a constant conversation with God and a joyful exchange of fellowship. And the best thing about this is that I don't struggle with the daily guilt of not 'making it to the secret place. Some would think that sounds like I'm waxing cold. Quite the contrary... The GOSPEL truth is I've never felt more alive, more in love with Jesus, more in tune with the Holy Spirit and more aware of His awesome presence surrounding me and moving in me. My love for God has deepened, I'm more effective in ministry than I've ever been and I am seeing greater spiritual fruit in my life. True, there will be times when I am drawn into prolonged periods of prayer and Bible study. But the times when these are the most effective is when they are *Spirit-inspired* vs. *self-initiated*.

Waxing Cold

Now let me clarify again; while it is true that God is never distant from us, it is very possible for us to *feel* distant from Him. However, feelings don't necessarily define reality. Remember, God doesn't leave us. He is always with us. Nothing can separate us from Him. Our emotions can deceive us and we cannot always trust them. We must live by faith. However, sometimes our emotions are good indicators of where WE are in our relationships. When we lose our emotional passion for God altogether we need to do a heart check. That's why it is important to take advantage of the gift of prayer. Please understand that Grace doesn't negate prayer and worship. Just like making time for our friends, spouse and other earthly relationships, it is vital to cultivate our friendship with God to stimulate our passion for Him. However, we don't spend time with God to keep His love from growing cold. We nurture our devotion for God to keep OUR love and faith from growing cold. We don't maintain God's love for us, but we can maintain our love for Him. The main thing to remember in all of this is that, when we let God's Grace work in our lives, the discipline of prayer will not be a *wearisome burden* to please God, but a *wonderful benefit* in our relationship with Him. See the difference?

Earning Points with God

Remember; we don't rack up points with God when we *show up* for Him in prayer. On the contrary, when we approach God in prayer, we in-effect *tune-in* to the right frequency. Disciplining ourselves in prayer is all about focus. It helps us to get a clearer perspective as to what God is doing in our lives. When we say, *"I'm listening God"* it opens a whole new world of possibilities for us. As we posture ourselves to hear from God we diminish the potential for confusion, doubt and worry to settle in. After all, it's not as important to talk to God, as it is to *listen* to Him. Too often we are so busy jabbering that we miss what God is saying altogether. Allowing God to speak first (and He will if we let Him) will *draw* the right thoughts, words and actions out of our spirits. A practical way to approach this when we pray is to first still our racing thoughts, settle our anxious hearts, take a deep breath, surrender ourselves and say, *"Speak Lord, for your servant is listening."* (1 Samuel 3:10) This is the key to an ongoing, healthy relationship with God. When God initiates prayer and worship, peace follows and as a result you won't pray out of anxiety. This is what *Grace-based* praying is all about! Religion will cause us to love and trust in our self-motivated and initiated prayers. Another thing to consider is this... If we don't learn to embrace Grace we will find ourselves putting our affections in things like worship, prayer, fasting, Bible study and the like. We aren't supposed to worship the worship. Prayer and all the other Christian disciplines can become idols in our lives and replace our first Love. We should never love prayer more than we love Jesus! Loving Jesus above all else, including the spiritual disciplines, causes us to be established in God's love for us and gives us the proper perspective of the purpose and practice of those disciplines. Friend, the *secret place* is not the discipline of having a certain *location* or a prescribed amount of time set aside for prayer. The secret place is JESUS!

"For YOU HAVE DIED and your life is HIDDEN WITH CHRIST in God."
(Colossians 3:3 NASB)

Our secret place is IN CHRIST. He is our hiding place and in the secret place of His presence He sings TO US.

"You are my hiding place; You preserve me from trouble; You surround
me with songs of deliverance. Selah." (Psalms 32:7 NASB)

To effectively rise to our fullest potential, we have to first die to our own striving so that the power of God may work in us. That is what Paul meant when he said...

"I have been crucified with Christ; and it is no longer I who live, but Christ lives in me; and the life which I now live in the flesh I live by faith in the Son of God, who loved me and gave Himself up for me." (Galatians 2:20 NASB)

Paul wasn't just talking about dying to an old life of sin. He was saying that the only way to die to *sin* is to first die to *self (the flesh)*. When we die to the flesh (self-efforts to be holy) and receive God's Grace by faith; Christ's power will work in us. The fact is Christians are going to sin. However, they will find themselves sinning less when they surrender the pride of self-perfection.

Since awakening to God's Grace, I feel like I have been born-again *all over again*. Granted, I still haven't mastered every weak area in my life. Yet, I can say with confidence that I sense God's strength at work in me and am experiencing greater breakthroughs in the areas where I otherwise struggled before. I have also discovered, through Grace, that although my righteousness is IN CHRIST, it doesn't mean I'll reach a state of perfect performance this side of Heaven. I am not perfect because of what I do or don't do, but because of what Jesus has already done. Now I can rest from my self-efforts to be *"perfect"* and simply *allow* the power of God to work in me.

"For IT IS GOD WHO IS AT WORK IN YOU, both to will and to work for His good pleasure." (Philippians 2:1 NASB)

"May the God of peace, who through the blood of the eternal covenant... equip you with everything good for doing his will, and may HE WORK IN US what is pleasing to Him, through Jesus Christ, to whom be glory for ever and ever. Amen..." (Hebrews 13:20-21 KJV)

Sin cannot have a hold on us when we die to ourselves. I'm telling you the truth! When we come out from under the premise of the Law that says we must obey to be holy but rather embrace our holiness by faith, we will begin to break the vise-grip that sin has on us (Romans 6:14). I refuse to believe that Christ died needlessly for me. Christ *died for me* that He might *live* in me.

"For if righteousness comes through the Law (self-effort), then Christ died needlessly." (Galatians 2:21 NASB)[37]

Paul's writings emphasized that if we get caught in the cycle of striving to do what's *right*, we eventually find ourselves doing everything *wrong*. When we fall into the pattern of trying to please God with perfect performance we annul the work of Christ. The only way to experience the power of Christ's resurrection is to die to ourselves.

"And be found in Him, NOT HAVING A RIGHTEOUSNESS OF MY OWN THAT COMES FROM THE LAW, BUT THAT WHICH IS THROUGH FAITH IN CHRIST—the righteousness that comes from God and is by faith. I want to know Christ and the power of His resurrection and the fellowship of sharing in His sufferings, becoming like Him in his death, and so, somehow, to attain to the resurrection from the dead."
(Philippians 3:9-11 NIV)

Paul was saying here that the only way we will ever know the power of the resurrection (overcoming a life of sin, guilt and condemnation) is to *lay down* our self-righteousness that comes by adhering to the system of the Law (self-effort) and *lay hold* of God's Grace through faith. Some scholars believe that what Paul meant by *"fellowship of sharing in His suffering"* was that he wanted to experience every level of Jesus' life *and death* in order to fully identify with Him. However, in context of the Grace message it means that he wanted to *die to himself* in order to *attain* Christ's resurrection power. We will never know resurrection to God's power unless we die to our own striving. If there is no death to *self* then there is no resurrection through *Christ*. In the passage above, the Greek word for *'attain'* is *katantaō*, which means to *'come into'* or *'arrive.'* Although we fall short of perfection we still attain perfection through Jesus! Much Bible teaching today is no different than what some world religions teach. World religions promote self-improvement or self-infliction to gain mastery over the flesh. Many preachers will promote the same principle: to attain favor with God we must strive for perfection through strict self-denial and self-discipline. Ironically, Buddha's last words before he died were, *"Keep striving."* Jesus last words before he died were, *"It is FINISHED!"*

We must WAKE UP to the fact that we cannot do enough good to transform ourselves into holy people. Holiness is a work that only the Holy Spirit can do. We don't become holy through human means. Holiness can only be *transferred* to us by the holy nature of God (2

Peter 1:4). It is His *work of holiness* through us not our *act of holiness* to Him that makes us holy. When we steadily *believe* and *receive* the word of promise that God's Grace is sufficient to transform us, that *promise* will build us up and sanctify (regularly renew and cleanse us) from all that would keep us from living a life of peace, freedom and victory. As we *freely* partake of the holiness of God's nature (without striving), our inclination toward sinful tendencies loses its power over us.

"And now I commend you to God and to the word of His Grace, which is able to build you up and to give you the inheritance among all those who are sanctified." (Acts 20:32 NASB)

Chapter 23

212 DEGREES

"The effective, fervent prayer of a righteous man avails much." (James 5:16 NKJV)

The temperature for boiling point is 212 degrees Fahrenheit. In our key passage above, the Greek word for *'fervent'* is *zeō* meaning, *"to boil with heat"* or *"be hot."* The Greek word for *'avails'* is *ischyo* which means, *to be strong in body, be robust, be in sound health, have power to perform extraordinary deeds, exert and wield power, have strength to overcome, be a force and be able.* In the past I've interpreted James 5:16 to say... *"The effective and fervent prayers of the righteous accomplish much."* In other words, if I pray with enough gusto, physical force, energy, intensity and volume, then my prayer will move the heart of God causing Him to rise to attention and do mighty things on my behalf. No my friend! Our fleshy ranting and raving produces nothing outside of the Grace of God. We can't perform miracles by lathered-up praying. Only God performs miracles! It is totally possible to pray peaceable and softly because the *prayers* of righteous people are heavily latent with substantial and significant power. You don't have to scream when you drop an atomic bomb. The atomic bomb has power *in and of itself* for mass destruction; all you have to do is drop it and KABOOM... The rest is history.

The same is true of our prayers. When a righteous man prays, his prayer is like an atomic bomb (regardless of how loud or how much energy is exerted). As I mentioned in the last chapter, when my grandmother was living, all she had to do was say, *"Our Heavenly Father"* and the whole room immediately became charged with supernatural electricity. My grandmother learned to rely on her relationship with Jesus, not her religious attempts to get His attention. She didn't trust in her great praying (as great as it was). She trusted Jesus and stood on all the authority of Heaven.

The NIV translation of James 5:16 is much more accurate than the NKJV... *"The prayer of a righteous man is powerful and effective."* James is in essence saying, *"The prayers of those who are made righteous by the finished work of Christ alone can stand confident knowing that their prayers are effectual and mightily wielding the power to perform extraordinary feats."* The truth is when we accept our righteousness as a finished work IN CHRIST we can rest in HIS power to work through our prayers. And the moment our prayers are uttered God's power is released. Those who know they are righteous get their prayers answered because they know who they are and whose they are.

"For the eyes of the Lord are over the righteous, and His ears are open unto their prayers." (1 Peter 3:12 NASB)

I've also read James 5:16 to say if we are *living righteously*, and have no sin in our lives then God will listen to us. However, all of us have sin issues that we are dealing with. I can hear some of you saying, *"No brother Tony! Not me! I've arrived; I don't have any sin in my life! I'm 99.9 percent perfect."* The truth is; if the Lord doesn't hear us when we have sin issues in our lives, then none of us would ever get our prayers answered *(just go ahead and admit it and deny the temptation to be religious)*. The Bible doesn't say that God hears the *religious* when they pray; it says God hears the *righteous* when they pray. Our holy living doesn't make us righteous. Only the blood of Jesus makes us righteous. We don't come to God by what we do *for* Jesus' name. We come to God IN Jesus' name.

"If you ask anything IN MY NAME, I will do it." (John 14:14 NKJV)

This scripture does not say (as many interpret it) that we have to *say* His name when we pray (although there's nothing wrong with that). We don't have to say, *"In Jesus' name, bless so-and-so and do this-and-that."* Beloved, this passage is not telling us to merely *say* His name. It's telling us that we are to *come* IN His name (in His righteousness). In other words, when we approach God, we are coming in HIS authority and power. Remember that being IN CHRIST qualifies us for all the blessings that belong to Christ (Ephesians 1:3). If He is blessed then we are blessed because we are IN CHRIST!

Many times people pray out of anxiety thinking that they are praying fervently. That is what I call *'fraying'* not praying. The scripture doesn't say to *"come fraying."* All God asks of us is that we make our petitions known without allowing anxiety to 'taint' our prayers (Philippians 4:6-7). The Bible is clear that when we fret or worry it adds nothing to our lives (Psalms 37:8). In fact, anxiety cancels the effect of our praying. In order to pray effectively, we must be at a place of peace. When we pray in fear we are not approaching God confidently. Confidence is huge factor when we pray.

"Therefore, do not throw away your confidence, which has a great reward." (Hebrews 10:35 NASB)

Did you see that? Confidence is what gets us the reward. The rewards of prayer are based on the level of our confidence. The reason we don't pray in faith is because we don't believe that God hears us. As a worship leader and songwriter, I am very attentive to the lyrics of many of our worship songs. I shutter when I hear lyrics that say, *"God can you hear me," "Please hear my prayer,"* or *"Please don't turn away from me."* Beloved, God ALWAYS hears the prayers of those whom HE HAS MADE righteous. You have to get this. When you do, you will pray *believing* that your prayers are being heard based on what God has already done. Look what happens when you know that God hears you…

"This is the CONFIDENCE WE HAVE IN APPROACHING GOD: that if we ask anything according to His will, HE HEARS US. And IF WE KNOW THAT HE HEARS US—whatever we ask—WE KNOW that we have what we asked of Him." (1 John 5:14-15 NIV)

The key is that we can approach God with *total* confidence that we have been made righteous. When we feel condemned it is hard for us to approach God confidently. Condemnation quenches the fire of our prayers; but when we are confident that God hears us, all of hell had better watch out! We must always pray from a place of Grace. God told us to come before His throne of Grace not the throne of scrutiny. Many times we feel as if we are coming before a God of *inspection*. My friend, God sees everything and yet still calls us to relationship. Besides, we will never be able to check off the checklist of good works because no matter how "good" we think we are we will always come up way short. We will never be able to approach God confidently if we come by any other way than by Grace. We don't ever have to come head down in shame. We know that our prayers will be answered because our faith is not in ourselves but in God's Grace. When we feel we have the right to have our prayers answered based on our good performance we will always be frustrated. God doesn't answer our prayers based on our good works. He answers prayers based on Christ's good works. Therefore, those who stand confidently in their righteous position IN CHRIST will have no problem believing that God hears them. When we know that God hears us we can rest assured that our prayers accomplish much. We must realize that God isn't waiting for us to arrive at the level of perfect performance before He listens to our prayers. God alone makes us righteous and because we belong to Him, He hears us. Amen!

"Do not fret or have any anxiety about anything, but in every circumstance and in everything, by prayer and petition definite requests), with thanksgiving, continue to make your wants known to God. And God's peace [shall be yours, THAT TRANQUIL STATE OF A SOUL ASSURED OF ITS SALVATION THROUGH CHRIST, AND SO FEARING NOTHING from God and being content with its earthly lot of whatever sort that is, that peace], which transcends all understanding shall garrison and mount guard over your hearts and minds in Christ Jesus." (Philippians 4:6-7 AMP)

Our prayers are dangerous to the kingdom of darkness. Even a prayer whispered rings like a sonic boom in the Heavens. It doesn't matter how much physical force we put behind our prayers. If we stand confident in our righteousness and rest on Christ finished work, we know that our prayers have the necessary force to move God to action. God would do anything for His children. And because we move the *heart* of God, He moves the *hand* of man on our behalf. IN CHRIST no *mountain* can stand before us and no *man* can stand against us! HALLELUJAH!

When you pray you must put on the mind of Christ. Christ is always acceptable to God and so this is how you approach Him. Therefore, when you pray, take a few moments to still your heart (Psalms 46:10) and begin to internalize your right-standing with God based on Jesus' finished work. When you do this, before long, confidence will start to rise within you and you will feel the power of your prayer begin to take effect. Make no mistake; sometimes I am extremely intense and passionate when I pray. Yes, many times I get loud to the point of shouting. However, it's not the shouting that makes my prayer powerful; it's the power of my prayer that makes me shout! HALLLUJAH! Conversely, many times my prayers are quiet. Yet I know that those prayers are just as powerful as the loud ones. Why... Because it's not how *much physical force that* I exert in prayer. Its how powerful God is through my prayers. God is not deaf! He hears us loud and clear at any volume.

I can also hear some of you saying, *"Well what about Psalms 66:18 (NIV) that says, 'If I had cherished sin in my heart, the Lord would not have listened?' "* The key word here is *"cherished."* If you cherish (love) your sin then it is obvious you haven't embraced the Grace of God. Those who embrace the Grace of God are fully aware when they sin and are disgusted by it. Righteous people hate sin! I hate sin because it gives the enemy access into my life. Living a life of righteousness means that we are continually submitting our sin issues to God, and pursuing a lifestyle of repentance before Him. Think about this: How can we live a lifestyle of repentance if we don't have any sin issues in our life? Being righteous doesn't mean that Godly people won't sin. The difference between those who have received the Grace of God and those who haven't is that they hate their sin. *Grace people* don't embrace their sin. They loathe it! This is the separating factor. Those who hate their sin are surely those whom God hears and answers. Just because we deal with sin doesn't mean God won't deal with us when we pray. Righteous people don't live in denial when it comes to their sin issues. However, those who are growing in the Grace and knowledge of Jesus refuse to come under condemnation and submit to defeat. Truly righteous people are confident that they can bring all their issues before the Father and receive the power to deal with their sin head on and overcome it through His Grace (Romans 6:14). No matter what you may believe this one thing is Gospel truth... Sin cannot stop God's Grace, but God's Grace CAN stop sin! Hallelujah

Once you get a revelation of your righteousness IN CHRIST, you will begin to see your prayer life change dramatically. You'll no longer pray from your own power. You will pray from your *position.* You are seated *with Christ* in Heavenly places and all of Heaven's resources are yours! For some reason we've come to think that we have to *"get-it-all-together"* before we approach God in prayer. Quite the contrary… Our prayers are effective, not because *we* have everything worked out, but because we know WHO has already worked it all out! Remember: We don't pray *for* the victory. We pray *from* the victory. Success in prayer comes from knowing our position IN CHRIST and will cause us to pray with passion and confidence.

"The righteous are as bold as a lion." (Proverbs 28:1 NIV)

Chapter 24

BLUE COLLAR GRACE

"He made Him Who knew no sin to be sin on our behalf, so that we might become the righteousness of God in Him."
(1 Corinthians 5:21 NASB)

Many Christians accept the false teaching that they must work towards righteousness. In other words, their right standing with God is something that they must strive for, rather than simply believe the moment they accept Christ they are made fully righteous by the blood of Jesus. When we stand firm that we have become the righteousness of God IN CHRIST, our works will prove it. Not the other way around. We don't work on our righteousness. God's righteousness works on us!

Recently I had the opportunity to minister at a church in Brooklyn, NY. After the service I went out to eat at a diner with the pastor, a Doctorate in Theology. Also, joining us for the evening was a professor of a well-known Seminary in New York City. As we stayed at the diner late into the early morning hours and discussed Grace in great depth regarding it's many complexities, the question arose as to why so many Pentecostals have such a hard time embracing the Grace message. After all, it is Pentecostals and many mainline Charismatics that have experienced the *"free"* worship experience through a divine encounter with God's Holy Spirit. Many times a 'Holy Ghost filled, tongue-talking' believer will tell you that God has set them *free* through this encounter. However, the liberty they speak of in relation to this experience is in direct opposition to their fundamental belief that they must work to maintain their righteousness. As we conversed on the subject into the early morning hours, it became clear to me that the reason why so many embrace the *works-based gospel* (as if those two concepts could even be put together in the same sentence) is that the message of works is concrete and based upon a set of rules or a code of ethics to adhere to. Therefore, the expectations are clear and all one has to do is simply follow the instructions (when in reality, following the Law to the 'T' is literally impossible).

The focus and the purpose of this book does not allow me the time to expound on this, but essentially Pentecostalism (from a historical perspective) has spread like wildfire primarily amongst the poor and working class social structures. Politically and socially, Pentecostalism originated in churches filled with people who were poor and oppressed and it has never forgotten those roots. Its early leaders were *working class Christians* with a very similar life experience to the people they led. Even to this day, Pentecostalism continues to spread in parts of the world where people suffer from poverty and injustice.[26]

Before I continue I must point out (in order not to appear snobbish) that I fully embrace the experience of the Spirit empowered life. I am not ashamed to be among those who have had the privilege of encountering the initial and ongoing power of the Holy Spirit through speaking in tongues, prophesying, witnessing miracles and the like. My spiritual heritage is deeply rooted in the Pentecostal faith and I make no apologies for it.[30] I am also not advocating that the working class mentality isn't bright enough or smart enough to grasp the truths of God's Grace in all its complexities. It amazes me how someone who is an auto mechanic can hear the strange sounds in a car engine, immediately assess the problem and proceed to repair the issue (such knowledge is too lofty for me). Know for certain that I am not being snide or slanderous in any way towards the working class. In fact, economically speaking I fit into the middle/working class category. I fully defend that working class people are extremely intelligent and in no-way am I insisting that they are inferior to any other group of people. The working class comprises the fundamental fabric and backbone of our society. I mean not to take anything away from the working class. In fact, I wholeheartedly concur with the British writer and apologist G. K. Chesterton who once said, *"The farmer who tends cabbage and stays home knows more of life than the so called world traveler who only sees the surface of things."*

Many people from all walks of life (including the intellectual, professional and working class) have adopted the 'gospel' of *righteousness by works*. The works based gospel has not been reserved to just the working class. However, historically speaking, Pentecostalism has been more widely accepted among poor and

236

working class societies (I hope you are starting to see the correlation here). By speaking of the working class, I'm only pointing out here that the blue-collar mentality is that of working hard for one's earnings. Therefore, the hard blue-collar work ethic that is ingrained in our culture trains many of us to believe that God's rewards come from *"running the race"* or *"enduring to the end"* *(Hebrews 12:1; James 1:12).* While this may be true in a practical sense as it applies to earthly success, it is totally the antithesis to the work of Grace. Grace is not *earned* through hard work; it is *received* by simple faith.

"And may be found in Him, not having a righteousness of my own derived from the Law, but that which is THROUGH FAITH IN CHRIST, the righteousness which comes from GOD ON THE BASIS OF FAITH."
(Philippians 3:9 NASB)

One of the main reasons that the *Grace without works* message is hard to receive amongst many people is because it is difficult to wrap the mind around an abstract concept like Grace. That's why Paul called it a mystery (Ephesians 6:19; Colossians 1:26) and that it must be embraced by simple faith (Romans 3:22; Ephesians 2: Philippians 3:9). However, although Grace is seemingly somewhat ambiguous to grasp by many, Paul yet carefully defends, through an extensive and detailed thesis (i.e. the book of Romans) the ministry of righteousness by faith through Grace. Many scholars agree that the book of Romans was not only a great Biblical work but was one of the greatest literary works of all-time. This is because of Paul's meticulous defense of the gospel of Grace. Even early history records that the book of Romans was required reading for those training to become Lawyers because of it's argumentative approach and definitive content. However, even though the concept of Grace is somewhat ambiguous to grasp, Paul carefully and methodically explained it in terms that most can grasp (contingent upon an initial acceptance by faith). Grace is not merely a doctrine that can easily be grasped by the working class or by anyone for that matter. Grace is a *person...* Jesus Christ. Having a relationship with a person is not based upon rules & regulations. I don't have a religion with my Heavenly Father. I have a relationship with my Heavenly Father. While there may be expectations for successful friendships, the complexities of having a relationship are not the same as solving a crossword puzzle, repairing a car, building a house or constructing a spaceship. Healthy relationships are based upon unconditional love, mutual understanding, constant affection, willingness to forgive and agreed-upon expectations.

The logical or common sense mindset finds it difficult to embrace Pauline Grace because it simply does not make sense. Grace is not logical! Therefore, it is difficult and often confusing for most to wrap their minds around the message of a faith-based relationship. The entirety of the Christian life stems from a belief system and is totally illogical as to confound even the most agnostic skeptic. How can the very Son of God, conceived by the Holy Spirit, be born through a virgin? Many think it ridiculous to think that it is easy to receive Grace. Receive by simply believing? Ridiculous! This is the problem with religion. Religion says in order to have Grace you have to please the Lord and then He gives more Grace. No and again I say no! Grace is given in order that we may experience God's good pleasure. To many it seems more logical that if you carefully follow the prescribed rules and obey all God's Laws then, presto... Results achieved! But *true and pure religion* says that only by Grace through faith can you experience the God-life, which is salvation in-full through Christ alone (Ephesians 2:7-9).

The Christian life isn't hard to live; it's IMPOSSIBLE! No one from any culture, creed or perspective can perfectly perform to the standard of the Law. Most of us can agree that we regularly fail (Proverbs 24:16) and James 2:10 tells us that if we fail at one point of the Law, we fail at all points. In other words, when you break one of God's Laws, you break them all! Paul based his explanation of Grace entirely on the truth that Jesus was sent to us because we were incapable of living up to our side of God's legally binding contract (Matthew 5:17) thus taking the responsibility for becoming righteous off of our shoulders and placing it upon Christ's shoulders. God makes us righteous by His Son's finished work alone. God started the process of redemption, righteousness and holiness in us, and it is He alone that is able to finish this work in us (Philippians 1:6; Hebrews 12:2). This is difficult to compute for the one who believes that only hard work *pays off.* Paul's exposition on Grace addressed the true *working class* society of his day: The self-righteous Jew who felt that *working* to achieve righteousness made perfect sense. That's why Paul says God's ways cannot be figured out (Romans 11:33; 1 Corinthians 2:14). The irony for many is that although they know that Grace is a free gift, they still find themselves striving to earn God's Grace. However, in order to be justified (Just-if-I'd never sinned), Grace must be *received* as a free gift not contingent upon working to *achieve* the sinless state. Simply put, God's righteousness must be received by faith..

"For in it the righteousness of God is revealed from faith to faith; as it is written, "BUT THE RIGHTEOUS man SHALL LIVE BY FAITH." (Romans 1:17 NASB)

"Now that no one is justified by the Law before God is evident; for, "THE RIGHTEOUS MAN SHALL LIVE BY FAITH." (Galatians 3:11 NASB)

Paul said this so many times that it would take a few pages just to write theses passages. Paul's constant repetition of this revelation gives evidence of the importance to grasp this truth (this is why I've also been so repetitive throughout this book). However, no matter how many times Paul emphasized it, receiving righteousness through simple faith is where many classical Pentecostals *fall out* with those who fully embrace the Grace message. The misconception is that since everything in life is achieved through hard work then so also is right standing with God attained and maintained by hard work and holy living.

The Pentecostal outpouring in the late 1800's into the early 1900's, beginning with the Azusa Street meetings and the Brush Arbor gatherings in the Hills of North Carolina, were preceded by one hundred years of holiness teaching and practice. The holiness faith was founded upon striving to *please* God through good works and a devout determination to live the holy life. In some circles, holiness people fell into the same error as the Pharisees: that we are made righteous by our piety and holy performance. Again, I am not advocating that we should not live holy and that we should have a sincere devotion to God. I am merely pointing out that these do not make us righteous. Rather, Grace gives us the power to live a life of consecration and dedication!

Rollin' On the River

I don't want to make the reader feel I am being unfair by singling out the Pentecostal faith. There is another extreme side to this story of Grace as well. Many denominations come from the perspective that being *saved* is all there is to the Christian faith and that experiencing the Spirit filled life is not for today's church. I categorically deny this extreme. On one side of the coin the *works-based* Grace message says that you must maintain your righteousness by self-effort in order to live the Spirit-empowered life. The other side of the coin says all that matters is being saved from your sins and going to Heaven. One extreme teeters on the left bank of the river while one hangs out on the right. The *balance* of these two extremes (and I don't mean a balance of the Law and Grace) is that not only are you *forgiven and saved* but you can also experience the *fullness of the Spirit* here and now. Grace is not merely a message of salvation *without* works but a salvation *that* works! Why hang out on either side of the murky riverbanks when you can splash around in the middle of the stream and get caught up in the exhilarating power of God's raging rapids of Grace? I'd rather be (as Creedence Clearwater Revival so eloquently put it) *Rollin' On the River!*

To All Working-Class Christians

Because Grace is such an abstract subject, there have only been a small handful of books ever written entirely on the subject of Grace. The many how-to books about overcoming depression, prayer, evangelism, self-improvement, holy living, and Christian discipline & service flood the bookshelves. These books are certainly great subjects to write and read about. However, when it comes to books on Grace, they are far and few between. Some books may touch or dabble on the topic of God's free gift of Grace, but because of the abstract subject matter and its controversial nature, most of the time it is either summarized, brushed over or simply avoided all together. There is also much emphasis on the word *"balance"* as to maintain the illusion that in order to maintain peace amongst both 'camps' we must mix a little Law with the Grace of God to avoid widespread sin amongst church people. This is a tragic because as I have pointed out in earlier chapters, when we teach a mixture of Law and Grace (even with the slightest subtlety) it cancels out the effects that Grace can have in the life of the believer (Galatians 5:4). Righteousness is a gift that is not earned. When you work you receive wages and the wages that are earned through self-effort are *'death'* (Romans 3:23). But the *gift* of God is eternal life for those who trust in Jesus and stand on the truth of God's Grace alone that makes them righteous. The truth is that the moment you receive Christ you are made righteous. As believer's we don't have to work to get righteous. We are already righteous and must learn to accept it and walk in it. Our own works never make us acceptable. We are acceptable to God through Jesus only! You may ask, "How do I receive it." Simple: You must simply ACCEPT it IN SPITE OF; in spite of your failures (past), your failings (present) and your failings yet to be. My friend, whether you believe that God loves and accepts you or not doesn't change the fact that He INDEED loves and accepts you. It's when you embrace His love and acceptance that the pain of your past ends and all the joys of your new life begin.

The Ox Pulls the Cart

As I close this chapter I want to make one thing abundantly clear. While I am proud of my Pentecostal heritage and living the Spirit empowered life, I do not attribute this glorious infilling to my holy living. The encounters I have had with the power of the Holy Spirit are work of God's Grace alone and are in no part a result of any good work that I have done. I do not earn the gift of the Holy Spirit because I *am able* to live Holy. I have the Holy Spirit to HELP *enable* me to live holy. I cannot live a holy life without the power of the Holy One working in and through me. I did not earn the Holy Spirit through my ability to be devout nor do I do anything ongoing to deserve it. The Holy Spirit is a gift that I simply receive by faith because I am in desperate need of it. Ever since receiving this wondrous work of Grace in my life I can tell you with no uncertainty that I have failed miserably at times. Yet, the Holy Spirit never leaves me abandoned. It is because of the love of God revealed through the power of the Holy Spirit that I am able to begin again each time and move forward. It is in times of great weakness that I have felt the strength of the Holy Spirit surround me and greatly encourage me. He has been my guide through some of the most dark and difficult times of my life when there was *nothing I could do* but trust in Him. After all, it's not a matter of what I can do but what God can do through me. Looking back I can boast of nothing but God's great love and the work of the Holy Spirit in my life.

We must all understand that any work of Grace in our lives is not a result of our prior doing. It is Grace's *doing* in our life first that empowers us to live for Him and to draw others to Him. If we put the ox before the cart it will result in a disastrous wreck. We can only attribute anything we are and anything we will ever do the praise of His glorious Grace.

"To the praise of the glory of His Grace, wherein HE HATH MADE US ACCEPTED in the beloved." (Ephesians 1:6 KJV)

Chapter 25

DISORDER IN THE COURT

"...And if anyone sins, we have an Advocate with the Father, Jesus Christ the righteous." (1 John 2:1 NASB)

Picture the scene of the chilly courtroom of your life. The Lawyers have arrived and are seated after completing litigation now preparing to give their closing statements. The case is air tight against the accused and the jury is smugly resolute, already arriving at a verdict before deliberation. The audience, with baited breath, expects a unanimous decision: a 100-percent pronouncement that the defendant is guilty as charged. The court stenographer and paralegal have presented their detailed transcripts to all parties involved. The prosecutor is totally convinced that the case will go in his favor. No stone has been unturned. Every shred of evidence points to the full conviction of the charged based on indisputable proof. All witnesses have been deemed credible and their testimony is irrefutably incontestable. The deafening tension and suffocating silence is unbearable. The entire gathering is on the edge of their seats. God, the Judge of the living and the dead, enters as the bailiff introduces Him and all are seated. Now look to the cowering defendant. The defendant is YOU and your fate looks bleak. Hopeless! You are GUILTY as charged for the crimes of murder, slander, theft, fraud, extortion perjury, adultery and too many more felonies to cite. Yes, you have committed every sin imaginable. You may say, *"How did I do all of this? I don't sin."* Oh but look again...

"You have heard that the ancients were told, 'YOU SHALL NOT COMMIT MURDER' and 'Whoever commits murder shall be liable to the court.' "But I say to you that everyone who is angry with his brother shall be guilty before the court; and whoever says to his brother, 'You good-for-nothing,' shall be guilty before the Supreme Court; and whoever says, 'You fool,' shall be guilty enough to go into the fiery hell... You have heard that it was said, 'YOU SHALL NOT COMMIT ADULTERY;' but I say to you that everyone who looks at a woman with lust for her has already committed adultery with her in his heart..." (Matthew 5:21-22; 27-28 NASB)

"Have you not made distinctions among yourselves, and become judges with evil motives... But you have dishonored the poor man... But if you show partiality, you are committing sin and are convicted by the Law as transgressors. For whoever keeps the whole Law and yet stumbles in one point, he has become guilty of all."
(James 2:4-10 NASB)

When you are angry with someone in your heart you are as guilty as if you had murdered him. When you lust after someone you bear the blame of committing adultery. When you call someone a fool or show partiality toward people you are guilty of slander and prejudice. When you lie, you commit perjury. When you speed in the car on the way home from work, you break the Law. When you yell at your kids, you abuse them. When you pilfer copies on the job you are a thief. When you call the guy who cut you off in traffic an "idiot" you're guilty of spiritual road-rage. Sin is sin and the Bible makes it clear that when you commit even one sin, you have committed all of them thus breaking the entirety of God's Law (James 2:10).

In God's eyes, when you imagine committing sin you are just as guilty as if actually committing it. The above passages in Matthew and James aren't singling out the sin of murder, adultery slander and prejudice. Jesus and James are simply introducing the principle of motive. God doesn't judge our sin alone but the *motive* of our sin. Some call this temptation (i.e. religious people who think they haven't committed sin they've just been *tempted*). Not so friend. When you imagine committing sin, you've already committed it. C.S. Lewis once said, *"If you look upon ham and eggs and lust, you have already committed breakfast in your heart."* Although this is a humorous anecdote on the subject, it illustrates the fine line between temptation and evil imaginations. However, we all know that we've crossed that *line* more often than we want to admit. I don't care how holy you think you are, or how long you've been serving God; you know you have crossed the *line* of sin (even recently). So if you're reading this and you think that you haven't sinned, don't turn up your "holier-than-thou" nose like the religious Pharisees. Be real here! Come to grips with your own failures and admit it because no one is without excuse (Romans 1:20).

Under the Old Covenant there were those religious Jews who had all the bases covered. They thought they were perfect and that they never *actually committed* sin. They thought so because they lived to every letter of the Law. It was like the ceiling was 7-feet high and they could jump up and touch it while some struggled to even do one good thing their whole lives. Think of all the people in the world (including yourself) who would not be allowed into Heaven if they could be righteous by their own works (i.e. rapists, murderers, thieves, fraudulent, delinquents, human traffickers, etc.). However, in the new covenant Jesus raised the ceiling to 30-feet. Now no one can reach it. ALL have sinned and are guilty as charged, including you and me (Romans 3:23). *Meanwhile, back in the courtroom...*

So now that you know you are guilty what do you do? Well, I'm sure you think that the camera is focused on you. However, the camera is still panning the room, slowly turning, and finally pausing and coming into focus on the defending attorney. His name is Jesus! All eyes are on Him! Jesus is your defense counsel! Talk about rigging the trial. Your defending attorney is the Judge's Son and He has complete and total favor with the judge.

"Even now, behold, my witness is in Heaven, and my advocate is on high." (Job 16:9 NASB)

As you glance across the courtroom you notice the prosecuting attorney satan, who appears to be a little nervous. According to the Tanakh (Jewish Bible) the Hebrew name for Satan is *HaSatan*, which means *prosecutor or accuser*. In the courtroom is also the defendant (you), the jury (the religious), the audience (the world), the Holy Spirit (The paralegal/court stenographer who inspired the message of Grace through Paul) and finally there's God, the Judge of the living and the dead. Then Jesus (your Advocate) asks if He may approach the bench for a sidebar and God the judge allows it (Hebrews 10:12). The microphones are able to pick up Jesus' whispering deliberation...

"God, my Father, the Good Judge (Luke 18:8), You appointed me to take the punishment for the defendant's sin. I have done just that. At Your will I was obedient to the point of death and submitted to Your purposes (Philippians 2:8). I have already paid in full, the penalty that You are requiring which is death. I have born all of his sins on My own body on the cross (Isaiah 53). I was bruised for his iniquity and his twisted distorted and demented behavior. I was lashed for his diseases and condemned in his place. I suffered his due judgment on the cross. I bore the harsh suffering of his shame with My very body. He has fully

repented, trusted in Me and committed his life into My nail-scarred hands. I have cleansed and forgiven him (1 John 1:7). He has My forgiveness forever (Colossians 1:14). All of his sins (past, present and future) are forgiven (Hebrews 1:12). As His representative I have declared him blameless and fully covered under My finished work. I was previously judged on His behalf and My sacrifice completely appeases Your wrath (1 John 2:2). Therefore, You have to let him go free because You are totally satisfied with My perfect sacrifice for him (Hebrews 10:10)."

At this, God the judge steadfastly looking at Jesus (not even glancing once in your direction) releases you and declares you "RIGHTEOUS! FREE OF ALL CHARGES!" Absolute pandemonium erupts! Complete DISorder in the court! The world is confused, the religious are enraged, the saints are overjoyed and satan is furiously foaming at the mouth (still trying to fight through the mob of angels that are jumping up and down in bedlam). Satan can't even get close to shake a finger at you, but see God the righteous judge; He is smiling! As the verdict is announced you are in utter shock and total disbelief. You lose control of your emotions and fall helplessly weeping into the outstretched arms of Jesus. It's almost as if God can't see you because you are completely wrapped up in the loving embrace of His Son. Grace has saved you. Now God will never look at you the same again because you are IN CHRIST. You are fully pardoned, never to receive the harsh sentence you deserved. Christ has become your redemption.

"But by His doing you are IN CHRIST Jesus, who became to us wisdom from God, and righteousness and sanctification, and redemption."
(1 Corinthians 1:30 NASB)

"In Him we have redemption through His blood, the forgiveness of our trespasses, according to the riches of His Grace."
(Ephesians 1:7 NASB)

You see (as covered previously) when someone in the Old Testament brought their sacrifice before the priest, the priest examined the lamb, and if the sacrifice was acceptable the sin of the *sin-ee* was imputed (passed into) the sacrifice and God's righteousness was passed onto the sinner (a trade-off if you will) deeming the person righteous. In light of our new covenant gospel of Grace, Jesus' sacrifice covers us forever, *once-and-for-all*.

"By this will we have been sanctified through the offering of the body of Jesus Christ ONCE FOR ALL." (Hebrews 10:10 NASB)

Grace Under Fire

Now, although we have been forgiven for our past, present and future sins; there will be some religious people who will think we have only been covered for our past sins only. When we fail or fall short they will accuse us and hold us liable for our *present* and *future* sins to be sure. But look what Paul has to say about this...

"Indeed, all who desire to live Godly IN CHRIST Jesus will be persecuted." (2Timothy 3:12 NASB)

Did you catch that? Paul didn't say that all who desire to live Godly will be persecuted. He said all who desire to live Godly IN CHRIST JESUS will be persecuted. Many church-going people won't revile you if you simply believe that Jesus saves you. It's when you believe that you are righteous through Christ alone and not by any effort of your own that the fiery arrows will fly. Paul was persecuted because he believed you could be righteous by being IN CHRIST, not by performing religious duties and adhering to empty traditions. Christians during Paul's day were being persecuted for their faith (not their works). To top it off, the persecution was originating from the Jewish leaders who were prompting Roman officials to carry out harsh brutality upon true *believers* IN CHRIST. They did the same thing to Jesus (the lovely person of Grace) and they sought to unleash the same cruelty to those who were departing by the hoards from the ancient system of the Law and turning to Jesus for salvation. It is no different today. Those who believe and proclaim the full message of God's Grace will face slander by religious people who believe you have to perform good works to be righteous. Those who accuse us are directly influenced by satan — The father of all accusation (Revelation 12:10). Be forewarned; as you progress in your knowledge of Grace you will eventually disappoint some who have stood behind you because of your similar backgrounds and viewpoints. But growing in Grace will also remove much deep-rooted insecurity that has caused you to strive for man's approval. So in the end it balances itself out. However, a word to the persecuted: we must still show love towards our adversaries. We most colorfully prove we have embraced the gospel of Grace, not in the way we respond to those accept us, but to those who reject us. Remember to give much Grace to the slanderer; for he will need it when his words backfire on him.

No Higher Court

No matter how harshly we are persecuted for declaring the truth of the gospel of Grace, the truth still remains: once God passes His judgment of NOT GUILTY upon us He cannot rescind His decision (Romans 11:29). We can never be tried again. However, long after our criminal trial has ended, our *accuser* will continue to tenaciously bombard God and us with false accusations, trying to condemn us, declaring that we are guilty and should be punished for our crimes. We will hear those accusing voices in our head. But, not to worry! Every time satan accuses us, God reverts to His original decision: NOT GUILTY BY THE BLOOD OF JESUS! At this, satan will persist, attempting to take his case to the court of appeals. But as he will discover, there is no such thing in Heaven's judicial system. There is no higher court than the Court of Heaven where God the judge presides. There is no other authority or jurisdiction that can overrule God's decree (especially the court of man). God's decree is that we are free! Hallelujah! The suspicions and opinions of others cannot change it. Even God HIMSELF cannot change His own ruling (Hebrews 6:18). He is bound by oath and by the sacrifice of His perfect Son, therefore accepting us into the beloved. In Heaven's jurisdiction instead of innocent *until* proven guilty we are innocent and *never found* guilty. HALLELUJAH! Jesus proves us innocent by His finished work. Finished means *finished, finito, fertig, fini, terminado, Nahting Moh (That's Mandrin Chinese).* Whatever language you speak the work is DONE! We can stand before God IN CHRIST totally vindicated FOREVER! When God asks us why we should be allowed into His Heaven, we can humbly say, *"Not by anything I've done but through Son, Jesus!"*

"Let us draw near (to God) with a true heart in full assurance of faith (not by our works), having our hearts sprinkled from an evil conscience, and our bodies washed with pure water. Let us hold fast the profession of our faith without wavering; for He is faithful that promised." (Hebrews 10:22-23 NASB)[37]

When God makes us righteous it is immutable. God's decisions are irreversible. The Greek word for *immutable* is *ametathetos,* which means: *not transposed, not to be transferred, fixed, and unalterable.* Look at what Paul has to say about our unalterable righteousness.

"Thus God, determining to show more abundantly to the heirs of promise the IMMUTABILITY of His counsel, CONFIRMED IT BY AN OATH. That by two IMMUTABLE things, in which it was impossible for God to lie, we might have a STRONG CONSOLATION, who have fled for refuge to lay hold upon the hope set before us:" (Hebrews 6:17-18 KJV)

There are two truths of God's Grace in this passage. First, it is impossible for God to lie. God's Word on the matter is sure and all His decisions are final. *Secondly,* and extremely vital to the realization of our righteousness IN CHRIST, is that *"we might have a strong consolation, who have fled for refuge to lay hold upon the hope set before us."* Our hope is that we are forever righteous because we have *fled for refuge* (IN CHRIST). Secondly, we are to have a *"strong consolation."* What is that consolation? The Greek word for 'consolation' is *paraklesis* meaning, *comfort, solace, refreshment, admonition and encouragement.* In John 15:26, the Greek word (paraklesis) is also a similar word for *"Helper."*

"When the HELPER comes, whom I will send to you from the Father, that is the Spirit of truth who proceeds from the Father, He will testify about Me." (John 15:26 KJV)

The Greek word for "Helper" is *parakletos.* Look at all the wonderful meanings...

One who comes to our aid to assist us

One who pleads our cause before a judge

Our counsel for defense, legal assistant, an advocate

One who stands in our place (an intercessor)

Notice the word *consolation* (paraklesis) in Hebrews 6 and the word *helper* (parakletos) in John 15 are powerful relative words in the Greek language. The usage of the word *helper* in John 15 pictures Christ being exalted at His Father's right hand, pleading (proving our case) with God for the pardon of our sins. This is beautiful! Another important implication of this word in the context of this verse is that the Holy Spirit will lead us to a deeper knowledge of the gospel truth, and divinely empower us with much needed strength to enable us to undergo trials and persecutions on behalf of the gospel (including satanic accusation and religious harassment for believing and proclaiming the Gospel of Grace). Jesus promised us the Holy Spirit would come as a *helper* (parakletos), running to our aid to substantiate God's final decision that our case is closed and can never be tried again. When we fail the Holy Sprit reassures us of the Father's love and encourages us to run to Jesus, not run away from Him. Satan always *condemns* us but the Holy Spirit always *confirms* us! At the same time Jesus, our Great High Priest, unceasingly makes intercession, pleading our case with irrefutable testimony (Hebrews 7-10). We never have to plead our case before God. We have adequate representation. Nowhere in the Bible does it say we have to *plead the blood*. Jesus pleads our case with HIS own blood and we never have to prove our innocence to God.

It is futile to make extra attempts through self-effort to substantiate our salvation. Although it is necessary to cooperate with God in order to fully experience the victorious life, it doesn't make us any more saved than we already are. Once we are made righteous we're as righteous as we'll ever be. Be assured; I believe in doing good works! However, we don't work here on Earth to win trophies in Heaven. Our reward is JESUS (and the people we bring with us)! Laying up treasures in Heaven (Matthew 6:19-21) doesn't mean doing good works in order to be recognized amongst the Heavenly throng. It means fixing our hearts on eternal things instead of the temporary, material matters of this earth and wholeheartedly seeking God's Kingdom agenda before all else (Matthew 6:33). This is how God enforces and establishes His Kingdom authority through our lives (Matthew 6:10). Besides, any crowns we receive will be cast at Jesus' feet because none of them will compare to the glory of beholding Him face to face (Revelation 4:10-11). When it comes to doing good works we should be the first in line! We SHOULD live holy, be kind, exercise restraint and show compassion. However, we're not ultimately motivated by *guilt* to be compassionate; rather we're authentically motivated by *compassion* to be compassionate. This is the difference between those who know they are righteous and those who aren't sure. Those who aren't convinced of their righteousness will always strive through some humanitarian effort to earn Heaven's indulgences. Good works don't make us more righteous; they attract a hurting world to the redeeming love of Jesus.

"Let your light shine before men in such a way that they may see your good works, and glorify your Father who is in heaven."
(Matthew 5:16 NASB)

Therefore, instead of trying to *finish* Christ's work, we need to rest IN CHRIST'S FINISHED work. We are made completely whole, thoroughly cleansed, fully atoned for, totally acceptable, well pleasing and perfectly blameless through the blood of His Son (Ephesians 1:4; 5:27; Colossians 1:22; Jude 1:24; Revelation 14:5).

A Cross Examination

Yes, God judges our sins; but when He judges them He does so through Jesus who already paid the full penalty for our sins upon the cross. Satan presents a valid argument. We ARE guilty. We HAVE sinned against God. His accusations are completely accurate. Satan rightly accuses us of our crimes against Heaven and humanity. However, when Satan finishes pointing out all the evidence against us, Jesus our advocate delivers His CROSS examination. Jesus stands with arms open wide, displaying the nail print scars on His hands and feet to His Father. No words suffice compared to the remarkable demonstration of His love. Jesus carries the proof of our innocence by the deep scars of love in His own body! And when He is finished presenting HIS case for us, justice prevails. God then weighs the evidence against the price Jesus paid on our behalf. God can only presume us innocent based on Jesus CROSS examination.

Front Headlines: NOT GUILTY!

Have you read Heaven's headlines today? The cover story says that you ARE found *Not Guilty*! The Good News is you're FREE TO GO and sin no more. However, if you sin, Jesus, your Advocate, continues to defend your innocence. And even though you case is completely closed, He is never off the case.

"My little children, I am writing these things to you so that you may not sin. AND IF ANYONE SINS, WE HAVE AN ADVOCATE WITH THE FATHER, JESUS CHRIST THE RIGHTEOUS." (1 John 2:1 NASB)

Friend, the Gospel is not the Bad News of sin and hell. The Gospel is the GOOD NEWS of Jesus and His Grace! I'm taking some creative liberty here; but I imagine if you were able to catch a glimpse on the walls in the courtroom of Heaven, you wouldn't find the symbol of the *scales of justice.* Rather you would find the new symbol of our righteousness: the CROSS! Accept the good news! Receive your FULL and ETERNAL pardon and stand fast in the liberty whereby Christ has made you free (Romans 10:16; Galatians 5:1).

CASE CLOSED!

Chapter 26

THE ELEPHANT AND THE FLEA

"Not that we are adequate in ourselves to consider anything as coming from ourselves, but our adequacy is from God." (2 Corinthians 3:5 NASB)

There is a very cute children's story that tells of an elephant and a flea crossing a bridge together. The flea is tucked safely away in the ear of the elephant as he pounds the planks across the deep river gorge. Upon reaching the other side, the flea euphorically squeals in the ear of his gigantic friend, *"My, didn't WE make that bridge shake"* (as if the flea had anything to do with it).

While this story is humorous it vividly illustrates that many believers actually think that they have something to do with *making themselves* righteous. The truth is (as Paul put it) none of us are adequate in ourselves. Our adequacy comes from God alone. We have NOTHING to do with it and God has EVERYTHING to do with it! It's Jesus + nothing. To think we have anything to do with our salvation is like a lightning bug claiming he has something to do with lightning. The believer's self-effort has nothing to do with his salvation. Some well meaning Christians say things like, *"God accepts me because I have a disciplined prayer life"* or *"I am more 'Godly' than others because I avoid doing this or going there!"* Our Holy living doesn't make us holy. Christ ALONE makes us Holy. We have NOTHING to do with it! We cannot say, *"God and I did it!"* Nonsense! We can't take one smidgen of credit for our salvation. There is no standard of righteousness apart from a saving faith in Jesus.

"But now APART from the Law the righteousness of God has been manifested... Even the righteousness of God THROUGH FAITH IN JESUS CHRIST for all those who believe..." (Romans 3:21-22 NASB)

People think that their holy behavior and good works help to make them righteous before God. When we accept Christ upon initial salvation we will never be anymore righteous than we are the moment we believe and receive God's free gift. No amount of self-effort will ever make you righteousness. We are not justified by our good works.

"By the works of the Law, no flesh will be justified in His sight..."
(Romans 3:20 NASB)

"Knowing that a man is not justified by the works of the Law, but BY THE FAITH OF JESUS CHRIST..." (Galatians 2:16 KJV)

Notice that Galatians 2:16 says, *"by the faith of Jesus Christ."* Even our *own faith* won't make us righteous. True faith is a gift that is given to us because our own faith cannot accomplish anything. Our faith is unreliable and unpredictable, full of holes and subject to our own self-doubt. I've always said that the problem with *Holy* people is that they leak (Get it? *'Holely'*). That's why God must pour His own faith into us in order for us to believe and receive the indescribable gift of righteousness...

"Thanks be to God for His indescribable gift!"
(2 Corinthians 9:15 NASB)

We aren't saved by *our* ability to have faith in God. When God says something about us, we must believe on HIS faith in us. We must take God at HIS Word at whatever He says about us, no matter how much suspicion we have in ourselves and our ability or inability to perform perfectly. What God says about us is all that matters, and when He says in His Word that we are righteous (Romans 3:22), we must believe it! It is mindboggling to think that God has more faith in us than we have in Him. This is the strength of God's faith! When we believe we are righteous and rest in the truth of God's faith in us, eventually we will start to see the fruit of good works in our lives. The moment we put our FULL trust in Jesus Christ we cross the impassable gulf from sin to righteousness. When we struggle with self-doubt about our righteousness it prevents us from experiencing the full joy of our salvation. That's why we must ask God to help us eradicate all doubt in Jesus' sufficiency to save and keep on saving us (Mark 9:24). When we are transported from darkness to light we don't come into a little bit of light dimly and then proceed into the fullness of God's light. The Bible declares we have come into the brightness of His full light.

"But you are A CHOSEN RACE, A royal PRIESTHOOD, A HOLY NATION, A PEOPLE FOR God's OWN POSSESSION, so that you may proclaim the excellencies of Him who has called you out of darkness into HIS MARVELOUS LIGHT." (1 Peter 2:9 NASB)

Notice that Peter, without qualification, told the churches scattered all throughout Asia that they were a royal priesthood, a holy nation and a people belonging to God. He didn't say that if they *measured up* to God's standard that they would be qualified to be God's possession. Not so! We are God's holy treasure the moment we put our trust in Jesus. We FULLY belong to Him. God doesn't call us His stepchildren and hide us in the coat closet away from the rest of His family. We are full-fledged members of His ROYAL family and He is not one mite ashamed of us. If God had a wallet He would parade our picture all over Heaven. We are close to His heart at all times. Note that the passage above doesn't say we are standing in His *mediocre* light. No! We are enveloped in His MARVELOUS light! Our Heavenly Father has put us on display with Heaven's spotlight fully beaming down on us. We are surrounded by the countenance of the brightness of His smiling face. He is proud to be seen with us even when we fail. We have access to all the privileges and benefits that come along with being in His royal family. By Grace, we are entitled to ALL of Jesus' inheritance.

"For ye have not received the spirit of bondage again to fear; but ye have received the Spirit of adoption, whereby we cry, Abba, Father. The Spirit itself beareth witness with our spirit, that we are the children of God: AND IF CHILDREN, THEN HEIRS; HEIRS OF GOD, AND JOINT-HEIRS WITH CHRIST." (Romans 8:17 KJV)

Righteousness is not attained by degrees nor do you become more righteous by 'scaling' the holiness ladder. You cannot be part righteous or half righteous. You are either righteous or unrighteous. There is no in-between. It cannot be said that there are some that are more righteous than others. When you believe and fully receive the atoning work of the cross of Christ you are made *fully* righteous. The reason for this is that when you receive salvation you take on Christ's righteousness (2 Corinthians 5:21; Philippians 3:9) and Jesus alone is fully righteous. To say He were only half or partly righteous would be equal to blasphemy. Now be assured, it is one thing to take a man out of the world, but it is an entirely different thing to take the world out of the man. However, just because there are traces and even some significant remnants of *'worldliness'* that still remain in us when we receive salvation and as we mature in Christ, it doesn't mean we are not righteous before God. When you are *born again* you become a brand new creation. In the natural, when you are born, you cannot be reborn a second time. The same is true of the spirit. When you are born again into God's family, you cannot be born again *again*. Once you are born again you are a new creation! Your Spirit has been made fully alive IN CHRIST (1 Corinthians 15:22) however your mind still wants to live like the *old you.* That's why your *'soulish' self* (mind, will, emotions) must be retrained to think as a new creation.

"And do not be conformed to this world, BUT BE TRANSFORMED BY THE RENEWING OF YOUR MIND, so that you may prove what the will of God is, that which is good and acceptable and perfect."
(Romans 12:2 NASB)

The Greek work for *"transformed"* is *metamorphoo meaning* to *change into another form.* It is where we get our English word *metamorphasis.* In other words, we change from *worldy* living to *holy* living by having our mind renewed. What do we renew our mind with? We refresh our thinking with who we are IN CHRIST. When we begin to understand that we are the righteousness of God IN CHRIST holy living will naturally result. To be sure, it is a process in which takes time as we progress into maturity. But the more we believe and speak what God and His word say about us the, more we will reflect the true nature of Christ and His righteousness!

Your New Husband

In Romans 7, Paul uses the illustration of marriage to further explain this idea of being transformed in your thinking when it comes to the Law and Grace. Many think this passage of scripture is a doctrine on marriage. However, we have to remember that the book of Romans is a detailed argument for the gospel of Grace. When read in proper context, Romans 7 specifically uses the marriage relationship to further explain our relationship to the Law and Grace.

"Or do you not know, brethren (for I am speaking to those who know the Law), that the Law has jurisdiction over a person as long as he lives? So then, if while her husband is living she is joined to another

man, she shall be called an adulteress; but if her husband dies, she is free from the Law, so that she is not an adulteress though she is joined to another man. Therefore, my brethren, YOU ALSO WERE MADE TO DIE TO THE LAW THROUGH THE BODY OF CHRIST, SO THAT YOU MIGHT BE JOINED TO ANOTHER, TO HIM WHO WAS RAISED FROM THE DEAD, in order that we might bear fruit for God." (Romans 7:1-4 NASB)

Paul says here that if your old man (the Law) is still alive (lording over you) you cannot marry your new husband (Grace). Once your old husband dies (the Law) then you are free to marry your new husband (Grace). Paul used this illustration to show that the Law and Grace can't live together under the same roof. You either live by the Law or live by God's Grace. The new husband (Grace) is loving, kind, patient, gentle, forgiving, generous, etc. The old husband (the Law) is a ruthless, abusive, demanding, harsh, rude, brutal, unbending, unyielding, obsessive-compulsive perfectionist (Galatians 3:24). Many Christians have a bad case of the *abused-wife-syndrome*. In other words, even after marrying their new husband (Grace) they find it hard to believe that He is a gracious and loving husband. That is why your mind must be retrained in the perfect Law of LIBERTY (James 1:25) so you will be able to accept and fully trust your new husband (Grace). Now, through Christ's finished work, the Law has lost its dominance over you. In effect the Law (your old husband) is dead. Grace is now your new husband. Once you have revelation knowledge that your new husband (Grace) is nothing like the rude, abusive husband (the Law) you were once so used to living under, only then you will learn to break free from all types of behavior patterns, unGodly temperaments and insecurities and be able to enjoy the freedom of love that your new husband (Grace) has for you. It may take awhile, but there is plenty of time to learn to be free as you enjoy your newfound relationship with your new husband (Grace).

This is a beautiful picture of the awesome work of Grace in our lives. While we may be righteous before God, we will still have the tendency to think and perform in those old mindsets. That is why we must be transformed in our thinking. We must first believe we are made holy apart from good works or self-effort to attain to righteousness. From this new mindset will flow the life of Christ and the power of God. We are free to run, free to dance, free to live in the forgiveness of Christ. That's why Paul said, "*IN HIM (Christ) we live and move and have our being."* (Acts 17:28). In other words, there is much margin to fail in God. The Bible tells us that Noah found Grace in God's eyes (Genesis 6:8). Think of this. Noah may have fallen but he fell in the ark. We don't walk a tightrope with God. He has set us on our high place (Psalms 91:14) in a wide-open field of Grace to run. When you fail, you don't fall off the ledge of a cliff and plunge to your rocky death below. When you fall, you fall IN JESUS, not out of Him. You don't fall in and out of righteousness every time you sin. Nothing can snatch you out of the arms of Jesus. You belong to Him. You are His beloved. Nothing or no one can separate you from the love that is IN CHRIST (Romans 8:39). God's righteousness is unconditional, unchanging and eternal. It is not based on whether or not we feel we deserve it, but on the basis of simple faith in Jesus. His righteousness is not for sale. God's righteousness has already been paid for through the suffering, death, burial and resurrection of Jesus. It is free and when we receive it by faith it exclusively becomes ours with no addendums, escape clauses or contract "breakers." Know for certain that as you did nothing to make yourself righteous (like the story of the flea), nor can you do anything to make yourself unrighteous. It is impossible to spoil what God started. That would be like saying you are capable of foiling God's plans. When God starts something He intends full well to finish it. God leaves no projects uncompleted (Philippians 1:6).

When your life is a mess, you can trust God to do what is necessary to make things right in your life. Besides, God perfectly orchestrates what He initiates even to the minute detail. God leaves no stone unturned. Many think that God is a cosmic handyman just running around fixing everything and repairing our mistakes. Not so! God knows what He's doing. When we give our lives to God we can trust Him to work everything out according to His perfect purposes. To rest in God's Grace you must believe that when you are made righteous, you are made righteous forever! People may remind you of your past and point to your failures but God will not.[2] He will only remind you of your future (Jeremiah 29:11). God forgets your sins permanently. When the devil tries to remind you of your past, you need only remind him of his future (Revelations 20:10). Instead of trying to jog God's memory of your sins, be settled in your spirit that He has forgotten them. This will fill you with new confidence to live your life in the freedom that Christ has fully paid for. Now to be sure, there still remains the life-long process of sanctification and purifying work in our lives. An elderly minister in his seventies once preached on the subject of temptation and lust. Being vulnerable, he told the congregation that someone once asked him, *"When do you eventually overcome lust and sexual temptation in your life?"* The preacher cleverly replied, *"When you die!"* There is a saying (for many people in their silver years) that there may be snow on the rooftop but there's still fire in the furnace. In other words, temptation is an ongoing issue to deal with at any age.

To Infinity and Beyond

Some time back I was sharing with my two children the awesome truth that once we are forgiven, God removes our sins as far as the east is from the west. Think about this... If you were to take off from this point and go east you would never return to point zero. It would go on for infinity. It is unimaginable for us to comprehend but once God forgives us, our sins get lost in infinity. As far as the east is to the west our sins past, present and future are permanently expunged.

> **"As far as the east is from the west, so far hath He removed our transgressions from us." (Psalms 103:12 KJV)**

Righteousness: Attribute and Gift

Righteousness is both an *attribute* and *gift*. Once we receive God's gift of righteousness, that gift is *attributed* to us. *Attributed* means, to be *certified, endorsed, qualified, accredited and approved.* God qualifies us simply by having faith in Jesus (Colossians 1:12 NASB). Therefore, if we believe and receive righteousness as a free gift then eventually it will manifest as an *attribute*. There is a powerful relationship to being *attributed* by God's righteousness and reflecting the *attributes* of righteousness. In order to reflect righteousness in our behavior we must believe in our righteous position. We will never experience the fullness of the victory we have IN CHRIST if we believe that our actions qualify us and make us more and more Godly. Many Christians wonder why life transformation doesn't flow out of them like it should. The answer to that is so simple that it will *blow* your mind. The reason many believers don't witness powerful effective life-change is because they don't believe rightly in God's view of them. Rather they accept the judgmental estimations and condemnatory evaluations of others. However, when you are confident that you are righteous based on God's assessment of you, then you will begin to naturally demonstrate the reality of it in your lifestyle. You will know what it means to stand strong and securely in the liberty whereby Christ HAS made you free (Galatians 5:1). When you believe correctly you will live correctly!

Reigning is Receiving

"Those who receive the abundance of Grace and of the gift of righteousness will reign in life through the One, Jesus Christ." (Romans 5:17 NASB)

Why it is that we Christians have such a hard time reigning in life? The answer is because we refuse to simply *receive*. Then *what* do we receive and *how* do we receive it? *Firstly:* We must receive abundance of Grace and the gift of righteousness. Imagine for a moment that you are a heart patient lying on the operating table and the doctor comes over to you. He tells you, *"Your new heart is being transported by helicopter in a cooler this very moment. Just sign this release form and the heart is yours."* You wouldn't take out a wad of money and pay him for it. You would immediately grab the pen and sign the release form. After all, hearts are hard to come by. Someone had to die to give you that heart. This is the way it is with receiving God's righteousness. Jesus died to give you His heart. All you have to do is take it. God's favor and blessings are yours for the asking. Reigning in life is not about *achieving* but *receiving* the abundance of God's Grace! Abundance is defined as *never running out, never sparse, having excess, overflowing.* We never teeter on the brink of running out of God's Grace. Whenever we sin, God's Grace super-abounds to overflowing.

"But where sin abounded, Grace did much more abound." (Romans 5:20 KJV)

"For if the ministry of condemnation has glory, much more does the ministry of righteousness abound in glory." (2 Corinthians 3:9 NASB)

Secondly: How do we receive the abundance of Grace and the gift of righteousness? By simply believing IN CHRIST'S finished work...

That's it! We don't have to comprehend it; we only need to receive it! I don't understand how *brown* cows eat *green* grass and give *white* milk. I just drink it! Likewise, it's so easy for us to go to a doctor whom we don't even know, let him poke and prod all over us, take a prescription from him with scribble we can't even read, drive to the pharmacy and hand it to a total stranger and let him fill the bottles with toxic chemicals we know nothing about. Then we simply take the medicine fully trusting it will make us well. Yet, we can't trust God at His word? *Newsflash...* You will never be able to fully wrap your mind around the awesome Grace of God! God's Grace is too amazing to comprehend. So what do we do when we don't understand it? We believe it anyway! A Moravian preacher once told John Wesley, *"Preach faith John... Preach it until you have it."* Leaning on our own understanding of the things of God causes us to question Him and thus prevents us from entering into the benefits of all that His finished work has provided for us. We don't need a detailed explanation of how Grace works. We just need to trust that it works.

"Trust in the LORD with all your heart and do not lean on your own understanding." (Proverbs 3:5 NASB)

Many still try to *help God out* with their efforts to be holy. However, in order to receive God's Grace we must believe in our right standing with God without doubting and resolve to live in that belief. We must consistently accept the fact that we are righteous apart from our own works and that nothing we do or don't do will separate us from the love of God (Romans 8:35-39). When we *relax* from our own efforts and simply *receive* God's Grace, we can enjoy our *relationship* with Him. Knowing that we have full *rights* to the favor of God empowers us to *reign* in life. To practically apply the process of living in God's Grace, simply remember these five keywords...

Relax
Stop striving to please God and rest in His Grace!

Receive
Trust Christ's finished work to keep saving you!

Relationship
Enjoy your friendship with God at all times!

Right

Freely accept the unmerited favor of God!

Reign

Experience the unlimited power of God's Grace!

"To the praise of the glory of His Grace, by which He made us accepted in the Beloved." (Ephesians 1:6 NKJV)

Chapter 27

GRACE SPEAKS OUT

"To Jesus the Mediator of the new covenant, and to the blood of sprinkling that speaks better things than that of Abel." (Hebrews 12:24 NKJV)

The first mention of blood is found in Genesis 4:10. Here God tells Cain that Abel's blood was crying out to Him from the ground where it was spilled by his murderous brother. What was Abel's blood saying? It was crying out for vengeance.[4] That is the premise of the Old Testament Law. The Law cried out for vengeance to those who failed to live up to it's standard of perfection. That's why the shedding of blood from animal sacrifice was constantly required. The Law required a payment for vengeance and that payment was death by slaughter. However, in our key passage, Jesus, the great high priest of our new and better covenant of Grace, shed His blood as a *once-and-for-all* sacrifice for our sins (Hebrews 8:6; 10:10). Jesus' blood speaks BETTER THINGS than that of the blood requirement of vengeance. Jesus' blood speaks forgiveness, eternal life, wholeness, redemption, healing, prosperity, joy, comfort, love, acceptance, deliverance, breakthrough, and victory! That is the sound of Jesus' blood! HALLELUJAH! The redeeming blood of Jesus has forever silenced the screams of vengeance. Jesus' blood won our victory! Now instead of fear and condemnation we can offer up praise in faith and our enemy cannot refute it (Psalms 8:2). When Jesus' precious, holy blood fell onto the cursed ground (where Abel's blood once cried) the ground was redeemed. Our sins have been forgiven once and for all (past, present & future). You will never hear Grace crying out, *"Vengeance!"* Rather, Grace proclaims forgiveness and pardon. In fact, God took the vengeance that we deserved and exacted it upon the avenger (the devil). God took the very blood of vengeance from His son (that we should have paid from our own veins) and used it to pay for our redemption and conquer the Devil. That is a powerful illustration of the awesome mercy of our Lord. You should be shouting right about now!

"Say to them that are of a fearful heart (those under condemnation), be strong, fear not, stand confident: behold, your God will come with vengeance, even God with a recompense (payment or reward); He will come and save you." (Isaiah 35:4 KJV)[37]

If you were to open today's mail and discover that you had been fully credited for your current mortgage payment, what would you feel? Relief? Joy? Peace of Mind? You would probably experience all of those and more. For certain you wouldn't be disturbed or distraught. You would be elated that you didn't have to pay the bill. That's exactly what our Heavenly Father did for us (Romans 4:3-11; 22-24). When we believed God He credited it to us as righteousness (considered us righteous). God didn't just pay some of the debt; He sent His own Son to be an OVERPAYMENT for every sin we have committed and ever will commit so that our hearts can be at rest fully assured that we do not have to fulfill the Law of vengeance and death. It was the sprinkling of Jesus Blood on our hearts that silenced sin's cries of vengeance. Now we can draw close to God with a clear conscience without EVER having to fear God handing us over to the avenger (satan).

"Let us draw near with a sincere heart in FULL ASSURANCE of faith, HAVING OUR HEARTS SPRINKLED CLEAN FROM AN EVIL CONSCIENCE and our bodies washed with pure water." (Hebrews 10:22 NASB)

The Bible tells us that vengeance belongs to God (Romans 12:19). This means that satan is prohibited from administrating and enforcing any form of vengeance upon the believer. Vengeance is off-limits to the devil and his demons when it comes to the life of the believer. God is in total control of the vengeance department and He took care of the vengeance issue by providing atonement (full payment) through His son Jesus. Our old landlord, Mr. Vengeance, can no longer come knocking to collect payment for our sins. Our debt to sin has been paid in full through the shed blood of Jesus!

The gospel of Grace is the Good News... It's the good news that declares *It's not what we do. It's what Jesus has already done* It constantly amazes me that although the payment for sin should have been mine, God sent Jesus to completely eliminate my sin-debt and now I can freely receive His favor and love. I believe this was the *"glad tidings of great joy"* that the angel spoke of in Luke 1:19. I deserved nothing good and holy from God, but Grace came through Jesus (John 1:17) and gave me favor undeserved. We owe absolutely nothing to Him. We are completely debt-free! Yet when we receive God's Grace, there will be something deep within us that desires to waste our lives for Jesus in worship and loyal obedience. Our best attempts at Christian service do not secure our righteousness. Only by Grace will we have the true passion to exhaust the rest of our days running after the One Whom our hearts adore. This is the power of Grace. God's Grace truly empowers us to be victorious in our *obedience-walk.* Grace is the silent force inside of us that causes us to loudly proclaim our righteousness both in word and in deed.

"I have proclaimed GLAD TIDINGS OF RIGHTEOUSNESS in the great congregation; Behold, I will not restrain my lips..." (Psalms 40:9 NASB)

And it came to pass afterward, that He went throughout every city and village, preaching and showing the GLAD TIDINGS OF THE KINGDOM OF GOD..." (Luke 8:1 KJV)

"We tell you the good news: What God promised our fathers." (Acts 13:32 NIV)

"How beautiful are the feet of them that preach the GOSPEL OF PEACE, AND BRING GLAD TIDINGS OF GOOD THINGS!" (Romans 10:15 KJV)

Mercy Speaks

God always speaks to His people from a position of Grace and mercy. When Moses spoke with the Lord, the Bible tells us that God spoke with Moses *face to face* as a friend (Exodus 33:11). Moses boldly entered the Holy of Holies and spoke with God in front of the Ark of the Covenant. The Ark of the Covenant was where the presence of God resided. The glory cloud (Hebrew = *kavod*) was the physical manifestation of His presence. God's pillar of fire would hover over the tent of meeting by night and His cloud would settle upon the tent during the day as a visible reminder that God was with His people (Exodus 40:38). We never have to fear for God is always with us. We don't need to do *any* amount of conjuring or religious babbling to summon God's presence, as so many worship teach and exhort.

Friend, God IS ALREADY WITH US and no amount of doubt or fear can change that fact (Isaiah 41:10). We don't worship to get God's presence. We worship from the place of His presence. Getting a revelation of this will change the way we worship. We worship God because He is with us, not to get Him to come to us.

When Moses spoke with God he would face the Ark of the Covenant and talk with God from between the Cherubim's wings. This was called the *mercy seat*. The mercy seat was literally the lid of the Ark. Angel's wings signal the arrival of God's presence and help usher us (carry us if you will) into God's light and glory, not to shoo us away. This is awesome! The place where God's voice was heard was from a place of mercy! God speaks in merciful tones to those who have received his forgiveness and mercy. God's judgment is not for the redeemed. It is solely reserved for those who reject His Son. Once a year the high priest would enter behind the veil and sprinkle blood on the top of the mercy seat signifying that the blood of sacrifice had atoned for the sins of the people. Jesus' blood not only covers, but completely takes away our sin (John 1:29). It was from this very place of mercy that God spoke to Moses and that mercy still speaks to us today! Jesus did not come to judge the world but to save it (John 3:17). The Hebrew word for *mercy seat* is *Kapporeth,* which means *to cover*. God not only speaks to us through Grace and mercy; He also completely covers and washes us in His mercy. Hallelujah!

Covered in Mercy[1]

To truly understand how we are *covered in mercy* we need to peer inside the ark for a moment. For in it is a powerful revelation of mercy that will forever liberate us. Understanding God's awesome mercy is a fundamental principle of Grace. As you open your eyes and gaze upon the ancient mystery of God's Grace, under the covering of the ark of mercy you will see three things:

The Golden Bowl of Manna

The Staff of Aaron

The Stone Tablets of the Law

The Golden Bowl of Manna

Manna represented God's faithfulness. The Children of Israel selfishly grumbled against God's provision of Manna. Nevertheless, every morning they would wake up and find the ground blanketed white with fresh bread from Heaven. What an awesome picture of Grace. So many times, the Children of Israel were so obstinate and stiff necked against the will of God yet God continued to show His everlasting mercy and provide for them each day. What a marvelous illustration of the Grace and mercy of our Lord. God gave His people *Heaven's food* to sustain, rejuvenate and revive them. This food had all the necessary nutrients, antioxidants and immune boosters to sustain them and keep them disease free. It contained the essential vitamins and minerals that no earthly food could compare with. It came straight from Heaven, not the cursed soil of our earth. God supernaturally supplied His people with sustenance from Heaven because they had to endure the unforgiving elements of the desert. Life is unforgiving. Most people don't show Grace and mercy. They want retribution (even some church folks). I've heard it said that church people are the best at kicking their wounded. Heartbreaking! However, God is not this way. Many times when we fail it feels as if we are cut off from God's forgiveness, However, no matter how we feel, God's forgiveness still falls freely and abundantly upon us. Manna was God's visible sign of constant Grace, mercy and forgiveness. Guess what: if you have Jesus, you have that bread of strength, forgiveness, mercy and Grace.

"I am the living bread that came down out of heaven; if anyone eats of this bread, he will live forever; and the bread also which I will give for the life of the world is My flesh." (John 6:51 NASB)

It is also important to note that the golden vase of manna also represented the rebellion of God's people against His loving provision. Yet although they rebelled, God's mercy covered them and continued to bless them in spite of their sin.

The Staff of Aaron

The staff of Aaron that had miraculously budded with almond branches, leaves and almonds represented God's appointed and anointed leadership. In Numbers 16 the sons of Korah began to think they were just as qualified as Moses to be the leaders of God's people. Their jealousy incited them to arouse a faction against Moses thereby causing much dissension in the camp. This angered God! So God told Moses to command Korah and the 250 rebels to stand outside the opening of their tents the next morning with golden censers of fire and incense. There, God would appear before the people to prove who was His appointed leader. When the sons of Korah came to the opening of their tents the glory of the Lord caused a great earthquake to swallow them and their whole company. Then look at the next thing that happened...

"The LORD said to Moses, 'Speak to the Israelites and get twelve staffs from them, one from the leader of each of their ancestral tribes. Write the name of each man on his staff. On the staff of Levi write Aaron's name, for there must be one staff for the head of each ancestral tribe. Place them in the Tent of Meeting in front of the Testimony, where I meet with you. THE STAFF BELONGING TO THE MAN I CHOOSE WILL SPROUT, and I will rid myself of this constant grumbling against you by the Israelites.' So Moses spoke to the Israelites, and their leaders gave him twelve staffs, one for the leader of each of their ancestral tribes, and Aaron's staff was among them. Moses placed the staffs before the LORD in the Tent of the Testimony. THE NEXT DAY MOSES ENTERED THE TENT OF THE TESTIMONY AND SAW THAT AARON'S STAFF, WHICH REPRESENTED THE HOUSE OF LEVI, HAD NOT ONLY SPROUTED BUT HAD BUDDED, BLOSSOMED AND PRODUCED ALMONDS. Then Moses brought out all the staffs from the LORD's presence to all the Israelites. They looked at them, and each man took his own staff. The LORD said to Moses, 'PUT BACK AARON'S STAFF IN FRONT OF THE TESTIMONY, TO BE KEPT AS A SIGN TO THE REBELLIOUS. This will put an end to their grumbling against me, so that they will not die.' Moses did just as the LORD commanded him. '"
(Numbers 17:1-10 NIV)

According to this passage, Aaron's staff also represented the rebellion of God's people against His leaders.

The Stone Tablets of the Law

The Ten Commandments represented God's commands (It also was a visible sign of the disobedience of the Children of Israel). It also represents our failure to live up to God's perfect standard of holiness.

It is also interesting to note that when the Philistines captured the ark from Jerusalem, and opened the mercy seat, God killed 50,070 of the men who were standing near the ark (1 Samuel 16:9 NIV). God did not allow anyone to physically touch or open the lid to the mercy seat, not because He wanted people to be afraid of Him, but in order to cover the sins of the people discouraging anyone from judging their failures. God is very serious when it comes to exposing the faults of others. Once we are forgiven, we are forever sealed until the day of redemption (Ephesians 4:30). We should never judge the faults of others. This puts us in a compromising position. If we pass judgment and refuse to release God's forgiveness towards others, we will be unable to fully experience the joy of His forgiveness (Mark 6:14-15).

Moses heard God from a place of mercy. This illustrates a powerful truth. When we hear the voice of God, it will always come in waves of mercy. Condemnation is the voice of the enemy. This is not to say that we won't genuinely feel remorseful when we sin. We should feel a sense of *undoneness* when we fall short. Truly feeling sorry when we sin is a positive indicator that we need restoration by God's loving Grace. However, overwhelming guilt, condemnation accompanied by a total sense of unworthiness is not from God. Remember when we fail, the Holy Spirit always tells us to run to Jesus! It is the devil that will tell us to run and hide (Genesis 3:7-10). When we fail, Grace is *shouting* out for us to run and fall into the loving arms of Jesus to receive His Grace, forgiveness and love.

Grace Shouts

"This is the word of the LORD... 'Not by might nor by power, but by My Spirit,' Says the LORD of hosts. Who are you, O great mountain? Before Zerubbabel you shall become a plain! And he shall bring forth the capstone with SHOUTS OF "GRACE, GRACE TO IT!"'
(Zechariah 4:6- NKJV)

When God speaks to us, He speaks in tones of mercy. The prophet Zechariah had a vision of the rebuilding of the temple. As God gave him this vision of the capstone being set into it's foundation, the angel of the Lord told him that the mountain would be moved by the shout of Grace. Often looming mountains of discouragement, disappointment, defeat, doubt, despair, depression, confusion and condemnation stand in the way of our God-given dreams. When this happens we often are prone to search for human options to solve super-sized solutions. However, the angel spoke clearly and said that *'with shouts of Grace! Grace!'* the mountains would be moved and the vision would come to pass. Did you notice that God told Zechariah to shout "Grace" *twice*? The formula for tough times is *Grace x 2 = Victory!* God gives us a double portion of Grace to tackle life's greatest challenges. The truth is we need much Grace much of the time. So often we try to work things out in our own strength. When we put our hands on the situation we leave no room for God to work. Grace in the practical sense means taking our hands off of it and letting God put His hand on it. Remember that when we work, God doesn't. Raising our hands in worship is simply saying, *"God I take my hands off of the situation and let you work it out."* Next time you raise your hands in worship think about it that way. Only God's Grace can do what we are incapable of doing because there will always be a God-sized mountain only God can move. When we strive by our own might and our own power to solve life's difficulties we often end up worse off than when we started. But when we allow the Grace of God to work, we will witness the miraculous. It's simple: When flesh shouts, the mountain is *flat unmovable*. When Grace shouts, the mountain is simply *flattened*!

"Truly I say to you, whoever SAYS to this mountain, 'Be taken up and cast into the sea,' and does not doubt in his heart, BUT BELIEVES that what he SAYS is going to happen, it WILL be granted him!"
(Mark 11:23 NASB)

Sometimes we make confessions but do not truly believe what we're saying. It's almost as if we are just quoting scripture thinking there's a magic formula involved. However, faith is not just quoting scripture. Faith is having a deep settled assurance (birthed only by the Spirit) that God will do what He says He will do. The reason *believing in the Grace of God* is so important is because it causes us to be settled on every promise in scripture. When we believe in God's Grace and trust that we are truly righteous apart from our works, it crosses into every area of our lives. We begin to have a deeper trust in God's Word on every issue. It's when we don't trust God's Grace and try to work every situation out that Grace has no effect (Galatians 5:4).

When we simply relax and trust God at His word it will produce a deep down kind of faith that cannot be mined out by the drills of the enemy. Faith isn't *tensing*. It's *trusting*. Therefore, We must trust in His word that says we are saved by Grace THROUGH FAITH. The word "saved" in Ephesians 2:8 has a much deeper meaning than just being saved from your sins. The Greek word for *saved* in this verse is *sozo*, which means...

To deliver from the penalty of judgment

To protect

Rescue from danger, injury or peril

To save or cure one's disease

To make well, heal and restore to health

That's why it is so important to constantly speak the Word of God. When we speak the Word our ears hear what we are speaking and sooner or later faith will come as a result of hearing the word spoken.

"So FAITH COMES from HEARING, and HEARING BY the word of Christ." (Romans 10:17 NASB)

Chapter 28

SUPERGLUED

"In Him, you also after listening to the message of truth, the gospel of your salvation, having also believed, you were sealed in Him with the Holy Spirit of promise."
(Ephesians 1:13 NASB)

When I was a young boy there was a T.V. commercial advertising superglue where the construction worker's hardhat was bonded to the support beam? I can still see him dangling there holding his hat and swinging back and forth. This commercial portrayed a man putting his trust in a synthetic compound that was sure to hold him in place. I don't think anybody was crazy enough to try that so we'll never know if it really worked (Somebody call 'Mythbusters'). If this man could put his life in the hands of human-made *superglue,* why is it so hard for us to believe that God's *supernatural-glue* of Grace will keep us from falling out of righteousness? God's Grace is the compound of love that cannot be broken.

"Whereby ye are sealed until the day of redemption."
(Ephesians 4:30 KJV)

The scripture above tells us that we have been SEALED UNTIL THE DAY OF REDEMPTION. That means from the moment we get saved, through the time in-between, until the end of time we are totally secure in our right-standing with God. Until means *until.* Nothing can break the bond that keeps us permanently fixed to God.

Greasy Grace

Many preachers give the disclaimer that they don't preach *greasy Grace* (meaning that the message of Grace isn't some *loosey-goosey* concept that permits us to live anyway we want to). Many times they will say this to immediately disarm the skeptic and to remove the tension that arises when the word "Grace" is mentioned. It amazes me that the lovely word of Grace causes such consternation. If you want to make people outside the church mad preach Law. If you want to make people inside the church mad preach Grace. Folks, the Grace of God isn't something that permits us to slip and slide in and out of a sinful lifestyle without repercussions. God's Grace is the eternal adhesive that binds us to God regardless of our imperfections and nothing can sever the bond of our righteousness IN CHRIST. Neither you nor God can break the seal between you and Him. O what a glorious truth! In our key passage, the Greek word for sealed is "*sphragizo*" which means...

To stamp with an official seal

To seal or affix (i.e. 'seal' an envelope)

Security from Satan

To keep confidential (to hide)

To keep in silence, keep secret

To mark a person or a thing

To prove, confirm, or attest a thing

To authenticate and place beyond doubt

IN CHRIST your salvation is sealed, hidden, proved, affixed, secure, confirmed and authenticated and nothing that satan or sin can do can ever snatch you from the arms of Jesus. When you accept, believe in and trust in the finished work of Jesus for your eternal salvation, it is as if God stamps His official insignia on your soul and seals it in an envelope not to be opened until the end of time when you see Him face to face. Until then, you are safe in His protection and no matter how hard you try you'll never be able jump out of His embrace. Besides, you can't keep your end of the bargain with God anyway. It is impossible for anyone of us to live out the full letter of the Law. That's why Grace has been given (not earned). If we could live flawlessly, then Jesus would not be necessary. Besides, righteousness isn't a contract drawn by us *toward God*; rather it is a covenant made by God *toward us*. As previously mentioned, if righteousness were a mutually binding contract depending on our fulfillment of it's clauses and amendments, then it wouldn't be Grace. We have FULL ASSURANCE that Jesus blood makes us righteous apart from good works or holy living (Hebrews 10:22-23). We don't live under the old legal system of contracts. We live under a new covenant of Grace that says we are forever sealed, fixed and bonded to God. What kind of salvation would it be if it were dependent upon my attitude or attributes to keep it? It would be a pretty weak salvation if you ask me. Why? Because I fail on a regular basis and if I fell in and out of salvation every time I sin, then it wouldn't' be a very trustworthy salvation.

What is that to You?

Many may ask, *"What about those who have turned away from God and fallen back into a sinful lifestyle? Are they still saved? Does God accept them? What about those who think Grace gives them a license to sin?"* Jesus gave us the answer to this question.

"Peter, turning around, saw the disciple whom Jesus loved following them; the one who also had leaned back on His bosom at the supper and said, 'Lord, who is the one who betrays You?' So Peter seeing him said to Jesus, 'Lord, and what about this man?' Jesus said to him, 'If I want him to remain until I come, WHAT IS THAT TO YOU? You follow Me!' Therefore this saying went out among the brethren that that disciple would not die; yet Jesus did not say to him that he would not die, but only 'If I want him to remain until I come, WHAT IS THAT TO YOU?' " (John 21:20-23 NKJV)

After rising from the dead Jesus appears to His disciples one last time before returning to His Father in Heaven. During his final discussion with his friends, Jesus tells them that they will suffer persecution and even martyrdom for the cause of the gospel. Peter begins to express his concern about John being excluded from those who will die for their faith in Jesus. That's where the above passage picks up with Peter in essence asking, *"If we are all going to die for You, why isn't John going to die?"* Peter thought it unfair for John not to have to suffer like everyone else. Jesus' answer is profound. He tells Peter, *"What is that to You? You follow Me!"* Notice the exclamation point after the word *'Me!'*

The essence of Jesus' answer to Peter's question is important when addressing the issue about others treating Grace as a license to sin. So many times we feel the need to control those *special cases* where immature Christians feel Grace gives them a license to sin. In our well meaning attempts to corral people into a 'sinless' lifestyle, we will add clauses and addendums to the gospel of Grace, telling them that they will fall out of salvation and that they will no longer be righteous if they sin. This is dangerous! Just because we can't comprehend God's Grace and the fact that we are made righteous apart from our own ability to live perfectly doesn't give us license to teach *another gospel* or add postscripts to the New Testament message of pure Grace.

'Hands Off' Policy

We must not worry about how people will receive the message of Grace. We must preach it the way Jesus lived and taught it and the way Paul wrote and proclaimed it. We must present the message of Grace, unfiltered, uncontested and unaltered and trust God's Grace to work in the lives of people no matter how immature or how Biblically illiterate they are. Think of it in these terms; many people conclude that God doesn't heal all the time. So does this mean we should stop preaching the full gospel message of divine healing if certain people aren't being healed? God's word tells us that Jesus forgives all our sins and heals all our diseases (Psalms 103:3) and that by His stripes we are already healed (1 Peter 2:24). What if people aren't receiving the baptism of the Holy Spirit with the evidence of power and spiritual gifts in their lives? Should we revise the message of the Spirit empowered life just because some aren't yet receiving the impartation of its truth? The issue here isn't that the message is skewed but rather the person is either unwilling to receive this gift from doubt, fear or misunderstanding of the purpose and power of the Holy Spirit.

The answer to these rhetorical questions is an emphatic "No!" We must continue to preach the truths of all of God's Word in spite of people's ability to comprehend or receive them. It is not up to us to make people understand and come into alignment with God's word. Only God can illuminate truth in the heart of the believer. In other words, we can bait the hook and cast the line but we can't make the fish bite. This is all extremely relevant and applicable to the message of the Gospel of God's Grace. We must continue to preach and teach the simplicity and purity of God's Grace, then take our hands off of people and let God work in their hearts to produce authentic life transformation. When we do this we will be shocked at how many people will come out of sin and live holy lives. God doesn't need our help to change other people. His policy for us is a *hand's off* policy. We must entrust the hearts of the people we minister to into God's capable hands and whenever we begin to worry about what people will do with the message of Grace, we must hear Jesus saying, *"What is that to You."* Instead of imposing strict standards of religion and obedience to a code of conduct, we must teach people to be extra sensitive to God and to be careful to obey the inner voice of the Holy Spirit in every situation. Urging people to stay on the side of Grace will open the door for God's power to produce good works and holy living in their lives. Paul put it this way...

"What I'm getting at, friends, is that you should simply keep on doing what you've done from the beginning. When I was living among you, you lived in responsive obedience. Now that I'm separated from you, keep it up. Better yet, redouble your efforts. Be energetic in your life of salvation, reverent and sensitive before God.

That energy is God's energy, an energy deep within you, God himself willing and working at what will give Him the most pleasure."
(Philippians 2:12-13 THE MESSAGE)

We need to let people work out their *own* salvation in direct relationship the Holy Spirit's leading. Paul told the Corinthian church that the devil himself (through the Judaizer's teachings) was subtly deceiving them away from the simplicity of their devotion to Christ.

"But I am afraid THAT, AS THE SERPENT DECEIVED EVE BY HIS CRAFTINESS, your minds will be led astray from the simplicity and purity of devotion to Christ. For if one comes and preaches another Jesus whom we have not preached, or you receive a different spirit which you have not received, or a different gospel which you have not accepted, you bear this beautifully." (2 Corinthians 11:3-4 NASB)

Legalism vs. Libertarianism

Two very important distinctions in the Grace message are legalism and libertarianism. We must understand these opposing viewpoints to better embrace the gospel. When you preach the *pure gospel* that says we are saved by Grace through faith, not of works (without boundaries, exceptions or controls) that is called *Libertarianism*.[16] When it is taught that we are saved by Grace *but also* must maintain our salvation by good works and sinless living, that is called *legalism*. Legalism advocates that we must not sin or we jeopardize our righteous standing with God. This is not the New Testament gospel (Paul called it preaching *"another Jesus"*). Legalism is accompanied by the fear that unless we preach Grace with stipulations, then we are throwing everything out of *balance*. It's, *"Yes Grace BUT we must also..."* or *"Yes, Grace BUT we must be careful..."* Fear causes us to attach warnings to the message of Grace. Simply stated: Legalism says, *"Grace, but..."* Libertarianism says, *"But GRACE!"*

When we try to coerce others into adhering to the standard of holy living out of fear that they will take license to sin, we fall into the tireless cycle of fear and control. Why? Control is a by-product of fear. We fear losing control of people so we impose extra addendums to keep them out of sin. Fear is the mother of all confusion. When we operate out of fear and control it only brings envy and strife. Envy and strife are the co-conspirators of confusion and evil, and where confusion and evil exists, sin will surely abound.

"For where envying and strife is, there is confusion and every evil work." (James 3:16 KJV)

Enforcing religious controls on people will prove ineffective to produce true holiness in them. People will comply with legalism to a point but will eventually rebel because the flesh can't keep up with the Law. The Law eventually runs the flesh down. That's the way God designed it. He created the Law to drive us to utter exhaustion in our own strength (Galatians 3:24). God's Grace alone totally extricates us from the harsh domination of the Law. Legalism is based on manipulation and control, which ultimately brings people back into bondage. Libertarianism however, liberates the believer to hear from God and respond to God's power. Living in this way leads the believer towards true life-transformation. If you are a pastor or leader and are trying to control people with legalistic teaching you should stop THIS INSTANT! Because the truth is you are not the Holy Spirit, nor can you do His job. In other words, you are not someone else's Holy Spirit. We have to allow God's Grace to work on the inside of people and genuinely influence them towards holiness and purity. We cannot clean people on the inside by adjusting them on the outside. Gods Grace works from the *inside out*. Legalism attempts to change people from the *outside in*, but in the end is entirely unsuccessful. When we express irritation, resentments or anger towards others for their seeming disregard for holiness it doesn't produce the fruit of righteousness in them. The only way we effectively influence people to live holy is to model righteousness from a heart of encouragement, patience, understanding and love.

> **"...Everyone must be quick to hear, slow to speak and slow to anger; for the anger of man does not achieve the righteousness of God."**
> **(James 1:19-20 NASB)**

Legalistic teaching actually backfires and causes people to rebel or even many times snowball into sin. The reason for this is that when you present Laws that attempt to hold people in 'check' it only arouses their curiosity and desire to sin.

> **"Once I was alive apart from Law; but WHEN THE COMMANDMENT CAME, SIN SPRANG TO LIFE and I died" (Romans 7:9 NIV)**

The victory is not in the working; it's in the yielding. By this I mean that when we yield ourselves to God's Grace we release the Holy Spirit to move deeply in us to transform us from the inside out. Surprisingly we will discover ourselves feeling extremely uncomfortable with certain activities that do not bring God honor and glory. Whenever we feel that something is offensive to God, it is because the Holy Spirit is working in us to avoid those things as not to give the devil access into our lives. Living by Grace is listening to the Holy Spirit and responding to His enabling power! There's no better way to live!

An Unbreakable Bond

Nothing can break the hold that God has on us. Our *unbreakable* bond with God *breaks* the power of sin and destroys the power of discouragement and disappointment (two leading factors that cause us to often plunge deeper into sin). When we live on the side of Grace, we experience the victory that overcomes the world. Jesus promised NEVER to leave or forsake us. In other words, we are stuck to Him. If Jesus forsook us based on our behavior we would all be hopelessly lost. David said when he soared like an eagle or made his bed in Hell, God was with Him (Psalms 139:8). Paul put it this way...

"For I am convinced that neither death, nor life, nor angels, nor principalities, nor things present, nor things to come, nor powers, nor height, nor depth, nor any other created thing, will be able to separate us from the love of God, which is IN CHRIST Jesus our Lord."
(Romans 8:38-39 NASB)

Jesus gave us a powerful promise and a solid assurance that once we come to Him, He will never cast us away. For those who feel Jesus will cast them out for their failures, they only need listen to His words.

"All that the Father gives Me will come to Me, and the one who comes to Me I will certainly not cast out." (John 6:37 NASB)

Chapter 29

HERE LIES WORKS

"O foolish man… faith without works is dead?"
(James 2:20 NKJV)

This verse is perhaps one of the most controversial passages in the argument between justification by works and justification by faith. James 2:20 is often misunderstood to mean that we are saved by faith *and* works. The term for this is called *synergism.* In other words, we must trust Jesus to save us but that alone is not enough. Many think in order to fully attain salvation they must add their own deeds of loyalty and good service. In order to justify this, many historical and mainline theological camps have classified Grace into two categories:

Positional Righteousness

We are saved through faith by God's Grace.

Practical Righteousness

We have a responsibility to maintain our right standing with God through ongoing good works.

If we accept that we are made righteous by *positional* AND *practical* righteousness, then we really don't believe that God's Grace *alone* saves us. We in fact hold to the view that we have *something to do* with our righteousness. There is no "and" in the equation of Grace. There is no 1 + 1 formula for righteousness. Two things don't make us righteous. Only one thing makes us righteous… FAITH IN GOD'S GRACE! James' intimate knowledge of Jesus as the *Person of Grace* gave him a unique and powerful platform in which to write this letter. Remember, that James was the brother of Jesus and experienced Grace as a person first hand. Jesus was the living example of Grace that James was writing about. Jesus Himself knew that He couldn't teach on Grace many times because of the mindset of His day. That's why He said in John 16:12, *"I have many more things to say to you, but you cannot bear them now."* Therefore, Jesus proclaimed the futility of the Law and the power of Grace both through *living* example and also by *teaching* parables (I.e. The Prodigal Son – Luke 15:11-32; Jesus' visit to Martha & Mary – Luke 10:38-42; Old & New Wineskins – Mark 2:22; Lazarus & the Rich Man – Luke 16:20-31; The Vineyard Owner – Mark 20:1-10, Etc.).

Just-if-I'd Never Sinned

A simple way to understand what justification means is to remember this simple phrase: *Justified = Just if I'd* never sinned. It also means *Just if I'd* always obeyed. When we are justified, God's Grace totally cleanses us and we stand before Him as never having sinned and in the perfect obedience of Christ. Of course we can do so only through the finished work of Jesus and not of our own good deeds. Only one sacrifice meets the requirements and that is the shed blood of Jesus. There are 5 aspects of justification:[12]

1. We are justified by *Grace* (Romans 3:24). We do not earn the right to be justified. We are justified simply because we believe. It's not about what we do for God. It's about what He has *already done* for us.

2. We are justified by *faith* (Romans 5:1). When we believe on the Son of God and repent of our sin we receive forgiveness and are justified (Ephesians 1:7; Colossians 1:14). Faith is how we accept and appropriate God's free gift of Grace.

3. We are justified by *blood* (Romans 5:9). The blood of Christ paid sin's debt entirely whereby God justifies the sinner by making him righteous (2 Corinthians 5:21).

4. We are justified by *God* (Romans 8:33). God alone makes us righteous and not the other way around. We don't make ourselves righteous! Please get this! It will set you free!

5. We are justified by *power* (Romans 4:25). The same power that raised Christ from the dead has raised us to good works (Ephesians 1:19-21). Good works are the results of a life that has been justified by God's power.

Did you notice that nowhere in any of the points above that it says we are justified by own effort? The bedrock, Biblical truth is that the work of justification is not accredited in anyway to our contribution. We must not indulge ourselves to believe that our salvation is attributed to any good we have done. Therefore, to sum this process up... *Grace* is the foundation for our justification and *faith* is how we receive it. The *blood* paid our inescapable debt, *God* is the one who justifies us and His *power* is the manifestation of our faith. Therefore, *works* will result.[12] Yet so many times we try to go through the whole process backwards. It's like trying to walk up a downward moving escalator. However, by trusting in our own works to save us we will never get to the top of the *justification escalator*. We must first step onto it receiving our righteousness by faith and thus move in the natural direction that Grace intended. Our works will never justify us. They are simply the outward sign that we have *true faith* in the Son of God. In other words, our good works are a natural *by-product* that we have faith. Faith cannot be seen unless our works show it. Faith in our *good* works, will not produce *God's* works. Thus, our faith is dead. When our faith is dead (having faith in the wrong thing) the result will be dead works. Simply put, good works are *visible* proof of the *invisible* working in us.

God Signs

Many born again believers struggle to show *God-signs* in their life failing to produce works that reflect true repentance. The truth is, if we aren't detecting *outward* indications of *inward* faith then it is a telltale sign we are putting our trust in our own behavior to earn favor with God. In other words we have become *self*-conscious rather than *Christ* conscious. When we are *self*-conscious we trust in ourselves resulting in 'dead' faith. This kind of faith begets worthless works. Remember, God justifies us the very moment we believe, thus making our faith and works inseparable. The first produces the second, and the second is the evidence of the first. We are justified by faith in God and the work of His Son thus demonstrating it by our works towards man. It's not rocket science people! I repeatedly emphasize that we are not saved by faith *plus* works! To accept this is to believe that the blood of Christ is not enough thus blaspheming the atoning work of the cross. Jesus' blood is sufficient payment for our righteousness! If it were possible to be saved by faith *plus* works, then Jesus would not be our Savior. In effect we would also need *another savior.* However, the whole of the New Testament (particularly the Pauline epistles) is crystalline: Jesus + Something = Nothing. We can't add any of our good works to the salvation equation. Jesus alone saves and keeps saving. Our salvation is based on the kind of faith that RESULTS in a life of good works. Works are not the *root* of our salvation; they are the *fruit* of our salvation. In other words, right *believing* is the cause and right *actions* are the effect. To show a life of real faith apart from good works is simply impossible. If you have faith in Jesus alone to save you, then your faith is living. If you have faith in your own works to produce righteousness, then your faith is dead. This is what it truly means when it says, *"Faith without works is dead."* Notice in our key passage (James 2:20) that Paul says we are *foolish* if we put our faith in our own works.

We must also address the question: *If I recite the sinner's prayer, does that alone produce faith in me towards salvation?* I have heard it said that nearly two-thirds of people that come forward for *"salvation calls"* end up producing no real significant life change. What could possibly be the reason for this? The answer: It is only *head* belief not *heart* belief. Head belief results in *dead* belief. Head belief involves no real surrender and therefore does not produce real transformation. It is not enough to merely believe in a moral existence of God. Although it is key in the salvation process it alone is not sufficient. Even the devil and his demons believe in God and are terrified of Him. However, they do not bow to Him nor obey Him. In other words, they do not have *real faith* in God. When we truly believe in the finished work of Christ we in effect lay all of our cards on the table and fully submit (body, soul and spirit) to the Lordship of Jesus Christ. This commitment in-turn results in a changed life. Full recognition of our need for a Savior ('Godly sorrow' as Paul calls it) will result in full and true repentance thus leading to a repentant *lifestyle* that produces the fruit of righteousness.

"Godly sorrow brings repentance that leads to salvation and leaves no regret... See what this Godly sorrow has produced in you: what earnestness, what eagerness to clear yourselves, what indignation, what alarm, what longing, what concern, what readiness to see justice done." (2 Corinthians 7:10-11 NIV)

We will never have peace with God by trying to earn His favor with works. This will cause us to feel as if we lose God's favor when we stumble. That's why Paul greeted the churches 13 different times in His writings using the words *"Grace and peace be unto you"* (See Romans 1:7; 1 Corinthians 1:3; 2 Corinthians 1:2; Galatians 1:3; Ephesians 1:2; Colossians 1:2; 1 Thessalonians 1:1; 2 Thessalonians 1:2; 1 Timothy 1:2; 2 Timothy 1:2; Titus 1:4; Philemon 1:3; 1 Peter 1:2; 2 Peter 1:2). These passages were more than just greetings. They were declarations that when you live on the side of Grace you will know the peace of God. When you realize you already have peace with God you can simply enjoy the benefits that come along with it. Grace and peace are synonymous. Where Grace is at work, peace is the result. Where Grace rules, peace REIGNS! Paul told the church at Philippi to *regularly rehearse* what He taught them about Grace and as a result they would experience the peace of God.

"The things you have learned and received and heard and seen in me, practice these things and THE GOD OF PEACE WILL BE WITH YOU."
(Philippians 4:9 NASB)

As we have already covered, Paul's ministry was to live, teach and publish the message of God's Grace (Acts 20:24). By *practice* Paul meant to simply receive and rehearse over and over in your heart your firm belief of the truth about God's Grace, and as a result the peace of God would manifest itself in the life of the believer. Paul was serious about helping people live free of condemnation and overcome a lifestyle of sin. As I mentioned before, even in the greetings of many his letters, Paul would immediately introduce the truth of God's Grace resulting in peace (Romans 1:7). Notice that Paul addressed the Roman church as *"Beloved of God"* and *"Saints."* The center reference in my Bible defines "saints" as *holy ones.* Surely, there were those in the Gentile Roman church that hadn't reached perfection yet (that would be all of them and ALL OF US to be exact). Besides that, the Gentile members of this Roman church were not raised in the traditions and practices of the Mosaic Law. Yet, because they believed in God, Paul called them "saints." Note that *sainthood* doesn't denote perfection. The moment we receive Christ through faith, we are *instantly* made saints (fully righteous) through Jesus blood. Hallelujah! In light of all of this we must *once-and-for-all* put to death our self-righteousness, receive God's free gift of righteousness by faith and stand firm in the liberty whereby Christ has made us free.

"It was for freedom that Christ set us free; therefore keep standing firm and do not be subject again to a yoke of slavery." (Galatians 5:1 NASB)

The True Sabbath Rest

Our freedom in Christ should produce a deep settled sense of rest. However, many Christians today spend most of their lives wrestling instead of resting. Throughout the Old Testament, the Children of Israel never really understood the full meaning of the Sabbath day rest. They were merely obeying the rule that they were not to work one specific day of the week (Exodus 20:8 NASB). To be sure, the Israelites stopped physically working one day a week, but they didn't stop striving to be righteous. Did you know you can be lying in your bed and still be working and laboring through self-effort to be Holy before God? It's called "being anxious" or "worrying." Worrying is working! Did you know that your worrying doesn't accomplish anything in your relationship with God...

"And which of you by worrying can add a single hour to his life's span?" (Luke 12:25 NASB)

You will never truly be at rest while living a life of self-effort. The Old Covenant Sabbath wasn't the *true Sabbath* that God intended for His people. Taking one day a week off of work was only a type and shadow or a living illustration of what Jesus would ultimately bring. There were many in Jesus day (particularly the Jewish leaders) that were offended and even outraged if anybody did any kind of activity on the Sabbath day (the Sabbath day was from sundown on Saturday to sundown on Sunday). The Jews were so steeped in their religion they couldn't even accept Jesus healing people on the Sabbath. Imagine that! They even despised Jesus and His disciples snacking on their "day-off" as they were passing through the wheat fields...

"Now it happened that He was passing through some grainfields on a Sabbath; and His disciples were picking the heads of grain, rubbing them in their hands, and eating the grain. But some of the Pharisees said, 'Why do you do what is not Lawful on the Sabbath?' And He was saying to them, 'THE SON OF MAN IS LORD OF THE SABBATH.'"
(Luke 6:1-3 NASB)

Jesus responded to His critics by telling them that HE was their Sabbath rest. In other words, the Sabbath is not a *day* of the week; it's a *person*. JESUS is our Sabbath rest and by trusting in His finished work alone we truly know what it means to live the Sabbath life... a life of REST! The Sabbath for us means a *life* of rest IN CHRIST. In this new Grace dispensation, The Sabbath rest for us is to lean on the free gift of righteousness given to us through the birth, death, burial and resurrection of our Lord and Savior Jesus Christ. Paul was constantly trying to nail this truth down. He stressed that the Children of Israel never really *got it.* The great paradox, according to Paul, is that we should diligently labor to *rest.*

"So there remains a Sabbath rest for the people of God. For the one who has entered His rest has himself also rested from his works, as God did from His. Therefore, let us be diligent to enter that rest, so that no one will fall, through following the same example of disobedience." (Hebrews 4:9-11 NASB)[9]

Did you catch that? Paul said that the Children of Israel *fell into disobedience* because they never recognized their true Sabbath. When we strive to be righteous and maintain our own holiness we end up falling into the ditch of disobedience. The basis of the Christian life is to rest upon the finished work of Christ and lay down our striving so that HIS power can work through us. The significance of Jesus death, and resurrection is applicable here. Just as Jesus was taken off of the cross and buried on the Eve of the Sabbath day, we must also die to our own works (as Christ did from His) and be buried with Him so that we may enter His Sabbath rest. The Sabbath rest for us is dying to our own works so that we may be resurrected to new life IN CHRIST. God also rested from His work on the seventh day of creation. This is what Paul meant in Hebrews 4:10 when he said, *"For the one who has entered His rest has himself also rested from his works, "as God did from His."*

Yoked to Jesus

"Come unto me, all ye that labor and are heavy laden, and I will give you rest. Take My yoke upon you and learn from Me, for I am gentle and humble in heart, and YOU WILL FIND REST FOR YOUR SOULS. For My yoke is easy and My burden is light." (Matthew 11:28 NASB)

It is understood in agriculture that it takes two oxen yoked together to pull a plow. One ox is known as the *draft animal* (older, more experienced and stronger) and the other is known as the *gelded cow* (untrained steer). The draft ox is used for its muscular power to haul heavy carts and plow large fields.[21] Even the dictionary refers to oxen as *beasts of burden.*[22] The older more experienced ox that *knows the ropes* is able by its training and strength to walk straight lines and keep the plow from tilting. However, in some cases, the farmer that guides the plow yokes a younger ox to the trained ox so it could learn from the older. The younger ox (locked on one side of the yoke) follows, while the stronger more experienced ox takes the lead. When Jesus said, *"Take MY yoke"* He WASN'T saying that His life is a yoke of slavery and if you're going to follow Him you have to be burdened down with heaviness and sorrow. No! What He was telling his disciples in this passage was that it was HIS yoke and HIS burden to carry. He was our *beast of burden* as it were. Isaiah 53:4 tells us that Jesus bore ALL our griefs and carried ALL our sorrows. When you think of the word *yoke* you immediately think of forced constraint and hard labor. However, when you consider Jesus' definition of yoke, it means a life of rest. What Jesus is asking of us in Matthew 11:28-30 is that we be latched to Him and His purpose for our lives. He promises to carry the burden and all we need do is stay connected to Him. If we are submitted to His will then His Grace will do the work as He leads us through life's difficulties toward our bright future in Him. It's when we decide to rebel that things get all out of whack. Jesus is simply asking us to quit resisting and cooperate with Him in order that He might guide us in His rest. There was an Old Testament Law that commanded the Children of Israel not to yoke a donkey and an ox together. So don't be a *stubborn mule* (you can insert the KJV word for *mule* to get a clearer picture).

"Thou shalt not plow with an ox and an ass together."
(Deuteronomy 22:10 KJV)

This vividly illustrates how we often act in relation to God's will for our lives. Sometimes we're just plain stubborn! The scriptures declare that God will never let go of us (Romans 8:35-39). We are forever in His grip. It's too strong to break. However, so often we *let go* of Him, meaning that we fight against His purposes. Although God is still holding on to us, we are nevertheless flailing and wagging about living a weary life of constant tension and flux. Life with God was meant to be like a harmonious dance. My wife and I once took ballroom dance lessons and our instructor told us (in his Brazilian accent), *"It takes an incredible amount of GRACE to dance with a partner."* What an amazing revelation! If the man (the guide) properly executes his positions and steps, he can charm and gently guide the woman (his partner) to perform her movements with elegance, poise, style and Grace. We need to let Grace take the lead in life's dance. As we embrace Jesus, transfer our weight to His, meet Him eye to eye and lunge with His every move, we get caught up in the amalgamation of His Grace and flow in effortless union with Him. When He moves, we move. When He works, we work. When He rests, we rest. We just simply lean on HIM and life becomes the dance it was meant to be.

The word *'souls'* in Matthew 11:28 is very significant in relation to this. Jesus tells us that if we join to His yoke we would find rest for our *souls*. The word *'soul'* in this passage speaks of our thoughts and emotions (the primary battlefield for our peace). The devil seeks to destroy us first in our minds and emotions. Therefore, in order to *receive* peace of mind we must *rest* on Christ's finished work. Receive and Rest! Interestingly enough, a specially designed neck yoke for connecting oxen was used to ensure that the two animals would do the same amount of work.[23] When we rest in Christ finished work, He does the work through us. We literally feel the very same strength of Jesus working in our lives to accomplish His full purposes in us! Jesus is asking us to exchange our yoke of slavery to self-effort and be joined to Him (a life of His joy, His peace and His strength).

Good *'ol'* Boys

In ancient Israel the sage-discipleship relationship (yoking or bonding of teacher and disciple) was a common practice in which a prophet would become a contemporary or mentor-figure for a select group of disciples (or *talmidim* as they were called) as they ascribed to learn the rabbi's ways. The Hebrew word for 'yoke' is *ol*. It is what the Jews of the first century Judea called a *system of teaching the Law.* Through the guidance of a mentor, a sage (student) would learn to interpret the Torah or the Talmud (The Old Covenant Law), understand its parables and apply them to his practical, everyday life. This is why Jesus picked twelve ordinary, eager youngsters to be his protégés (not the middle-age men we stereotypically picture them to be).[24] The Old Covenant rabbis of Jesus time would have rejected these men because they didn't fit the typical *"cream of the crop"* for those normally chosen to be in a rabbi's inner circle. However, Jesus loves to take the rejected and turn them into revolutionaries. In other words, Jesus took a bunch of *good 'ol' boys* and transformed them into world shakers!

In Acts 15:10 the Apostles speak of the Law as a yoke of bondage upon the shoulders of the disciples. This supports the idea of what Jesus was saying, when He said, *"Take MY yoke upon you and learn from ME."* Jesus (our teacher and mentor) wants us (the student) to come out from under the burden of the living under the Law and learn (under His tutelage) how to live life in the fullness of His Grace.[25]

Too Fat for the Yoke

"And it shall come to pass in that day, that his burden (Midianite oppression) shall be taken away from off thy shoulder, and his yoke from off thy neck, and the yoke shall be destroyed because of the anointing. (Isaiah 10:27 KJV)[37]

The word *'yoke'* in this passage refers to the Midianite oppression that had troubled God's people for years. However, this verse was ultimately prophesying that the Messiah would come and break the oppressive yoke of slavery that holds the world in bondage to sin. Many think that the word *'anointing'* in this passage means to be *filled with the power of the Holy Spirit.* This is true in a sense, but it is not the literal rendering of this particular scriptural context. The Hebrew word for *'anointing'* is *shemen,* which means *fatness.*[34] If an ox is too fat his neck won't fit into the yoke or either the yoke around his neck will break. When we feed on the goodness of God's Grace, it supersizes our heart to the point that it eventually shatters the yoke of slavery into smithereens. God's Grace literally SUPERSIZES us!

No More a "Law Man"

To all of this we must decide once and for all how we want to live our lives. Do we wish to murk about in the quagmire of self-righteousness to please God or do we want to shine in the light of His favor knowing that we are already His chosen treasure and most prized possession?

Cutting ties with the flesh means losing our dependency upon self-efforts to maintain relationship with God. We can be forever liberated from chains of legalistic fervor and set free to skip in the Sun of God's unending and abounding Grace. We need only make the choice.

"What actually took place is this: I tried keeping rules and working my head off to please God, and it didn't work. So I quit being a "Law man" so that I could be God's man. Christ's life showed me how, and enabled me to do it. I identified myself completely with him. Indeed, I have been crucified with Christ. My ego is no longer central. It is no longer important that I appear righteous before you or have your good opinion, and I am no longer driven to impress God. Christ lives in me. The life you see me living is not "mine," but it is lived by faith in the Son of God, who loved me and gave himself for me. I am not going to go back on that. Is it not clear to you that to go back to that old rule-keeping, peer-pleasing religion would be an abandonment of everything personal and free in my relationship with God? I refuse to do that, to repudiate God's Grace. If a living relationship with God could come by rule-keeping, then Christ died unnecessarily."
(Galatians 2:19-22 THE MESSAGE)

Kick Back & Relax

"Who being the brightness of His glory, and the express image of His person, and upholding all things by the word of His power, when He had by Himself purged our sins, sat down on the right hand of the Majesty on high." (Hebrews 1:3 NKJV)

Did you know that Jesus is not scurrying and worrying about how everything will turn out in our lives? He's kicking back in His Heavenly throne with a steady confidence in us. And like Jesus, we need to be ruling not grueling. In Old Testament times there were no chairs in the tabernacle. The priests worked around the clock with not a second to waist to finish their tasks. But Jesus, our great high priest finished the work for our salvation and is now seated on the right hand of the Father in Heaven. And we are also seated with Him (Ephesians 2:6). Yet so many don't realize it and continue to work on their righteousness. My friend, we need to remember our position in Christ as being seated in His power and authority and enjoy our rest in Him. Therefore, it's time to die to our works and come alive in the power of Grace. We need to have a funeral for our self-righteousness and lay it to rest once and for all; and the epitaph should say...

Here lies works; my old man self
That got me nowhere fast
And now my soul can R.I.P.
By Grace I'm free at last.

Chapter 30

THE GRACE REVOLUTION

"…These who have turned the world upside down have come here too." — Acts 17:6 NKJV

John Huss (1372-1415), the famous Czech Catholic priest of the Renaissance period, is considered by many Theologians as one of the greatest Protestant Reformationists of all time. Huss was burned at the stake by the Roman Catholic Church for (what they considered) teaching heresy (see page 324 for further study). Huss believed that everyone of that time should be able to own his or her own copy of the Bible and even have the freedom to protest the Catholic Church. He also believed (along with other contemporaries of his time) in salvation by Grace through faith in Jesus Christ alone. You may also be interested to know that some of Huss' more radical followers (the Taborites) rejected any teaching that was not Biblically founded. Eventually these Taborites became one of the first Protestant *charismatic* communities known as the Moravians, who sent more missionaries throughout Europe than any other Protestant denomination in history. The Roman Catholic Church considered Huss' teachings extremely heretical and revolutionary. As a result, he was eventually excommunicated, condemned by the papacy and burned at the stake for his radical views, thus proving that all who want to live Godly IN CHRIST JESUS will be persecuted (2 Timothy 3:12).

Revolutionaries always march uphill! Huss' last words as he was stripped of his clothes and tied to the stake were, *"In a hundred years, God will raise up a man whose calls for reform cannot be suppressed."* That person of course was Martin Luther who nailed his famous *95 Theses of Contention* to the church door at Wittenberg 102 years later. Luther's *'95 Thesis'* was one of the finest written arguments against the Catholic church, defending many Biblical truths including the gospel of salvation by Grace through faith in Jesus and not of works.[13]

After declaring this *prophecy*, according to tradition, the bishop responsible for Huss' execution is said to have made the statement, *"Over my dead body."* Almost 100 years later, tradition records that as part of Martin Luther's confirmation into priesthood, he embraced the grave of this certain bishop. Huss' prophecy had come to pass. God had raised up such a man *over the bishop's dead body!* Revolutions are started by revolutionaries. When a person's life is turned around, they turn other people's lives around. Truth is, having a revelation from God does not do near as much as having a REVOLUTION with God!

A Lot of Hot Water

To fully understand our key passage in Acts we need to go a few verses back to pick up on the story.

"Now when they had passed through Amphipolis and Apollonia, they came to Thessalonica, where there was a synagogue of the Jews. Then Paul, as his custom was, went in to them, and for three Sabbaths reasoned with them from the Scriptures, explaining and demonstrating that the Christ had to suffer and rise again from the dead, and saying, "This Jesus whom I preach to you is the Christ." And some of them were persuaded; and a great multitude of the devout Greeks, and not a few of the leading women, joined Paul and Silas. But the Jews who were not persuaded, becoming envious, took some of the evil men from the marketplace, and gathering a mob, set all the city in an uproar and attacked the house of Jason, and sought to bring them out to the people. But when they did not find them, they dragged Jason and some brethren to the rulers of the city, crying out, "These who have turned the world upside down have come here too. Jason has harbored them, and these are all acting contrary to the decrees of Caesar, saying there is another king—Jesus." And they troubled the crowd and the rulers of the city when they heard these things. So when they had taken security from Jason and the rest, they let them go." (Acts 17:1-9 NKJV)

Paul and Silas had come to the Greek city of Thessalonica and found a Jewish synagogue there. So they stayed for three weeks and preached Christ (with the demonstration of the power of God) to these Jews. And look at what he preached...

"For you recall, brethren, our labor and hardship... WE PROCLAIMED TO YOU THE GOSPEL of God." (1 Thessalonians 2:9 NASB)

During Paul's three weeks in Thessalonica, he preached the gospel. The gospel for Paul was the good news of God's Grace (Acts 20:24; Romans 1:16). Why then did Paul stay so long to expound on the revelations he had received. It was because religious bondage runs deep and it takes awhile to dig people out of the mud of self-righteousness. By boldly preaching the gospel of Grace, Paul and Silas got in a lot of hot water with the Jewish leaders. You see; the Jews were envious of the response that Paul and Silas were receiving. In fact they were so outraged that they attacked the house of Jason where they were thought to have been staying. Yet, they were unable to find Paul and Silas so they came and dragged Jason and some of the others into the streets to make them a public example by stoning or flogging. The Jewish leaders accused them of treason: that they were declaring another King other than Caesar (religious people will stop at nothing to prevent the gospel of Grace from spreading even resorting to lying, slander and false accusation).

The main reason the Judaizers were furious because the Gospel of Grace puts all the attention on the *person* of Grace (Jesus), not on religious *personalities.* One thing is certain; the religious leaders of Paul's day could not help but recognize one powerful truth about them... They had *turned the world upside down* with the gospel of Grace. When we begin to preach the pure gospel of Grace we will start a gospel revolution that will turn the world upside down. It's time for ministers of the gospel to quit trying to make religious people happy with them. The fear of man is a minister's worst enemy. Those we fear the most are the ones we will strive to please the most. It's time to shake off the fear of man, get dangerous and preach an uncontaminated gospel that releases the FULL POWER of God that sets people free (1 Thessalonians 2:4). If you haven't gotten into some hot water lately from your preaching maybe it's because your preaching isn't bringing any heat. Are your sermons so soft and politically correct that they're not ruffling any feathers. My wife once told me that the words of a true prophet will never be popular. So quit trying to be popular and preach the uncompromised gospel that frightens satan and frees the sinner! The gospel of Grace isn't safe but it sure is sweet. It will stir up a bee's nest but that's where the honey is! The last-days church must not adopt the view that we are self-made men. We have not progressed so far or become more enlightened to believe that a particular formula added to the work of

Grace is necessary to maintain our hold on the precious gift we never merited in the first place!

The Grace Based Church

"And the congregation of those who believed were of ONE HEART AND SOUL; and not one of them claimed that anything belonging to him was his own, but all things were common property to them. And WITH GREAT POWER the apostles were GIVING TESTIMONY to the resurrection of the Lord Jesus, and abundant Grace was upon them all. For there was NOT A NEEDY PERSON AMONG THEM, for all who were owners of land or houses would sell them and bring the proceeds of the sales and lay them at the apostles' feet, and they would be distributed to each as any had need." (Acts 4:32-35 NASB)

The first century church was recognized as a church that was empowered by *"abundant Grace"* (some translations render it as *"great Grace"*). A church that is committed to declaring the full message of the gospel of Grace will demonstrate the following 4 characteristics:

Unshakable *Partnership*

Unquenchable *Passion*

Undeniable *Proof*

Unstoppable *Prosperity*

Unshakable Partnership – *"one heart and soul"*

Any church that preaches the pure Gospel of Grace will be so powerfully linked together that they will be inseparable. The definition of a *partner* is a person who is associated with others as a full contributor of all their resources in a joint venture who shares in all their risks and profits. A 'partner' is also a nautical term that describes a framework of timbers fastened around a hole in a ship's deck, to support the mast. In other words, the fulfillment of a vision is determined by the strength of the framework of its partnership. Grace is what empowers true partnership. The first century was a church that thrived no matter what forces or persecution came against it and was able to experience exponential growth and expansion because of it's commitment to proclaiming the gospel of God's Grace. Partnership is much more powerful than unity. With *unity* everyone believes in the same thing but *partnership* is *believing in* and *acting on* a common cause no matter what the cost. The church in the book of Acts was of *"one heart and soul"* that were willing to give their lives for what they believed in. God's Grace releases power to endure and persevere through all adversity. The church here in Acts 4 experienced a mighty move of God's Spirit in response to their communal commitment to preaching the pure gospel of Grace. A church that ministers in the power of God's Grace will be unshakable!

Unquenchable Passion – *"with great power"*

As previously mentioned, the Greek word for *"power"* in Acts 4:32-35 is *dynamis,* from which we get our English word *dynamite.* The word *dynamis* means the following: *strength, power, supernatural ability, power for performing miracles, moral excellence of soul, the influence that comes as possessing great wealth or resources and the force of a great army.* When we are full of Grace and the Holy Spirit we will make dynamite impact. The fuse of dynamite ministry is lit by the spark of Grace! When God's Grace falls mightily upon the church, she will march forward into her destiny perform miracles, display great moral influence in communities and government, possess authoritative influence that comes with having great wealth and be effectively mobilized to establish and enforce the Kingdom of God on this earth. The supernatural surged through the early church with amazing results under the influence of Grace and the power of the Holy Spirit. The Holy Spirit always endorses the message of Grace. In fact, Grace and Holy Spirit power are synonymous with each other. The ministry of Stephen is one great example of this kind of synergy.

"And Stephen, FULL OF GRACE AND POWER, was performing great wonders and signs among the people." (Acts 6:8 NASB).

The disciples had been with Jesus (the Person of Grace) and that Grace empowered them to proclaim His resurrection with *"great power."* (Acts 4:13). The early church regularly experienced powerful conversions amongst the people. After being mightily baptized in the Holy Spirit, Peter (the one who bitterly betrayed Jesus) was the one who preached the first evangelistic sermon after Jesus ascension. His message was only three-minutes long and as a result 3,000 people were saved and added to the church (Acts 2:41). God's Grace so impacted Peter's life that it turned him into one of the most effective evangelists of His time. It's interesting to note that fifty days after the Exodus from Egypt the Law was revealed. This day is known to the Israelites as Shavu'ot or the Feast of Pentecost. Ironically on this day 3000 people died from the curse of their disobedience (Exodus 33:28). This is why the Lord wanted the Children of Israel to commemorate this day: to remember that the Law crushed and consumed them in God's wrath as a result of their defiance and rebellion. However, on the day of Pentecost (the time of the New Covenant of Grace) when the Holy Spirit was fully released, 3000 people were saved. That's what the scripture means when it says the letter (Law) kills but the Spirit (Grace) gives life.

"Who (Jesus) also made us adequate as servants of a new covenant, not of the letter but of the Spirit; FOR THE LETTER KILLS, BUT THE SPIRIT GIVES LIFE." (2 Corinthians 3:6 NASB)

When the church fully embraces the gospel of Grace, we will be an unstoppable force, revolutionizing our communities, our cities, and the nations of the world. Grace turns the world upside down.

Undeniable Proof – *"giving testimony"*

The Greek word for *"testimony"* is *martyrion* from which the word *martyr* is derived. Other meanings are...

A witness in a legal, historical and ethical sense

One who is a spectator of anything

Those who, by genuineness of their faith IN CHRIST are willing to endure suffering and ultimately death

The gospel that the early Church suffered for was not just preaching Jesus, but also declaring that we are made righteous by faith in Him apart from our works! This same Grace must have a grasp on us! When we are empowered with the Grace of God, we will be made viable witnesses to the resurrection of Jesus, even if it means suffering and ultimately dying for the cause of the gospel. We will be credible to the world because they will see the convincing power of God Grace upon us. Another translation renders the word *"testimony"* as *"witness."* A credible witness in court **possesses** substantial and uncontested evidence; **presents** a powerfully compelling & convincing argument; **persuades** the defense beyond a reasonable doubt and ultimately **proves** the case. Being witnesses to and becoming recipients of God's Grace makes us powerfully persuasive in convincing others that Jesus is alive and well on planet earth. Wholeheartedly receiving the Grace of God into our lives produces the characteristics of true disciples who intimately know the heart of God. In other words, although we haven't actually seen Jesus the world will see Jesus in us. Oh how the world needs to see Jesus in us.

Unstoppable Prosperity – *"not a needy person among them"*

God's Grace is not just for our spiritual application. God's Grace covers every area of our lives (spiritual, physical, social, physiological, emotional, etc.). The early church was prospering in generosity to the extent that there was ample supply to cover every need. Not only that but God's Grace unleashed supernatural provision to finance the spreading of the gospel of Grace worldwide. Can you imagine a 21st century church flowing in this kind of supernatural provision? In today's failing world markets, the Church can rise above the coming tidal wave of economic collapse. God's people have always prospered in time of famine (I.e. Genesis 45:4-11). Our way to prosper is to receive abundant Grace. Many churches today are in great need of financial breakthrough. I truly believe that when we move in the power of God's Grace and teach it rightly that God's favor will be upon that people. God wants His people to prosper in order that they might spread the gospel to the ends of the earth (Deuteronomy 8:18). There isn't a thing God won't do for the church who will arise and proclaim the pure gospel of Grace; that when fully demonstrated, will heal the brokenhearted, proclaim liberty to the captives, recovery of sight to the blind and set oppressed and broken people free.

"The Spirit of the LORD is upon Me, because He has anointed Me to PREACH THE GOSPEL to the poor; He has sent Me to heal the brokenhearted, to proclaim liberty to the captives and recovery of sight to the blind, to set at liberty those who are oppressed..."
(Luke 4:18 NKJV)

Notice Jesus didn't say, *"I come bringing the Law that will set you free."* No! He came as our revolutionary bringing a whole new way to freedom. Through His birth, life, death and resurrection He proclaimed the good news of Grace declaring to all generations the only way to true righteousness (John 1:17; John 14:6). Faith in God's Grace is the only way to salvation, righteousness, freedom, blessings, peace, power, healing, prosperity, joy and abundant life.

"The thief comes only to steal and kill and destroy; I came that they may have life, and have it abundantly." (John 10:10 NASB)

Some say the church is too religious to embrace the real Grace message. If that were true then it would be a hopeless cause to stand for the gospel of Grace. However, I once heard it said that no cause is lost if there is but one fool left to fight for it. I have made a vow to God that I will be the "fool" who will stand for a true Grace revolution no matter the cost.

Chapter 31

FROM HERE TO HAPPY

"Pilate said to them, 'Then what shall I do with Jesus Who is called Christ?'" (Matthew 27:2 NASB)

Pilate's question is a question all of us must answer. After hearing the message of God's marvelous Grace, what will you do with this truth you have come to discover? The truth you have heard will set you free if you will simply believe and receive it. It is a free gift. You can cease from your weary efforts to try and please God and simply allow the light of His shining countenance that is already smiling upon you to light your way.

"For you were formerly darkness, but now you are Light in the Lord; walk as children of Light." (Ephesians 5:8 NASB)

Please don't be like the countless thousands who are still working to be righteous and earn favor with God! If you are a believer you are already right with God and are entitled to all His blessings. Therefore, simply trust IN CHRIST alone. Come to Jesus and let Him take your heavy yoke of slavery and give you His joy and peace. *No Jesus, then no peace... But know Jesus and you'll know peace.* God's Grace always brings peace!

"GRACE to you AND PEACE from God our Father and the Lord Jesus Christ." (1 Corinthians 1:3 NASB)

North Gate, South Gate

Many of you, before reading this book, have developed false mindsets over the years and have come to believe in certain things that have shaped the way you relate to God which in turn effects the way you live your life. However, now you have the choice to return the way you came or go out by another way: a true and living way.

But when the people of the land come before the LORD at the appointed feasts, HE WHO ENTERS BY WAY OF THE NORTH GATE TO

301

WORSHIP SHALL GO OUT BY WAY OF THE SOUTH GATE. And he who enters by way of the south gate shall go out by way of the north gate. NO ONE SHALL RETURN BY WAY OF THE GATE BY WHICH HE ENTERED BUT SHALL GO STRAIGHT OUT." (Ezekiel 46:9 NASB)

In ancient times, when people came to Jerusalem to worship God during the appointed celebrations and feasts, they were not to exit the city the way they entered it. If they entered by way of the north gate they were to leave by way of the south gate. If they came in by way of the south gate they were to exit by way of the north gate. What gate did you enter this book and what gate shall you leave by? Will you return to the aggravation of self-efforts to please God? Do you desire to continue your futile attempts to earn favor with God through the flesh? Or will you choose to lay down your works and receive His free gift of Grace that makes you righteous apart from your works? The former is only frustration and failure. The latter is peace and prosperity!

Are You Bored Again?

What is your Christian life like right now? Are you born-again or are you *bored-again?* I tell the truth... Jesus isn't boring, so I will never make Him that way! Jesus did not save you to be bored. The Christian life is full of adventure and surprises. Yet if you live your life with the *plow* of self-works in your hand, you'll never know the joy of swinging from the *vines* of Grace.

Before you pray the prayer at the end of this book you must make a decision. You can either pray believing what you are about to say, or you can close the book now and crawl back to the life of slavery you've always known. The choice is yours! However, if you want to leave by way of the *south gate* of your life and enter a whole new way of living, God's very best is just within your reach. In fact, in God's Grace, all good things NEVER come to an end. I speak the truth; you cannot even begin to imagine what is about to unfold in your life. If you will just lay down, once and for all, your self-efforts to please God and take up His free and most wonderful gift of righteousness, your life will never be the same. Through God's Grace you can become the person you always thought you could never become.

"For you have not passed this way before." (Joshua 3:4 NASB)

Give Grace a Chance

It's time to say goodbye to your past and reach out to take hold of the awesome things God has for you. It's time to give Grace a chance. You have a brilliant future waiting just around the corner. God's plan for you is nothing short of spectacular!

"For I know the plans that I have for you,' declares the LORD, 'plans for welfare and not for calamity to give you a future and a hope."
(Jeremiah 29:11 NASB)

The decision you are about to make and the prayer you are about to pray will transport you to another dimension in your relationship with God that you never, in your wildest dreams, thought possible. Everything is about to change for you. Get ready to be amazed!

"Because of this decision we don't evaluate people by what they have or how they look. WE LOOKED AT THE MESSIAH THAT WAY ONCE AND GOT IT ALL WRONG, as you know. We certainly don't look at Him that way anymore. Now we look inside, and what we see is that ANYONE UNITED WITH THE MESSIAH GETS A FRESH START, IS CREATED NEW. THE OLD LIFE IS GONE; A NEW LIFE BURGEONS! Look at it! All this comes from the God who settled the relationship between us and Him, and then called us to settle our relationships with each other. God put the world square with Himself through the Messiah, giving the world a fresh start by offering forgiveness of sins. God has given us the task of telling everyone what He is doing. We're Christ's representatives. God uses us to persuade men and women to drop their differences AND ENTER INTO GOD'S WORK OF MAKING THINGS RIGHT BETWEEN THEM. We're speaking for Christ himself now: Become friends with God; He's already a friend with you."
(2 Corinthians 5:16-20 THE MESSAGE)

So, are you ready for your life to be changed forever? Are you ready to let go and let God take over? Then don't just *say* this prayer... PRAY this prayer and believe what you are praying...

Dear Heavenly Father, I am tired of my old life. I am tired of constantly trying to make things right with You in my own strength. I know now that You came to offer me a way of living that always is becoming new. Your goodness, Your mercy and Your GRACE have led me here and I don't want crawl back to the trash of my past. I reach my arms straight out to you and embrace a new life of Grace. I lay down my self-efforts to maintain my righteousness and simply accept my right standing with You. I know You accept me and I don't need to do anything to make You love me more, be pleased with me or consider me Your own. I ALREADY belong to you. I fully turn from the things that are causing me to stumble and I place them in your hands. I am already perfect in You. Because I am now IN CHRIST, I am everything He is in this world! I accept my forgiven status IN CHRIST and choose by faith to receive full righteousness. I am thankful that by Your blood I have forgiveness of sins and my repentance is forever sealed in Your finished work. I now will walk in newness of life and know that I will never be the same. I am forever grateful for this breathtaking journey of Grace!

Your Grace has saved me and will keep on saving me. I no longer have to maintain my righteousness by perfect behavior. It is impossible for me to live up to your perfect standard anyway. Therefore, I trust that Your Grace empowers me to overcome sin. I will no longer live under the harsh demands of the Law. I will live by the PERFECT LAW OF LIBERTY and embrace the life of the New Covenant. I clearly see by Your Word that I AM THE RIGHTEOUSNESS OF GOD IN CHRIST. I am not becoming more righteous. I HAVE BECOME Your righteousness. Because I am IN CHRIST I am as righteous as I'll ever be!

All my sins, past, present and future are forgiven and condemnation no longer has a hold on me. I may not be able to change the past, but I can surely change my future. Therefore, when satan (my enemy and accuser) exaggerates my failures I stand IN CHRIST as fully righteous facing forward in my right standing with God. I will not dwell on what is wrong about me. Rather, I will listen to the Holy Spirit tell me what's right about me! When satan reminds me of my past I will remind Him of His future (Revelation 20:2-3). My great High Priest, Jesus Christ, ever lives to intercede for me and defends my case. By all the evidence presented IN CHRIST I have been declared NOT GUILTY! His blood forever makes me clean. When I fail I will not run away from You. I will run TO

YOU. I will not go out and start living a life of sin. My old nature is dead and I am alive IN CHRIST. Therefore, I do not want to sin! When I fall I will fall into Your arms of Grace. You will never let me go!

I am very aware that I may struggle in Your will for my life at times but I am sealed in Your clasp and nothing can break the bonds of that love. I am Yours forever! Because I have received Your Grace I will freely give it. I will cease judging people from a perspective of self-righteousness. I will hurt with the hurting and have a broken heart for the broken. I will not see Your people as they act, but as they are... as You see them... A finished work IN CHRIST! Your power is constantly changing me and I will be a life that shouts and sings of your Grace. I will declare from the rooftops the marvelous works of Your Spirit in my life. As a result, the fruit of Your Spirit will naturally manifest in me without forcing it to grow by my own efforts. I will produce abundant fruit because I am deeply rooted in Your righteousness! As I simply surrender to Your Grace and abandon myself to a lifestyle of worship, the flame of my devotion will burn like a raging inferno of passion to declare Your praise and live for Your renown! No one will ever be able to take away this marvelous revelation of Grace. I will be a revolutionary proclaiming the gospel of the good news of what Your Grace has done and will do. I will never go back to what I was. I am a new creation! I am Your awesome work of Grace...

I am your GRACEWORK!

About the Author

For nearly three decades Tony Sutherland has served on staff in the local church as well as traveled extensively around the world stirring in hearts everywhere a passion for God's presence and a powerful Grace awakening through his music, teaching and preaching. Tony has captured the unique ability to effectively reach a wide diversity of people in today's church. His dynamic ministry style crosses denominational and cultural barriers impacting children, youth, young adult, middle age and seniors. Congregations large and small are refreshed by his passion for Jesus. Along with his busy traveling schedule, Tony has served on staff as a Worship Leader at Free Chapel's main campus in Gainesville, GA under the ministry of Pastor Jentezen Franklin for the past ten years.

Having over a quarter-century combined experience in various ministry areas including: worship, youth & children, church planting, associate pastor, and an expansive itinerate ministry in evangelism and foreign missions (to name a few), Tony is well equipped to address the life of the local church on numerous levels. Along with these, he has also ministered in hundreds of established and thriving churches as well as young, church plants around the world, consulting a plethora of pastors from every size congregation, cultural background, denomination and Christ-centered church movement. His extensive research and hands-on involvement in helping to develop church environments is an invaluable resource for growing ministries desiring to adopt a culture that is entirely Christ-centered with a Christ centered, Spirit-led paradigm.

Tony is also an accomplished songwriter having written songs with and for artists such as Israel Hougton, Micah Massey, Ricardo Sanchez, Ce Ce Winans, The Katinas, Mandisa, Phillips-Craig & Dean, Bishop Paul Morton, David & Nichole Binion, Ashmont Hill, Daryl Coley, Myron Butler, Ron Kenoly and many others.

Tony resides in the North Atlanta area with Sherri, his beautiful wife of 25 years and their two amazing children, Asher and Anna.

Appendix I

EARLY REFUTATIONS OF GRACE

This section is provided for a brief historical reflection of the ensuing arguments over the centuries against the gospel.[18] During the proliferation of Lutheranism in the 1500's the Roman Catholic Church harshly and even violently reacted to the proponents of the Grace message. Martin Luther, considered to be a major spearhead of Protestantism, believed and taught that salvation is attained by Grace through faith in Jesus Christ alone. Therefore, in hopes to put a stop to the widespread teachings of the likes of Luther and many others, the Catholic papacy convened *The Council of Trent* (December 13, 1545 through December 14, 1563) in attempts to refute the doctrines of these reformers.

The canons listed in this section are those created by the Council that adamantly oppose the gospel of justification by Grace through faith *(I have also cited the scripture references that contradict that particular canon).*[19] At the end of each canon note where the word *"anathema"* is used. This word was taken from Galatians 1:8-9 (KJV) and used to justify that the *curse* came from Holy Scripture and therefore came from God. Anyone who disagreed with the following canons and any other doctrines set forth by the Council were under the curse of *anathema* and therefore deemed as unsaved, damned to perish in the eternal flames of torment and immediately excommunicated from the church. As a result of the Council's decisions, many Protestant reformers were brutally tortured and even executed for their convictions.

CANON 9: "If any one says, that by faith alone the impious is justified; in such wise as to mean, that nothing else is required to co-operate in order to the obtaining the Grace of Justification, and that it is not in any way necessary, that he be prepared and disposed by the movement of his own will; let him be anathema."

Contradicting Scriptures:

"Therefore by the deeds of the Law there shall no flesh be justified in his sight: for by the Law is the knowledge of sin... Being justified freely by his Grace through the redemption that is in Christ Jesus... Therefore we conclude that a man is justified by faith without the deeds of the Law." (Romans 3:20,24,28 KJV)

"For by Grace are ye saved through faith; and that not of yourselves: it is the gift of God." (Ephesians 2:8 KJV)

"Not by works of righteousness which we have done, but according to his mercy he saved us, by the washing of regeneration, and renewing of the Holy Ghost." (Titus 3:5 KJV)

CANON 12: "If any one shall say that justifying faith is nothing else than confidence in the dIvine mercy pardoning sins for Christ's sake, or that it is that confidence alone by which we are justified... let him be accursed"

Contradicting Scriptures:

"But as many as received him, to them gave he power to become the sons of God, even to them that believe on his name." (John 1:12 KJV)

"Therefore we conclude that a man is justified by faith without the deeds of the Law... For what saith the scripture? Abraham believed God, and it was counted unto him for righteousness." (Romans 3:28; 4:3 KJV)

"Wherefore he is able also to save them to the uttermost that come unto God by him, seeing He ever liveth to make intercession for them. For such an high priest became us, who is holy, harmless, undefiled, separate from sinners, and made higher than the heavens; Who needeth not daily, as those high priests, to offer up sacrifice, first for his own sins, and then for the peoples: for this he did once, when he offered up himself." (Hebrews 7:25-27 KJV)

"For the which cause I also suffer these things: nevertheless I am not ashamed: for I know whom I have believed, and am persuaded that he is able to keep that which I have committed unto him against that day." (2 Timothy 1:12 KJV)

CANON 14: "If any one saith, that man is truly absolved from his sins and justified, because that he assuredly believed himself absolved and justified; or, that no one is truly justified but he who believes himself justified; and that, by this faith alone, absolution and justification are effected; let him be anathema."

Contradicting Scriptures:

"For what saith the scripture? Abraham believed God, and it was counted unto him for righteousness... Therefore being justified by faith, we have peace with God through our Lord Jesus Christ." (Romans 4:3; 5:1 KJV)

CANON 23: "If any one saith, that a man once justified can sin no more, nor lose Grace, and that therefore he that falls and sins was never truly justified; or, on the other hand, that he is able, during his whole life, to avoid all sins, even those that are venial, – except by a special privilege from God, as the Church holds in regard of the Blessed Virgin; let him be anathema."

Contradicting Scriptures:

"He that believeth on the Son hath everlasting life: and he that believeth not the Son shall not see life; but the wrath of God abideth on him... And this is the will of him that sent me, that every one, which seeth the Son, and believeth on him, may have everlasting life: and I will raise him up at the last day... And I give unto them eternal life; and they shall never perish, neither shall any man pluck them out of my hand." (John 3:36; 6:40; 10:28 KJV)

"That as sin hath reigned unto death, even so might Grace reign through righteousness unto eternal life by Jesus Christ our Lord." (Romans 5:21 KJV)

"These things have I written unto you that believe on the name of the Son of God; that ye may know that ye have eternal life, and that ye may believe on the name of the Son of God." (1 John 5:13 KJV)

CANON 24: "If any one saith, that the justice received is not preserved and also increased before God through good works; but that the said works are merely the fruits and signs of Justification obtained, but not a cause of the increase thereof; let him be anathema."

Contradicting Scriptures:

"O foolish Galatians, who hath bewitched you, that ye should not obey the truth, before whose eyes Jesus Christ hath been evidently set forth, crucified among you? This only would I learn of you, Received ye the Spirit by the works of the Law, or by the hearing of faith? Are ye so foolish? having begun in the Spirit, are ye now made perfect by the flesh... Stand fast therefore in the liberty wherewith Christ hath made us free, and be not entangled again with the yoke of bondage. Behold, I Paul say unto you, that if ye be circumcised, Christ shall profit you nothing. For I testify again to every man that is circumcised, that he is a debtor to do the whole Law." (Galatians 3:1-3; 5:1-3 KJV)

CANON 30: "If any one saith, that after the Grace of Justification has been received, to every penitent sinner the guilt is remitted, and the debt of eternal punishment is blotted out in such wise, that there remains not any debt of temporal punishment to be discharged either in this world, or in the next in Purgatory, before the entrance to the kingdom of heaven can be opened (to him); let him be anathema."

Contradicting Scriptures:

"Therefore being justified by faith, we have peace with God through our Lord Jesus Christ." (Romans 5:1 KJV)

"And you, being dead in your sins and the uncircumcision of your flesh, hath he quickened together with him, having forgiven you all trespasses; Blotting out the handwriting of ordinances that was against us, which was contrary to us, and took it out of the way, nailing it to his cross." (Colossians 2:13-14 KJV)

CONCLUSION:

From Jesus' day until now, the vengeful spirit of religion (blatant or subtle) still exists and operates in church movements worldwide. At the same time the truth of the gospel continues to reverberate, sending shockwaves throughout the earth that we are saved by Grace through faith in Jesus Christ alone! The scriptures loudly proclaim that we can do nothing to substantiate our justification through self-effort. Our eternal righteousness is secured only through Christ's finished work. Only when we receive the revelation and believe the truth of Christ's sovereign work of Grace in our lives, will we begin to align ourselves rightly to His purposes and thereby experience the fullness of the victorious life promised to us!

Religion has had its *field day* and the time has come to trumpet the sound of freedom to the four corners of the earth for the release of the captives. Liberty is at hand! The multitudes still enslaved by satan's spell must be awakened. In this final hour of history will you rise and be counted amongst this unstoppable force of *Grace carriers* heralding salvation and hope to deliver?

Souls wait...

Appendix I

ARMINIANISM AND CALVINISM

The arguments from the two main *camps* of Arminianism and Calvinism consistently surface whenever the subject of Grace is discussed. Therefore, to give the layperson a general understanding and historically doctrinal perspective, I have provided a brief description of the five points of each view.[29] It must be clearly understood that this book was not written to endorse any one side of these arguments nor to force my opinions, but rather to help enlighten you to God's heart of Grace. However, as you review each of the five points you may discover what side (or sides) most strongly supports your philosophy. When asked how he reconciled the two "camps" Spurgeon said, *"What need is there to reconcile friends."* Therefore, as you compare these viewpoints you should use them simply to help guide you in further study. Arminianism and Calvinism is not the foundation for our understanding of Biblical Grace. These are only theological suppositions to the Christian faith. The only sure source for revelation to experience God's Grace is the inerrancy of the Bible, the leading of the Holy Spirit and wisdom from Godly leadership.

THE FIVE POINTS OF ARMINIANISM

Free Will or Human Ability

Although human nature was seriously affected by the fall, man has not been left in a state of total spiritual helplessness. God graciously enables every sinner to repent and believe, but He does not interfere with man's freedom. Each sinner possesses a free will and his eternal destiny depends on how he uses it. Man's freedom consists of his ability to choose good over evil in spiritual matters; his will is not enslaved to his sinful nature. The sinner has the power to either cooperate with God's Spirit and be regenerated or resist God's Grace and perish. The lost sinner needs the Spirit's assistance, but he does not have to be regenerated by the Spirit before he can believe, for faith is man's act and precedes the new birth. Faith is the sinner's gift to God and his contribution to salvation.

Conditional Election

God's choice of certain individuals unto salvation before the foundation of the world was based upon His foreseeing that they would respond to His call. He selected only those whom He knew would of themselves freely believe the gospel. Thus, election was determined by or conditioned upon what man would do. The faith which God foresaw and upon which He based His choice was not given to sinners by God (it was not created by the regenerating power of the Holy Spirit) but resulted solely from man's will. It was left entirely up to man as to who would believe and therefore as to who would be elected unto salvation. God chose those whom He knew would, of their own free will, choose Christ. Thus, the sinner's choice of Christ, not God's choice of the sinner, is the ultimate cause of salvation.

Universal Redemption or General Atonement

Christ's redeeming work made it possible for everyone to be saved but did not actually secure the salvation of anyone. Although Christ died for all men and for every man, only those who believe on Him are saved. His death enabled God to pardon sinners on the condition that they believe, but it did not actually put away anyone's sins. Christ's redemption becomes effective only if man chooses to accept it.

The Holy Spirit Can be Effectually Resisted

The Spirit calls inwardly all those who are called outwardly by the gospel invitation; He does all that He can to bring every sinner to salvation. But inasmuch as man is free, he can successfully resist the Spirit's call. The Spirit cannot regenerate the sinner until he believes; faith (which is man's contribution) precedes and makes possible the new birth. Thus, man's free will limits the Spirit in the application of Christ's saving work. The Holy Spirit can only draw to Christ those who allow him to have His way with them. Until the sinner responds, the Spirit cannot give life. God's Grace, therefore, is not invincible; it can be, and often is, resisted and thwarted by man.

Falling from Grace

Those who believe and are truly saved can lose their salvation by failing to keep up their faith, etc. However, all Arminians have not agreed on this point; some have held that believers are eternally secure in Christ--that once a sinner is regenerated, he can never be lost.

THE FIVE POINTS OF CALVINISM

Total Inability or Total Depravity

Because of the fall, man is unable of himself to savingly believe the gospel. The sinner is dead, blind, and deaf to the things of God; his heart is deceitful and desperately corrupt. His will is not free, it is in bondage to his evil nature, therefore, he will not--indeed he cannot--choose good over evil in the spiritual realm. Consequently, it takes much more than the Spirit's assistance to bring a sinner to Christ--it takes regeneration by which the Spirit makes the sinner alive and gives him a new nature. Faith is not something man contributes to salvation but is itself a part of God's gift of salvation--it is God's gift to the sinner, not the sinner's gift to God.

Unconditional Election

God's choice of certain individuals unto salvation before the foundation of the world rested solely in His own sovereign will. His choice of particular sinners was not based on any foreseen response or obedience on their part, such as faith, repentance, etc. On the contrary, God gives faith and repentance to each individual whom He selected. These acts are the result, not the cause of God's choice. Election therefore was not determined by or conditioned upon any virtuous quality or act foreseen in man. Those whom God sovereignly elected He brings through the power of the Spirit to a willing acceptance of Christ. Thus God's choice of the sinner, not the sinner's choice of Christ, is the ultimate cause of salvation.

Limited Atonement or Particular Redemption

Christ's redeeming work was intended to save the elect only and actually secured salvation for them. His death was a substitutionary endurance of the penalty of sin in the place of certain specified sinners. In addition to putting away the sins of His people, Christ's redemption secured everything necessary for their salvation, including faith, which unites them to Him. The gift of faith is infallibly applied by the Spirit to all for whom Christ died, therefore guaranteeing their salvation.

Irresistible Grace or The Efficacious Call of the Spirit

In addition to the outward general call to salvation, which is made to everyone who hears the gospel, the Holy Spirit extends to the elect a special inward call that inevitably brings them to salvation. The external call (which is made to all without distinction) can be, and often is, rejected; whereas the internal call (which is made only to the elect) cannot be rejected; it always results in conversion. By means of this special call the Spirit irresistibly draws sinners to Christ. He is not limited in His work of applying salvation by man's will, nor is He dependent upon man's cooperation for success. The Spirit graciously causes the elect sinner to cooperate, to believe, to repent, to come freely and willingly to Christ. God's Grace, therefore, is invincible; it never fails to result in the salvation of those to whom it is extended.

Perseverance of the Saints

All who are chosen by God, redeemed by Christ, and given faith by the Spirit are eternally saved. They are kept in faith by the power of Almighty God and thus persevere to the end.

Endnotes

1. Adapted from Prince, Joseph. *Destined to Reign*. Tulsa, OK: Harrison House Publishers, 2007.

2. Adapted from Johansonn, Paul. *Free by Divine Decree*. Grandview, MO: Oasis House, 2009.

3. Wommack, Andrew. *Grace, The Power of the Gospel*. Tulsa, OK: Harrison House Publishers, 2007.

4. Inspired by a teaching from Joseph Prince, 2009. www.josephprinceministries.org

5. Dater, John. *How Jesus Died* (The Final 18 Hours) DVD/Video. Trinity Pictures Ltd.

6. Adapted and revised from Chuck Missler's Study Notes on the Book of Romans. God TV, 2009.

7. Adapted from a teaching by Pastor Jentezen Franklin, *Failure Isn't Final*. Gainesville, GA: Free Chapel, 2009.

8. Bickle, Mike. *Passion for Jesus*. Lake Mary, FL: Creation House, 1993.

9. Direct quote from a teaching by Pastor Robert Morris, Senior Pastor, Gateway Church, Southlake, TX. www.gatewaypeople.com

10. For further study, Hypothalamus, *http://www.biologyreference.com/Ho-La/Hypothalamus.html*

11. Vaxa Research. Hypothalamus Function. *www.incrediblehorizons.com/balance-Hypo%20function.htm*

12. Farstad, Arthur L. *Believer's Bible Commentary*. Nashville, TN: Thomas Nelson Inc., 1995.

13. For further study, "Biographical sketches of memorable Christians of the past" *http://justus.anglican.org/resources/bio/7.html, and "John Huss" http://www.theopedia.com/John_Huss.*

14. Note that Jeremiah 29:11 says our future is bright and Romans 11:29 says our righteousness is irrevocable. The reverse references are uncanny. No casual coincidence. Our destiny is bright and our salvation secure.

15. I have purposely and repeatedly capitalized 'IN CHRIST' to help reinforce the profound revelation of Grace.

16. Paul was careful not to send a mixed message to others about what it meant to have liberty (1 Corinthians 10:23 NIV).

17. The World Book Encyclopedia (1993) Vol. E, p. 78

18. This section is not intended to single out the precious saints affiliated with the Catholic Church. Many Catholics are embracing God's Grace and as a result are experiencing an outpouring of revival.

19. Adapted from Council of Trent: Canons on Justification. *http://www.carm.org/religious-movements/roman-catholicism/council-trent-canons-justification*

20. I purposely have not capitalized the words *"devil," "satan"* or *"hell"* as to reinforce my lack of respect for his name and position.

21. The Poultry Connection. Poultry Youth Program, Oxen Training. *www.poultryconnection.com/forums/archive/index.php/t-403.html*

22. *http://dictionary.reference.com/browse/beast+of+burden*

23. Dr. Drew Conroy, Ox Yokes: Culture, Comfort and Animal Welfare. Common Ground: Moving Forward with Animals. World Association for Transport Animal Welfare and Studies (TAWS). TAWS/TAA/BVA workshop, Silsoe Research Institute: UK, April 2004. *www.taws.org/TAWS2004/TAWS04-Conroy-040419-A4-all.pdf.*

24. Follow The Rabbi, *www.followtherabbi.com/Brix?pageID=1855*

25. P'nei Adonai, Resources for Walking in the Presence of God, Yoke. *http://penei.org/concepts-yoke.shtml.*

26. Pentecostalism. (Last updated February 2, 2009). *http://www.bbc.co.uk/religion/religions/christianity/subdivisions/pentecostal_1.shtml#section_.*

27. Ironically, Revelation 15:3 declares that we will sing the *song of Moses* (the father of the Law) to testify of the awesome Grace of God.

28. Wilson, Pete. No Strings Attached. *http://withoutwax.tv/2010/06/07/no-strings-attached/comment-page-1/#comment-40915.*

29. Steele, David N. & Thomas, Curtis C. *Romans: An Interpretative Outline.* Pages 144-147. P.O. Box 817, 08865 Phillipsburg, NJ. P&R Publishing Co. 1963. ISBN 978-0-87552-443-6. www.prpbooks.com. Reprinted by permission from the publisher.

30. Spirit filled people are no better or Godlier than anyone else. While it is true that the gifts of the Spirit more enable us to overcome in this life; it is inevitable that Spirit empowered people are just as susceptible to fall short and even fail miserably at times. No matter what level of spiritual maturity we think we are, we should never be deceived into thinking we are impervious to temptation nor be disillusioned when we fall into sin.

31. In correspondence to 1 Timothy 4:1 (NASB), I want to address a similar passage found in Hebrews 10:26-27 (NASB), *"For if we go on sinning willfully after receiving the knowledge of the truth, there no longer remains a sacrifice for sins, but a terrifying expectation of judgment and the fury of a fire which will consume the adversaries."* Essential to an accurate interpretation of this passage, we must understand the historical conditions and context in which it was written. The clear purpose of Paul's Letter to the Hebrews was to address quite specifically Jewish Christians who were considering returning to Judaism after *"receiving the knowledge of the truth"* (v.26) and *"after being enlightened"* (v.32) by God's Grace through faith in Jesus. This was being termed as the *apostasy.* Paul wasn't scolding those who where trading their newfound faith for a life of immorality, debauchery and lasciviousness. Rather, he was appealing to those who were flocking back to the synagogues in reaction to the wave of persecution hurled against them from the religious leaders. Paul admonishes the new converts to stand firm in the face of intimidation and public scrutiny and to endure the great *"conflict of sufferings"* imposed upon them for their decision to depart from Judaism (I.e. v.34 seizure of property). In fact, Paul unflinchingly confirms the Pharisaical culprits responsible for the apostasy as *"the adversaries"* (v.27). The *adversaries* were those Jewish legalists who fought him *tooth & nail* throughout his Grace campaign (1 Corinthians 16:9, Philippians 1:28; 3:2). *"Sinning willfully"* (v.26) also refers to the Judaizers (See 12:3). Thus, in an attempt to stop the *desertion* and prevent these new converts from being coerced back into slavery to the Law, Paul reminded them that the system of sacrifices was incapable of

granting them salvation. This explains Paul's statement, *"there will remain no more sacrifice for sins"* (v.26). All throughout Hebrews, Paul painstakingly and eloquently illustrates that Jesus is our great High Priest – the *once and for all* sacrifice for sins. Therefore, if these Jewish Christians returned to the futility of works then they would once again be enslaved under condemnation of the Law (v.27). This explains Paul's warning, *"How much severer punishment do you think he will deserve who has trampled under foot the Son of God and has regarded as unclean the blood of the covenant by which he was sanctified and has insulted the Spirit of **Grace**?"* (v.29) According to Paul, choosing the Law over Grace was the same as trampling God's Son underfoot (v.29). Note: This commentary on Paul's statements does not even slightly support a deliberate lifestyle of sin. People who continue to willfully commit sin *without conscience* will answer to God for their actions. However, it must be clearly understood that Hebrews 10 should never be taken out of context in order to coerce people to avoid sin or else be subjected to eternal punishment. Employing these scriptures and others like it, by means of manipulation and fear tactics, is ultimately unsuccessful at motivating people to maintain a holy lifestyle. The only sure way to produce real life transformation is through the spirit and admonition of Grace. **Important Note:** It is not for anyone to decide what will happen to habitual sinners. Therefore, we must pray for them and resign all verdicts to God trusting that He is a good and righteous judge (Psalms 96:13; 98:90; 2 Titus 4:1; 4:8; Hebrews 10:30). For those who have accepted Christ; their sins have already been judged and punished by God in Jesus own body. The believer has been pardoned and is not subject to the condemnation and imputation of sin.

32. Quote by Bishop Dale C. Bronner

33. What is Biblical Numerology? CARM (Christian Apologetics & Research Ministry) *http://carm.org/what-biblical-numerology*. Excerpt (Bullet #5). The number 5 has been referred to as symbolic for Grace. Israel came out of Egypt in ranks of 5 (Exodus 13:18). David picked up 5 smooth stones to fight Goliath (1 Samuel 17:40). The holy anointing oil was pure and composed of five parts (Exodus 30:23-25).

34. See Isaiah 10:27 (ASV)

35. A very close friend and contributing endorser to this book, who is also a Licensed Professional Counselor (see endorsements), often refers her clients to the further study of God's healing Grace. She has counseled many individuals who regularly experience things such as severe depression, grief, obsessive-compulsive tendencies, acute anxiety, self-

harm (i.e. cutters) and many other psychological disorders (which in her professional opinion and deep spiritual conviction) are directly related to condemnation and fear. Almost all of her patients who have fully embraced and grasped the revelation and implications of the Gospel of Grace (along with continued professional counseling sessions) have been able to discontinue their use of prescription anti-depressant medicine and are fast on the road to full recovery today. Grace really works!

36. Tchividjian, Tullian. *Jesus + Nothing = Everything.* Wheaton, IL: Crossway Books, 2011.

37. Parenthesis Author's Emphasis

Other Great Resources from
www.tonysutherland.com

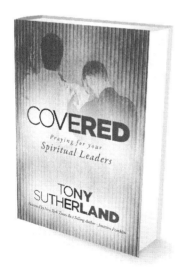

41731152R00185

Made in the USA
Charleston, SC
10 May 2015